Citizen's Guide to
P3 Projects

Citizen's Guide to
P3 Projects

A Legal Primer for **Public-Private Partnerships**

Ernest C. Brown, Esq., PE

iUniverse

CITIZEN'S GUIDE TO P3 PROJECTS
A LEGAL PRIMER FOR PUBLIC-PRIVATE PARTNERSHIPS

Interior Graphics/Art Credit: Marla Aufmuth- Photographer

iUniverse books may be ordered through booksellers or by contacting:

iUniverse
1663 Liberty Drive
Bloomington, IN 47403
www.iuniverse.com
1-800-Authors (1-800-288-4677)

ISBN: 978-1-5320-8999-2 (sc)
ISBN: 978-1-5320-9000-4 (hc)
ISBN: 978-1-5320-9001-1 (e)

Library of Congress Control Number: 2020900645

Print information available on the last page.

iUniverse rev. date: 01/27/2020

CONTENTS

INTRODUCTION

America's infrastructure is in trouble.

The roads, bridges, dams, and pipelines that we rely upon as the backbone of our economy are up to one hundred years old and are grossly inadequate for our growing population and societal objectives. Our Federal Government, states and localities lack the financial resources to make the necessary investments to restore, enhance and properly maintain our public infrastructure.

In the past decade, Public Private Projects, or "P3s" have emerged as a new design, build and financing alternative. A P3 or Concessionaire Agreement is a cooperative agreement between a public agency and private entity for the design, construction, finance and management of a project or service used by the public. P3's can provide private investment funds and offer ordinary citizens the opportunity to advocate for creative local projects.

The P3 approach has resulted in the construction of hundreds of exceptional projects in the United States, Canada, and abroad. They offer great opportunities for new investment and can be catalysts for successful project development. In 2018, the Trump Administration announced its Building a Stronger America program, a plan to promote $1.5 trillion in new infrastructure programs, largely funded by P3 investment. In fact, there is bi-partisan support at all levels of government for implementing P3s to save our rapidly aging infrastructure.

As recently observed in the Harvard Business Review:

> [I]t's no surprise that there is renewed interest in public-private partnership (P3) projects, where businesses supplement public investment in return for reaping rewards such as tolls and fees. ("What Successful Public Private Partnerships Do," Elyse Maltin, January 8, 2019).

In sum, the voting public is distrustful of raising property taxes or otherwise financing urgently needed projects with increased gas taxes, user fees or bonded indebtedness. Thus, we desperately need private investment vehicles such as P3s to make our roads, bridges, airports and hospitals safe. We simply can't fund the repair and expansion of our core infrastructure without these types of innovative finance solutions.

That is why P3s are so promising in fixing our infrastructure

> *The material covered in this P3 Legal Guide should be considered general information and guidance regarding these innovative projects. The reader is advised not to take any specific actions based upon the general observations and suggestions in this general survey of the law without consulting an experienced P3 attorney or law firm.*

CHAPTER 1

PROJECT CONCEPTION

1.01 Why Do We Need P3 Projects?

The P3 approach can be an exceptional method for pursuing urgently needed infrastructure projects, especially when government budgets are grossly inadequate.

While the United States economy has largely recovered from the 2008 financial crisis, the aging of the boomer generation, growing public retirement expenses and hostility to new taxes has impacted state and local budgets, restricted government services, curtailed investment, affected bond ratings and deferred maintenance. As a direct result, American infrastructure is crumbling faster than it is being repaired or replaced. And it requires a fresh approach to avert major safety risk to the public.

A 2016 study by Syracuse University concluded through dozens of owner and Concessionaire interviews for US-based projects that there is a significantly higher likelihood of meeting cost and schedule objectives under P3 models compared with traditional public sector project delivery where a project is owned, managed, and financed by government.

The Government Accountability Office (GAO) defines a public-private partnership as "a contractual agreement formed between public and private sector partners, which allows more private sector participation than is traditional. These agreements usually involve

1

a government agency contracting with a private company to design, renovate, construct, operate, maintain, and/or manage a facility or system."[1] That is why many consider P3 the future of infrastructure.

On April 15, 2019, the Build America Bureau of the US Department of Transportation further endorsed P3s:

> Early involvement of the private sector can bring innovation, efficiency, and capital to address complex transportation problems facing State and local governments. The Bureau provides information and expertise in the use of different P3 approaches, and provides TIFIA and RRIF loans, Private Activity Bonds (PABs), and INFRA Grants to facilitate P3 projects.

> Overall, 65% of U.S. roads are in poor condition and 25% of U.S. bridges are in need of significant repair or are unable to handle the current volume of traffic.[2] The Federal Highway Administration (FHWA) estimates that to eliminate the nation's bridge backlog by 2028, we would need to invest $20.5 billion annually, while only $12.8 billion is being spent currently.

Throughout the United States, there have been increasing numbers of well-publicized bridge collapses, such as the I-35 Bridge Collapse in Minneapolis, weather catastrophes in the Gulf States, widespread power outages and wildfires in the Western United States, the failure of the Orville Dam Spillways in California, and other public facility failures that have taken many lives and disrupted local economies.

---

[1] Associated General Contractors of America (AGC), "AGC White Paper on Public-Private Partnerships: The Risks and Opportunities" p. 2.

[2] U.S. Dep't of Transportation, "Beyond Traffic 2045: Trends and Choices," available at http://www.dot.gov/sites/dot.gov/files/docs/Draft_Beyond_Traffic_Framework.pdf.

In New York State alone, the American Society of Civil Engineers estimates that $9.3 billion is required just to replace or repair deficient highway bridges.

A November 11, 2019, review of federal data and reports obtained by the Associated Press under state open records laws identified 1,688 high-hazard dams rated in poor or unsatisfactory condition as of last year in 44 states and Puerto Rico. About 1,000 dams have failed over the past four decades, killing 34 people, according to Stanford University's National Performance of Dams Program.

There are thousands of people in this country that are living downstream from dams that are probably considered deficient given current safety standards," said Mark Ogden, a former Ohio dam safety official who is now a technical specialist with the Association of State Dam Safety Officials. The association estimates it would take more than $70 billion to repair and modernize the nation's more than 90,000 dams.

"Most people have no clue about the vulnerabilities when they live downstream from these private dams," said Craig Fugate, a former administrator at the Federal Emergency Management Agency. "When they fail, they don't fail with warning. They just fail, and suddenly you can find yourself in a situation where you have a wall of water and debris racing toward your house with very little time, if any, to get out."

At the same time, local and state governments have limited enthusiasm for funding new projects or maintaining existing ones. While taxpayers may be willing to pay more for the public services they expect, they are concerned with the government's ability to raise and spend money efficiently. In view of the very substantial budget deficits and the looming 'debt bomb' of unfunded municipal pension plans, P3s will be increasingly important.

And the money is there to fix these problems. The private investment market dwarfs the public finance market. It is more robust as capital is attracted to higher returns. However, P3 projects must promise a significant and stable return on investment (ROI) to make them attractive to private investment.

Among the benefits of P3s on large projects is their ability to attract large international design and contracting organizations with access to

3

capital, technical innovations, group purchasing, licensed technology and information processing capacity beyond the capabilities of most state, local and municipal governments. These competitive efficiencies in the private sector can result in dramatically lower costs to the public on such projects.

In addition, they provide a grassroots opportunity for community groups to create projects. Such projects can seize community interest, market opportunities and exploit new technologies.[3] In this context, P3s are not just a source of funding, but a sophisticated financing and procurement methodology for projects of all sizes. The people of the United States are willing to pay for infrastructure, one way or another.

The P3 pricing method encompasses the design, construction, operation, and maintenance of a project for twenty to thirty years, if not more. Accordingly, the projects tend to be awarded on a best value basis where initial price is a major, but not the only, factor.

In fact, P3 projects are typically awarded based upon life cycle costing. As such, the long-term energy costs, maintenance, operational expenses and financing methods are taken into account. This is in stark contrast to creating a fanciful but inefficient design then awarding the construction contract to the lowest cost construction bidder – a system that ignores the costs of running the facility after the initial cost of construction. A good P3 creates value and efficiency by incorporating all future costs of operations into the package price of the facility.

In a P3, the private firms invest equity upfront to help pay for the efficient design and construction costs of the project. They seek competitive rates of return on stable investments.[4] Those returns are typically paid through tolls on the constructed facility or by annual payments from the public partner. P3 teams must look at a broad set of costs, including estimating the value of delivering of a project, estimating the lifecycle costs, and the expected project revenues, and the value of transferred risk.[5]

---

[3] Drew Thompson, "Building Bridges," Constructor Magazine (Nov./Dec. 2014), quoting Ernest C. Brown, Esq., PE.

[4] U.S. Dep't of Transportation, "Beyond Traffic 2045: Trends and Choices," p. 174.

[5] Id.

In 2014, the Committee on Transportation and Infrastructure of the US House of Representatives created the "Panel on Public-Private Partnerships". The Panel concluded that P3s have the potential to deliver high-value, complex projects more efficiently than traditional procurement and financing mechanisms.

That federal study displayed little imagination regarding the potential for using P3 on smaller projects. They gave the prevailing view that exists in many large organizations that as the number of extremely large projects was limited, P3s were appropriate for only a small portion of national infrastructure needs.[6] The opposite is true. P3s can become a substantial contributor to the improvement of the aging US infrastructure – for small, medium and mega-sized projects.

The Association for the Improvement of American Infrastructure (AIAI) has a similarly optimistic view. A Washington, D.C. based non-profit organization established to further P3 education and legislation, AIAI believes, "… [E]ffective and well-planned advocacy can provide legislative leaders with the knowledge they need to make informed decisions about all of the benefits of public-private partnership-economic development, life cycle cost savings, risk transfer and accelerated project delivery."[7]

A P3 approach allows local decision makers to evaluate the entire costs of a project, current and future, which makes it an effective and potentially universal planning tool for prudent government agencies. As such, P3s ensure the continued operation and maintenance of existing infrastructure with predictable future costs to the public partner. Such a method of analysis should arguably be used as a benchmark for all public projects – whether they proceed with a P3 structure or not.

The P3 approach also takes inspiration from the Silicon Valley model of blending money and business skills from the private sector

---

[6] Committee on Transportation and Infrastructure, "Public-Private Partnerships: Findings and Recommendations of the Special Panel on Public-Private Partnerships.," (U.S. House of Representatives, 113th Congress, September 2014), p. 9.

[7] AIAI Brochure, "We Are Ready to Work! Advocating for Public Private Partnerships" Association for the Improvement of American Infrastructure, p. 2, Dec. 5, 2013.

with the governmental backbone of public services to solve major problems. As a result, state and local governments are actively working to improve their existing legal frameworks and seeking higher levels of participation from private industry in order to provide needed services.

Again, there is wide, bi-partisan support for P3 projects. In response to the nation's deteriorating infrastructure, President Obama launched the Build America Investment Initiative on July 17, 2014.[8] The initiative was aimed at increasing private funding for public projects and did not include any increase in the use of federal funds.

The Federal Highway Administration (FHWA) also published a Model P3 Core Toll Concessions P3 Contract Guide, part of the agency's efforts to develop standard model P3 contracts for use by state and local transportation officials.[9]

However, these projects are not bulletproof. As Elyse Maltin recently warned in the Harvard Business Review:

> [M]any P3 projects go off the rails. For example, a European Union review of nine such projects launched between 2000 and 2014 found seven were late and over budget. A U.S. interstate highway project near Indianapolis was found to be 51% over budget and two years past the proposed completion date. These highly publicized travails not only make P3 projects a public nuisance (or more), they create big political hurdles to overcome the next time a much-needed infrastructure project requires outside funding.[10]

In fact, while there are specific types of projects for which a P3 is especially suited —such as roads, bridges, hospitals, public libraries and

---

[8] See §1.10 of this manual for further discussion of the Build America Investment Initiative.

[9] U.S. Dep't of Transportation Federal Highway Administration, "Model Public-Private Partnerships Core Toll Concessions Contract Guide," (Sept. 2014), available at http://www.fhwa.dot.gov/ipd/pdfs/p3/model_p3_core_toll_concessions.pdf.

[10] Elyse Maltin, "What Successful Public-Private Partnerships Do" available at https://hbr.org/2019/01/what-successful-public-private-partnerships-do

day care facilities; there are some projects where a P3 approach would simply not make sense, such as municipal police or the provision of other sensitive governmental services.

P3s can take more up-front resources to evaluate and procure than conventional projects and private financing costs can be higher than the costs of municipal bonds where they are available.[11]

But, this approach is growing steadily. P3 investments so far account for only a small portion of overall investments. Between 2007 and 2013, $22.7 billion of public and private funds were invested in P3s, about 2 percent of overall capital investment in the nation's highways during that same period.[12] So, there is a lot of room for innovation and efficiency that should result from wider use of this public investment strategy.

In many economists' views, upgrades to highway and transit systems, public schools, the electric grid, sustainable energy, 5G cellular service, and universal internet access are vital to make the United States truly competitive in the global economy.[13] Investment in infrastructure creates jobs and stimulates economic growth over the longer run; as well as creating jobs in the near-term in the construction sector and beyond.[14]

The President's Council of Economic Advisors and the National Economic Council suggest that investment in transportation infrastructure will continue to support strong job growth in the construction industry as well as in manufacturing, retail trade, and professional and business services.[15]

In the words of Matt Girard, president of the American Road & Transportation Builders Association (P3 Division), "Anything that

---

[11] U.S. Dep't of Transportation, "Beyond Traffic 2045: Trends and Choices," p. 173.

[12] *Id.*

[13] Ernest C. Brown, California Infrastructure Projects: A Legal Handbook for Successful Contracting & Dispute Resolution §1.1 (Brian Hunt 2012).

[14] U.S. Dep't of Treasury Office of Economic Policy, "Expanding our Nation's Infrastructure through Innovative Financing," 2, (Sept. 2014), available at https://www.hsdl.org/?view&did=806659

[15] National Economic Council and President's Council of Economic Advisors. An Economic Analysis of Transportation Infrastructure Investment. Washington, D.C.: The White House, 2014.

removes hurdles to allow for P3s to be more prevalent – to be another tool in the toolbox for state agencies – is obviously a good thing."[16]

President Trump has been inconsistent in his support of P3s.

> When President Donald Trump announced his campaign pledge to upgrade the country's infrastructure, he endorsed public-private partnerships (P3s) as a way to help finance and build the $1 trillion worth of projects subject to his proposal. He said he would leverage the power of P3s to turn $200 billion of public dollars into $1 trillion of investment, refurbishing crumbling infrastructure without emptying public coffers. But just a year later, he had soured on the idea, telling a group of legislators in 2017 that private financing of public infrastructure isn't likely to work and that P3s are "more trouble than they're worth." Construction Dive, October 25, 2019.

President Trump's enthusiasm for P3 financing appeared to further wane in 2019. According to the Wall Street Journal, the change surfaced after Speaker Nancy Pelosi (D-Calif.) and Senate Minority Leader Charles Schumer (D-N.Y.) announced they reached a tentative agreement with Trump to spend $2 trillion on an infrastructure package.

In the meeting, Trump reportedly referred to his administration's previous infrastructure plan, which called for public-private partnerships, as "so stupid" and argued that he was never supportive of the model because "you get sued." He blamed the past plan on his former top economic adviser Gary Cohn.

The Journal further reported,

> GOP lawmakers, concerned that Democrats will propose raising or implementing new taxes, argue that

---

[16] Tom Ichniowski, "Obama Seeks to Spark More Private Infrastructure Financing" available at https://www.enr.com/articles/7026-obama-seeks-to-spark-more-private-infrastructure-financing?v=preview

going with public-private partnerships could help them stretch federal spending for infrastructure projects.

Top House Republicans say they want public-private partnerships to stay on the table as an option for financing a sweeping infrastructure overhaul, despite criticisms from President Trump.

House Minority Leader Kevin McCarthy (R-Calif.) and House Minority Whip Steve Scalise (R-La.) both said [in response] that public-private partnerships could be a smart move to pay for any proposed infrastructure package.

"We ought to look at every option to see if those kinds of partnerships help us build more roads and help meet the needs of communities," Scalise told reporters. [Wall Street Journal, May 2, 2019].

P3 arrangements pair public entities with private investors to create projects that range from toll roads and highways to airports, government buildings, schools and universities. They are seen as an innovative way for municipalities to get much-needed infrastructure upgrades without cutting corners or breaking public taxpayer-funded budgets. Most P3 contracts are for Design-Build, fixed budgets and fixed schedule work, according to a recent position paper from the Design-Build Institute of America.

One of the hurdles of getting P3 interest on smaller projects has been the high transaction costs – particularly the legal and financing aspects - for P3 projects. The prevalence of "bespoke" concession agreements for the larger projects vary widely by agency and jurisdiction. This makes the negotiation and closing of Design-Build and financing transactions overly expensive for smaller projects.

A welcome change has been the trend to developing benchmark P3 contracts, such as the US Department of Transportation's "P3 Guidebook," as well as its just-released "Public-Private Partnership (P3) Procurement: A Guide for Public Owners" (June 2019). There is also a set of standardized P3 contracts and procurement documents published by the Federal Highway Administration Center for Innovative Support.[17]

Along these lines, the Author was Chairman of the P3 Committee of the ConsensusDocs Taskforce, a broad consortium of more than 40 leading engineering and construction professional organizations. The P3 Committee's effort resulted in publication of both of these standard ConsensusDoc agreements:

ConsensusDocs 900 Standard P3 Agreement and General Conditions

ConsensusDoc 910 Operations and Maintenance Agreement (O & M).

The O & M Agreement is suitable for use on P3, Design-Build Plus, and other standalone engagements where an O & M component is part of the overall contracting structure.

The Engineers Joint Document Committee (EJDC) has similarly released their version of a P3 Concession Agreement. (EJCDC P3-508 Public-Private Partnership Agreement.)

This type of standardization of P3 contracts for hospitals and other vertical projects has been routine in Canada for more than a decade. The Concessionaires, Design-Builders and bankers have become familiar with these sets of documents and they have accelerated their hospital, governmental offices and public works construction projects.

A keen understanding of the implications and costs of public infrastructure projects is essential to American democracy and the shape of our future. The expansion and maintenance of public infrastructure should not be solely the jurisdiction of the government. It is a collaboration that requires the participation of local citizens and private industry.

The construction of public infrastructure involves making tough choices about civic priorities. The public trough is not limitless. It takes

---

[17] https://www.fhwa.dot.gov/ipd/p3/toolkit/publications/procurement.aspx

careful stewardship of public funds to meet the essential public needs of transportation, safe water, education, law enforcement, and healthcare.

P3 development is an opportunity to stretch the public funds further by recognizing and balancing the true life cycle costs of public projects and by using the financing tools available to private industry to efficiently deliver services to residents.

A knowledgeable citizenry and involved investment community will ensure that public projects are economically efficient and responsive to public needs, whether the need is schools, parks, marinas, sports arenas, convention centers, public buildings, highways, hospitals, schools, water and wastewater treatment facilities, and conveyances, or even public golf courses or sports fields. These facilities can provide an exceptional and healthy life for our children and a beautiful, pleasant environment.

The use of P3s greatly increases the transparency of these public investments. The true costs of a public project range far and wide, although the ultimate cost is buried in reports and ledgers of accounts not readily available to the public. The winning bid figure read at bid opening and reported in news accounts of the project cost is merely a down payment on the realistic project cost.

When projects go forward without a clear commitment on costs, the price of construction can escalate and leave taxpayers paying back bonds, even without a project in exchange. For example, a new jail was budgeted at $220 million for construction in Wayne County, Pennsylvania. It has gone so far over the $300 million of authorized bond financing that the county may abandon the project altogether after issuing $200 million in bonds.[18]

Such surprises in cost can extend into the operations and maintenance (O&M) phase, most of which are not eligible for grant funding. According to a Brookings Institute report, O&M has represented only 8 percent of total federal grants since 2000.[19]

However, O&M represents more than half of the total spending on infrastructure and, in some areas, such as mass transit and aviation,

---

[18] Marlon A. Walker, "As $300M Wayne County jail project runs into trouble, board in charge seldom meets," Detroit Free Press, June 6, 2013.
[19] Barry Bosworth and Sveta Milusheva, "Innovations in U.S. Infrastructure Financing: An Evaluation" 3-4 (The Brookings Institution, 2011.

the proportion is two-thirds or greater.[20] Local governments may have the incentive to build new infrastructure, but they often do not have the expertise or resources to effectively operate or maintain completed projects. Over the last decade, state and local governments have often lost the trust of the public by under-representing the true, long-term costs of operating and maintaining buildings, hospitals and civil infrastructure.

Comparatively, a P3 project forces the consideration of a single price tag for the entire construction, including a fixed price for the future maintenance and operational costs. This figure allows the public to decide whether the project is worth it or not. It does not let public advocates hide the real costs of the project. When P3s are carried out in an efficient manner, they have been shown to lower the total costs of the project, including operation and maintenance, for taxpayers.[21]

The Author wants the reader to be able to make highly informed decisions about project evaluation, planning, construction management, risk identification and prevention, finance, and contracting. This guide arms the reader with a practical knowledge of the landscape, organizational structure, opportunities, and governing law of Public-Private Partnerships.

1.02   P3 Projects in the United States

Although there has been a recent resurgence of P3 financing in the United States, it is hardly a novel approach. This financing practice has been used for hundreds of years in Europe, often framed as the granting of "concessions." It has decades of use in developing countries where governments often do not have the cashflow or creditworthiness to float government debt for major projects.

In reality, since the Eighteenth Century, the granting of private concessions for public projects has been a vibrant force in propelling the growth of infrastructure in the United States. These include major

---

[20] *Id.*

[21] U.S. Dep't of Treasury Office of Economic Policy, "Expanding our Nation's Infrastructure through Innovative Financing."

toll roads, canals, ferries, bridges, cable car and municipal railroad lines. And, of course, the transcontinental railroads.

In fact, one of the first U.S. Supreme Court cases involving public works was the 1837 dispute between the City of Boston and two private infrastructure companies. It was a classic battle between two competing bridge ventures, creatively named, *The Proprietors of Charles River Bridge v. The Proprietors of Warren Bridge.*[22]

In 1785, the State of Massachusetts legislature had granted plaintiffs, Charles River Bridge Company, a concession to build a bridge across the Charles River connecting Charlestown and Boston.[23] At the time, the only means of crossing the river was by ferry, the operation of which would no longer be necessary upon completion of the bridge.[24]

In exchange for the right to build the bridge and collect tolls, the Charles River Bridge Company agreed to pay Harvard College an annual fixed sum for a period of forty years as compensation for the loss of annual income from the ferry service that resulted from the construction of the bridge project.[25] The bridge project was successful and continued to charge high tolls despite its profitability.[26]

In 1828, the Massachusetts legislature authorized the Warren Bridge Company, the defendants, to build a second bridge across the Charles River.[27] This second bridge was built in close proximity to the Charles River Bridge and was set to be toll free once its construction costs were paid and its agreed-upon profit was achieved.[28]

The Charles Bridge ownership brought suit against the upstart Warren Bridge Company, arguing that their only source of revenue, the bridge tolls, would be destroyed by the new toll-free bridge nearby.[29] Charles Bridge alleged the City's act of incorporating defendants' new bridge (and its Design – Build – Operate – Transfer - Finance

---

[22] 36 U.S. 420 (1837).

[23] *Id.*at 423.

[24] *Id.*

[25] *Id.* at 424.

[26] *Id.* at 427. Understandability, given they were a monopoly service.

[27] *Id.* The Warren Bridge was demolished in 1962 and replaced by the Charles River Dam.

[28] *Id.*

[29] *Id.* at 428.

approach) impaired the obligation of their contract with the plaintiffs and specifically alleged that it constitutionally violated their property rights by impairing their right to collect tolls.[30]

The Supreme Court evaluated whether the subsequent state law would unconstitutionally divest contract rights. The Supreme Court expounded on the commendable pluck, enterprise, and great risk undertaken by the original bridge builders in constructing the first bridge in New England over tidal waters and near the sea. However, the Court observed that the rights to the original bridge were derived entirely from the act of the state legislature where the plaintiffs were incorporated.[31] It found the plaintiffs' right to cross the Charles was not exclusive and not constitutionally impeded by the defendant's development of a competing bridge.[32]

The underlying lessons of this 182-year-old case still apply in today's public-private partnership sector. The moral of the story: it is important to read the fine print of your concession agreement. An obvious missed point was failing to secure either exclusive rights of access and right-of-way, or an agreement for compensation if a competing project was approved.

In San Francisco, the original bridges and ferry services were largely provided by concessions granted to private operators of those facilities.

On February 5, 1923, the Board of Supervisors of Contra Costa County, east of San Francisco, exerting power conferred by state legislation, passed ordinance No. 171 granting to the Rodeo-Vallejo Ferry Company a franchise to construct and for 25 years to operate the (first) Carquinez bridge.[33] On June 4, 1923, the same board granted to the Delta Bridge Corporation, a similar franchise for the construction and operation of a bridge across the San Joaquin River near Antioch, between the counties of Contra Costa and Sacramento.[34]

---

[30] *Id.*

[31] *Id.*

[32] *Id.* at 430-431.

[33] SC-B *Supra* at 948. The Author was Project Counsel for the third incarnation of this bridge, now named for Mr. Al Zampa, a legendary Bay Area bridge ironworker.

[34] *Id.*

Each ordinance provided that, on the expiration of the franchise, the property rights, including title to the bridge, reverted to the adjacent counties. The Antioch bridge was opened in January, 1926, and the Carquinez in May, 1927.[35] These were early DBOT projects.

In 1927, a privately-sponsored truss-lifted span opened between Newark and Menlo Park, south of San Francisco, then another private bridge, a causeway with draw-span joining San Mateo and Hayward.

As late as 1930, "The Bay Cities Bridge Corporation, a spin-off of the American Toll Bridge Company, was proposing a rail and highway causeway between Alameda Island and the Santa Fe and Southern Pacific rail yards on Sixteenth Street in San Francisco."[36] As the famous California historian Kevin Star observed, had there not been a Great Depression, the bridges across the Golden Gate and the Oakland – San Francisco Bay might have been all public-private partnerships.[37]

The clash of public private partnerships and the setting of bridge rates again came before the US Supreme Court in 1939.[38] This time, it was a West Coast Project. The bridge company that had built the aforementioned private bridge across the Carquinez Straits (the first one) asserted that the local rail commission's rate setting procedure violated the due process clause of the Fourteenth Amendment. It further alleged that the order set rates that were confiscatory.[39] The US Supreme Court affirmed the rail commissions order that subsequently reduced tolls across the appellant's bridge.

So, rather than a new and untested finance tool– public private partnerships have been successfully used in the United States for more than two hundred and thirty years. And in California for nearly a hundred years!

---

[35] SC – C Supra at p. 948.

[36] Kevin Smith, *The Life and Times of America's Greatest Bridge*, Bloomsbury Press (2010).

[37] *Supra* at 54. Kevin Star often objected to the Author calling him famous, but he certainly was.

[38] SC- *American Toll Bridge Co. v. Railroad Commission of California, et al.,* No. 704, 307 U.S. 486 (1939).

[39] *Id.*

1.03   Successful P3 Projects

The National Council for Public-Private Partnerships (NCPPP) gives awards each year for successful P3 Projects. These are their enthusiastic descriptions of 2019 award winners:

Hill Farms – Wisconsin State Office Building:

The new Hill Farms State Office Building created a more efficient use of shared space by allowing the State of Wisconsin to consolidate seven State of Wisconsin agencies, including anchor tenant, the Department of Transportation (WisDOT), into one state owned property in lieu of scattered smaller leased spaces. This over 5-year process, which started with the development of a Custom Proposal and P3 Development Agreement, was the result of a double joint venture in both the Developer — Gilbane Development Company and Summit Smith Development and contractor roles –Gilbane Building Company and CD Smith Construction ("Smith Gilbane").

Through the combination of a purchase and sale agreement and Design-Build-finance arrangement that leverages the state's existing asset (land) and the market's potential (growing demand base), Smith Gilbane:

> Delivered WisDOT's new facility and a 1,700-space parking garage on a turn-key basis, below budget and ahead of schedule, saving the WisDOT and the taxpayers of Wisconsin millions of dollars in capitalized interest alone; and

> Will deliver a vibrant $300M mixed use development consisting of 450 residential units, up to 450,000 SF of office and medical office space, a 200-room hotel, up to 200,000 SF of retail including a 50,000 SF Grocer, Restaurants and Other Destination Services and 2,600 parking spaces over 2 phases.

Working with HGA as architect, Smith Gilbane and WisDOT's facility incorporates concepts that merge "form and function" to engage visitors, enhance productivity of the building's occupants and meet the public's expectation for a government office facility that streamlines services while reducing operating expenses.

In addition to the direct social and economic impact realized by delivering WisDOT's new facility, Smith Gilbane expects to have an even greater impact as it delivers Madison Yards, the $300M mixed-use place-making component of the project.

Overall, the project was completed 3 months ahead of schedule and on budget in January 2018, allowing reduced Capital Interest Expenses to the State of Wisconsin.

Paine Field, Snohomish County Airport, State of Washington

Paine Field in Snohomish County, Washington is the first privately funded, built and operated passenger terminal in the U.S. as a result of a uniquely structured public-private partnership (P3).

Enormous economic growth in the Seattle region led the push in Snohomish County, Washington (population appx. 800,000) to support new passenger airline service at its local airport, Paine Field. Paine Field is the site of the largest Boeing manufacturing facility but prior to the Paine Field P3 did not have passenger service.

Paine Field is the first U.S. airport with a privatized commercial airline passenger operation within a publicly-owned airport. This unique P3 arrangement allows Snohomish County to focus on what it does best—operate an airport that is designed around the needs of Boeing's manufacturing plant—while ensuring a first-class passenger experience.

The original elements of the project included not only the unique P3 arrangement, but the genuine partnership between Propeller and County officials designed to fulfill passenger needs and to avoid conflicting with Boeing's needs.

Biosolids Drying Facility, Great Lakes Water Authority

The Great Lakes Water Authority (GLWA) awarded a contract to NEFCO to design, build, and operate a biosolids processing facility to augment the processing capacity of GLWA's wastewater treatment plant. The facility features technologically advanced air pollution, noise, and odor control systems to ensure that NEFCO is a good neighbor to the community.

Benefits from this contract include significant cost savings over the current biosolids management practice, capital cost savings by NEFCO providing dewatering at a significant cost reduction versus a centrifuge capital project that was planned, more efficient staffing, and a facility that greatly reduces impacts to the local community.

NEFCO's Detroit facility began operations in the fall of 2015 and is currently the largest biosolids processing facility in North America.

A comprehensive list of US P3 Bridge and Highway Projects provided by the US Federal Highway Administration is reproduced in Appendix A.

US Airports have also strongly embraced P3s for development and finance.

As reported by a recent Levelset.com briefing paper:

- Denver International Airport
  The City of Denver recently agreed on a $1.8B P3 project on the Denver International Airport. This is not the first time the Denver airport has done a P3 project – just one year ago

a commuter rail project was completed using the P3 format. This P3 will improve security and modernize the layout of the ticketing and entryway.

- La Guardia
  In June of 2018, LaGuardia entered into a $4B P3 to completely overhaul a terminal. Under the project, their private partner will also complete infrastructure and an entryway.

- Kansas City
  The Kansas City International Airport is currently reviewing P3 proposals to build a new terminal. Four groups bid on the $1B project.

- Los Angeles - World Airports
  Fluor Corporation is leading the LAX Integrated Express Solutions (LINXS) joint venture which was selected in January 2019, by Los Angeles World Airports (LAWA) to Design-Build, finance, operate and maintain the Los Angeles International Airport (LAX) automated people mover (APM). This P3 project, the first for LAX, has a contract value of $2.7 Billion. The 2.25-mile APM will include a total of six stations — three that connect parking, a rental car center and the Metro to airport terminals and three that connect the Central Terminal to other airline terminals. (Businesswire, February 1, 2018.)

Two transit projects in Washington, DC and Los Angeles are employing P3 on their multi-billion dollar transit projects:

Washington Metro – Purple Line

The Washington DC Metro project has announced they will use P3 financing for the expansion of the $2.65 Billion Purple Line.
According to the FHWA,

> The Purple Line Project is a 16-mile, 21-station light rail transit line that will connect several communities

in Maryland, from Bethesda in Montgomery County to New Carrollton in Prince George's County. The corridor is located along the Capital Beltway near Washington, D.C., in a densely populated area with continued commercial, institutional, mixed-use, and residential development. The Project will include five major activity center stations (Bethesda, Silver Spring, Takoma-Langley Park, College Park, and New Carrollton) and 16 smaller stations that serve residential communities, commercial districts, and institutional establishments. It will also provide direct connections to three branches of the existing Metrorail system, all three MARC commuter rail lines, and Amtrak's Northeast Corridor line. Although the Project will provide direct connections with Metrorail and MARC, it will remain physically and operationally separate.

MDOT and MTA entered into a public-private partnership (P3) agreement on April 7, 2016 with a special purpose company comprised of several leading design, construction, and maintenance firms to facilitate delivery and amplify performance of the asset. Under the terms of this agreement, the private partners will accept risk from MDOT and MTA in exchange for availability payments, and they will complete five third-party projects that will complement the completed Purple Line.

The Purple Line Project is primarily intended to address severe traffic congestion and improve mobility for transit-dependent neighborhoods, providing for an east-west transit option to complement the north-south option currently available through the existing Metrorail system and MARC lines. The Project is expected to reduce travel times by approximately 40% and eliminate approximately 17,000 auto trips per day.

LA Metro - Sepulveda Transit Corridor

As reported by Kim Slowey of Construction Dive on Nov. 10, 2019, the Sepulveda Transit project in Los Angeles will also be considering the P3 model:

> The Los Angeles County Metropolitan Transportation Authority (Metro) has issued a Request for Proposals (RFP) in order to find up to two contractors that can assist with the planning and design of the $9 billion to $14 billion Sepulveda Transit Corridor. The cost of the project will depend on which route the Metro chooses.
>
> The chosen contractor(s) will perform predevelopment work, including determining the overall concept and identifying potential transportation modes, for a fixed guideway transit line from the San Fernando Valley to Los Angeles' Westside and then eventually to Los Angeles International Airport. After the development phase, the winning team will have the opportunity to bid on the construction phase through a public-private partnership, although plans to use that delivery method could change.
>
> The agency expects to be complete with its evaluation of route alternatives by the end of this year and plans to both select the contractor(s) and identify preferred routes for an environmental review by the summer of 2020.

These major projects show P3 gaining wide approval for U.S. Projects.

1.04 Traditional Barriers

Starting in the mid-1800's, the emergence of public works statutes emphasizing competitive bidding of military equipment and civil engineering projects created a chilling effect on new P3 projects. The U.S. Congress got the ball rolling on these competitive bidding statutes during the Civil War in response to concerns over widespread graft and favoritism in granting procurement contracts.[40]

It is true that the open and competitive bidding of public works projects has driven down the costs of construction and rewarded the most efficient contractors. However, these statutes created artificial barriers to project creativity and finance innovation that are now embedded in federal, state, and local public works statutes and bureaucratic rules.

The standard, 1950's era, public works approach required the public entity and its consultants to fully design a project, provide a fully approved and static set of plans and specifications to the contracting community, and award the construction effort to the lowest responsive and responsible bidder. Upon completion, the public agency was expected to maintain the facility, bearing whatever the cost of operations might turn out to be until it became physically or technically obsolete.

The problem is that any design errors, omissions or problems with constructability are the responsibility of the public entity who by law impliedly warrant the plans to be correct and without substantial errors or omissions.

Where the geotechnical investigation or building plans were not adequate, perhaps due to lack of investment in those efforts, the agency was expected to experience and thereafter absorb the resulting project delays and costly claims.

Fortunately, the P3 approach is disrupting these hidebound traditions. The majority of state legislatures now permit the use of Design-Build contracting using a single entity, a method now used on the largest US public construction projects. These same legislatures are adopting innovative P3 statutes to allow private investment, life cycle design and O & M services on a competitive and cost-effective basis for state and local agencies.

---

[40] *E.g.*, The Civil Sundries Appropriations Act of 1861.

1.05   Project Concept

The P3 approach recognizes that breathtaking innovation can spring from any corner. A P3 project may be initiated by a community leader, a local businessperson, or an educational, entertainment, or recreational sports community. It can be submitted as an unsolicited proposal to a city council, county supervisors, and airport commission, or a regional fairgrounds board.

In the case of out-of-date prison facilities and their healthcare systems, the impetus for large capital projects might stem from local rulings of United States Federal Judges directing the State to meet enhanced standards of cell habitability, inmate safety and health care.

The use of a P3 project can help communities assess the accurate, long-term costs to the community of such an endeavor. The use of private investment can measure its economic viability. In other words, a shiny new project idea not be a viable public expenditure.

Instead, far less glamorous projects — such as youth softball parks, safe highways and emergency services centers — may benefit from a P3's highly-focused, local attention.

Every elected public body is expected to be community-oriented, environmentally sensitive, and budget conscious. However, the citizens are the root of all political power and influence. In essence, a P3 is a way to crowd-source a project. A grass roots effort can create a project with long term benefits for the entire community.

The World Bank sees such community-rooted projects as a worldwide opportunity. They have recently drafted "A Guide to Community Engagement for Public-Private Partnerships" (Draft - June 2019). As stated in this draft guidance, the benefits of early and sustained community involvement in the planning process for such innovative projects yields these benefits:

- deliver services valued by the community;
- keep tariffs and other user charges to an affordable and fair level;
- involve communities in solutions to any problems that emerge;
- attain and sustain support from communities,

- manage expectations so they are realistic and achievable,
- manage risks and mitigate the potential for disagreements;
- reduce the prospect of delay and disruption.
- more sustainable;
- more resilient to change;
- more efficient and
- more likely to attract good private partners and affordable financing.

These principles obviously apply to any P3 project in the United States.

1.06   Traditional Delivery Approach

In order to determine if a P3 Project is appropriate, it must be thoughtfully compared with other project delivery alternatives. Federal, state, and local agencies employ a variety of methods for project development and execution. A "Project Delivery System" is an overall pathway for project conception, planning, evaluation, design, financing, construction, and start-up. The P3 project delivery option is therefore only one of many choices available for designing, financing and executing public projects.

Obviously, public entities vary widely in their resources and capabilities. The best delivery approach provides quality services to the public taking into account agency resources that are available. A construction project requires cash, financing, planning, supervision, risk management, design and construction, administration, operation, and maintenance. When these resources are not available in the public agency, a P3 delivery approach can often accomplish the project in a creative and highly efficient manner.

It is therefore useful to contrast P3 with two established delivery systems:

[A] Design-Bid-Build

The traditional Design Bid Build approach starts with engaging an internal agency design team or private design firm (A/E) and then, much later, selecting a general contractor (prime contractor) through competitive bidding. In this well-traveled approach, an independent architect or engineer consults from concept through defining the owner's program, and into schematic and final design, including the preparation of "Construction Documents." In some circumstances, the construction community is allowed to provide input on the design, but typically, this is rare.

The owner then advertises for interested general contractors and issues a fixed set of plans and specifications. The owner solicits multiple bidders, answers a few questions during the bidding period, then awards the work to the lowest responsible, responsive bidding contractor, and construction thereafter begins. Issuing a request for bids on a quality set of complete plans and specifications with substantially complete permitting may also result in the lowest bid price from the construction contractors

This approach gives the owner absolute control and legal responsibility for the design because the Designer is either employed or hired directly by the owner. The procurement does not proceed until the owner is satisfied with the design.

A variation of this multi-party process is Integrated Project Delivery (IPD). In that process, the design firms, the general contractor and major subcontractors collaborate with the owner earlier in the process. The construction team members share their knowledge about constructability, cost trends and innovative products and materials with the owner, A/E firm and Construction Manager.

In IPD, the owner and project participants collectively share in the overruns or underruns of budgets. This is true, regardless of poor estimates or individual fault of the participants. The IPD does not attempt to share the long term life cycle costs of the facility or optimize the energy or maintenance costs of the project.

[B] Design-Build

The Design-Build method involves the selection of a single private entity for design and construction services. Thus, a single firm is largely responsible for all aspects of a project. Typically, a public entity will hire a consulting architect or engineering (A/E) firm to conduct early studies and develop a Front End Engineering Design (FEED). Then, a Design-Build contractor is selected to provide the final design and construction of the project.

A large general contractor is typically the lead entity and employs architects or engineers (directly or in partnership) for the design and contract administration phase. The construction company then performs the construction phase of the project.

A variant of this contracting method is the long-established "EPC" methodology – where engineering, procurement and construction management is performed by a single company. These EPC contracts are often enormous and risky megaprojects performed by such industry giants as Bechtel and Fluor (where the Author served as Corporate Counsel) and often on a reimbursable cost-plus fee basis.

In rare instances, an A/E firm may act as the leader of a Design-Build team, providing the overall management and design services and retaining a contractor for the construction phase. A/E firms are not typically the lead firm as they generally lack proper licensing for contracting and the smaller firms have difficulty supplying an adequate balance sheet, bond capacity or insurance limits.

An exception is AECOM, a global engineering firm whose purchase of Tishman Construction Corp., Hunt Construction Group and Shimmick Construction corporation for an aggregate of more than $500 million, allow it to conduct large Design-Build projects throughout the United States and beyond.

In all cases, the Design-Build team will be contractually responsible for all aspects of the project, including the design, construction, procurement and project warrantees.

The Design-Build methodology can provide great savings in cost and time because the entire project is managed and constructed by a single entity, thereby eliminating the difficulties of an owner dealing with multiple fragmented design and construction parties.

However, it does not incorporate future project costs into its business model. Further, companies like Fluor and AECOM have indicated a strong interest in exiting the fixed price market on large and complex construction projects, where design and permit disputes with owners can radically increase costs, create long delays or even bring a project to a halt.

1.07 P3 Project Delivery

P3 is really a family of delivery methods. The common theme is the involvement of private parties taking on traditional public roles such as project conception, finance, design, startup, operations and maintenance.

As of this writing, P3 projects are largely initiated by a governmental entity issuing a request for a competitive proposal after the project concept has been largely agreed upon. At that point, there are a limited range of conceptual and design options for the project.

There are distinct benefits of considering alternative proposals, or even completely unsolicited proposals, where the offeror has the core concept, performs preliminary design and secures a path to financing prior to submission to the public agency.

A private partner may also be given responsibility for many project delivery elements such as environmental studies, land acquisition, procuring permits, revenue projections, and fare collection. These later tasks come with substantial risks to the Concessionaire, as the public agency generally has stronger tools, such as political leverage, local knowledge, and a police force (e.g. fare evasion) to accomplish these inter-governmental aspects of a project.

The typical P3 Model envisions the Concessionaire designing, building, financing and operating a facility with a long-term contract with the public entity. Availability payments are tied to the Concessionaire's performance, including such issues as facility availability, operating hours, building temperature, humidity and noise levels, maintenance frequency, cleanliness and safety. However, there are many other types of P3 or similar delivery systems that may not include comprehensive project finance or a complex formula for availability payments.

These are a few examples:

[A] Design-Build Operate

The Design-Build Operate (DBO) approach combines Design-Build with an operations and maintenance contract. The public partner pays for design and construction as it is completed and a fixed fee for the O & M services thereafter.

DBO requires a single point of accountability from design through operation. The public partner retains ownership of the underlying assets, the operating revenue risk or surplus operating revenue, but passes off the need to train staff to operate the infrastructure and may be able to reduce the influence of politics from the facility's capital improvement program.

Allocating life-cycle responsibility for a project to a Design-Builder avoids several criticisms of the Design-Build method. Many of the decisions that impact life-cycle costs are made in the initial construction investments. Operational responsibility gives the private partner incentive to plan for economical operations and maintenance over the entire operations period.

At the time a Design-Build Operate project is awarded, the public partner knows the cost of providing the infrastructure services to the public for the duration of the contract.

The facility capabilities, quality, and scope of services defined by the procurement contract must be carefully drafted because the private partner is only obligated to provide those services at the specified quality for the agreed period of contract operations.

An example of a Design-Build Operate project is the Seattle Public Utilities Cedar Treatment Facility, which provides 70% of Seattle's drinking water and was completed in 2004.[41] Seattle Public Utilities awarded CH2M Hill a contract to design, permit, build, and operate for up to twenty-five years.[42] The Design-Build contractor assumed the technological risk of designing and building the largest ultraviolet light treatment plant in the United States.[43]

[B] Design-Build Operate Transfer

A Design-Build Operate Transfer (DBOT) occurs when a private entity builds a complete project on allocated land with the understanding

---

[41] The National Council for Public-Private Partnerships, "CH2M Hill Seattle Cedar Water Treatment Facility."

[42] *Id.*

[43] *Id.*

that the government will make long-term lease payments for the use of a successfully completed project.

Should the private entity fail to deliver and operate a facility that meets the specific performance standards mandated by the government, the government is under no contractual obligation to make payments to the private entity towards operations fees or the capital components of the facility. One option is to have the private party operate the facility and give the government the right to purchase the facility at the end of the lease term. Aspects of this approach may be characterized as *privatization* or *outsourcing* by project opponents.

Private firms engaged in wastewater treatment that have design, construction management, and plant operations expertise have long actively pursued DBOT projects. They have more experience with permitting, federal regulations, high tech patented processes, facility design, construction, mass purchasing, and daily operations than most public facility owners.

By applying industry expertise, worldwide buying power, access to global capital, and the diversity and quality of the staffs of these large enterprises, the public entity can achieve large cost savings. The public reaps the benefits of the decreased costs and avoids large capital expenditures.

This is extremely useful to local public entities that are either strapped for cash or lack bond financial capacity, or where the public does not approve outright funding for key facilities. The government commitment is to make fixed lease payments. The expected variations in electricity, natural gas, or other facility resources may be reimbursable costs passed through to the government or hedged through long term supply contracts.

Some local agencies and labor unions see DBOT arrangements as passing too much managerial authority and decision-making responsibility to a private entity. Thoughtlessly crafted agreements may bestow too much power over essential public services, in contravention of the public trust. Further, public unions are not pleased to see public jobs converted to private enterprise employment without comparable public sector retirement or fringe benefits.

However, the economies of scale can make DBOT a popular approach for smaller public agencies with limited technical or financial resources that would otherwise be unable to finance vital services for their communities.

An example of the "own" variant of P3s is the Heights Student Housing at Montclair State University in New Jersey. The project was developed pursuant to the public private partnership provisions in the New Jersey Economic Stimulus Act of 2009.[44] The housing contains 1,978 beds, common areas and a food court. The private Developer that constructed the facility will own, operate, manage, maintain (and profit from) the project for approximately 40 years.[45]

[C] Lease Leaseback

In Lease Leaseback arrangements, the private partner is granted a long-term lease of public property, which the private partner develops. The private partner then leases the improved property back to the public partner, effectively allowing the public partner to buy it back with the improvements through installment payments.

The George Duekmejian Courthouse Building in Long Beach, California, was built on property owned by the state. It is often called a P3, but it is more properly viewed as a lease-leaseback project.[46] The private funding approach was selected after a state bond measure for the project failed to garner support in the legislature.[47]

The Long Beach Courthouse property will revert to the state in 35 years.[48] But if the state defaults on its obligations, the private Developer may evict the state and operate the project for commercial use until expiration of the lease.[49]

---

[44] "New Jersey Economic Stimulus Act of 2009," NJ STAT. ANN. 52:27D-489a.

[45] Ronda Kaysen, "Public College, Private Dorm," The New York Times (Jan. 24, 2012).

[46] Enabling legislation is Government Code §§ 70371.5 and 70391.

[47] William G. Reinhardt, "$492 Million Long Beach Courthouse P3 Opens the Door for Social Infrastructure," Public Works Financing, 1 (Dec. 2010).

[48] Seth Eaton and William D. Locher, "Give PPPs a Chance," 26, Los Angeles Lawyer (Jan. 2009)

[49] Reinhardt, 2 (2010).

[D] Bond Financing for Private Transport

In the past, Industrial Revenue Bonds were a major source of funds for private development that had a positive economic impact. Shopping malls, car dealerships and other sales and use tax generating businesses benefited from low, public interest rates.

In recent years, project financing programs have been expanded to assist specific private projects, such as the LA – Las Vegas Bullet Train, a project sponsored by an affiliate of Virgin Trains USA.

On October 23, 2019, the Board of Directors of the California Infrastructure and Economic Development Bank (IBank), authorized a $3.2 billion tax-exempt, fixed-rate revenue bond issuance to help DesertXpress Enterprises LLC, build a high-speed train from Victorville, California, to Las Vegas, Nevada. As stated in the official IBank Press Release, "The high-speed rail will allow passengers to travel from Southern California to Las Vegas. More than 130 miles of the rail line will be within California and is projecting to remove an estimated 4.5 million car trips annually, which could eliminate 645 million pounds of carbon emission from the I-15 corridor. The project is expected to create more than 15,750 construction jobs as well as employ more than 400 people once the rail system is operational."[50]

This project seeks to provide swift transit between Las Vegas and Los Angeles and promote regional tourism to both international entertainment capitals.

1.08   Success Factors in P3 Projects

[A] Owner Expectations

The public entity's primary concerns in developing infrastructure are primarily governance, public safety, utility, long-term durability, and efficient use of the taxpayers' money. Contracts must be structured to

---

[50] Kim Slowey, "California approves $3.2B bond for Virgin's $4.8B bullet train to Las Vegas" available at https://www.constructiondive.com/news/california-approves-3b-bond-for-virgins-45b-bullet-train-to-las-vegas/566575/

balance the public owner's oversight responsibilities with the latitude of the Concessionaire to effectively meet the project's goals without conflicting direction or undue interference. This is necessary to ensure that the project meets both the needs of the public and investors in a financially efficient manner.

During the early planning stages of a project, the key goals and objectives are identified and prioritized.

The complementary goals of speed of construction, ease of operation, inspiring design, technical innovation, national expertise, local content, proven technology, and cost efficiency can rarely be reached simultaneously. Project priorities must be made at the highest levels of the client organization and will largely determine the success of the project.

P3s have been used to finance, build, operate, and/or maintain bridges, highways, rail lines, water and wastewater plants, schoolhouses, courthouses, and government offices. These facilities are built with proven technologies and with criteria for success that can be easily established and measured.

The first concern in analyzing risk is whether the P3 Project at hand is legally authorized by state or federal legislation. Thirty-six states? authorize P3 Projects of some variety, either horizontal projects (such as highways and bridges), vertical projects (such as courthouses, schools and hospitals), or both.

A detailed analysis of these state statutes is regularly updated by the Federal Highway Administration and the August 16, 2018 edition (most recent) is reproduced in Appendix B.

A map of these jurisdictions is found at the FHWA Innovative Project Development (IPD) website.[51]

A complex project may be a candidate for a P3 solely because of a need for financing. The need for substantially larger investments in public projects has moved legislatures to supplement the traditional Design Bid Build model through P3-enabling legislation. However, if the public owner is only interested in the financing and is unwilling or

---

[51] "States and Territories with Enabling Statutes for P3s as of August 2018, available at https://www.fhwa.dot.gov/ipd/p3/legislation/

unable to relinquish substantial design and operational authority to the Concessionaire, the project will likely fail.

Operation and maintenance of facilities can be expensive and have unpredictable costs. Using a P3 for operations and maintenance can create predictable public entity payments or no payments if tied to a revenue source, like tolls. However, few Concessionaires wish to take the fare box risk, as it is based upon estimates of growth and economics that may prove wrong.

The owner should have realistic expectations with respect to its level of influence over the design and operations of a project. The price of a P3 has the potential to be lower in part because the Concessionaire is granted the authority to exercise its discretion to exercise cost-saving and schedule opportunities while satisfying the contract requirements.

The owner gives up subjective preferences in the design process and certainly in the construction process. Even in design bid build projects with substantial portions of the design performed by the public entity's in-house staff, changes in the design or construction operations cost money and time.

The owner may pay for changes in order to make subjective design choices, but as the project proceeds, the owner has less and less influence over the outcome and making changes becomes progressively more expensive. From a contractor's perspective, the owner should make their design choices and set operational standards prior to the award of the P3 contract.

When the government defers to the P3 Team, the Concessionaire has the freedom to make appropriate cost-saving choices in a number of areas:

[1] Construction Costs

Project costs may be lower because of the working relationship between Designers and constructors established from the beginning of the project. This may lead to the incorporation of more economical design features and the application of cost-saving construction methods. However, it is important to understand that P3 contracts are like any other agreement; if one party breaches, there will be claims and disputes, but on a more limited basis.

[2] Team Atmosphere

Projects may proceed more efficiently because Designers and constructors are members of the same "team." The interface between Designer and constructor, which is often adversarial within Design-Bid-Build environments, may become more open and foster a cooperative exchange of ideas to produce a profitable project.

Owners frequently can maintain non-adversarial roles in P3 projects, particularly when they are satisfied with their original design specifications and allow the P3 Concessionaire and its Design-Build contractor to creatively accomplish the project within those parameters.

[3] Efficiency

Construction efficiency may be improved because design efficiencies can be woven throughout the construction process. Additionally, the Designer, as a member of the Design-Build team, can participate directly in resolving design issues that surface during construction.

Operational inefficiencies can be identified during the design process. Over the duration of operations, even small improvements in daily operations can yield substantial savings.

[4] Critical Flaw Analysis

The P3 team has a greater chance of seeing critical flaws early in the design stage, at which point they can still be avoided or mitigated. These flaws comprise a broad array of design, construction, and operational risks that a joint team is better prepared to address than a Designer alone. A third-party Designer's ideas may become cast in stone (or concrete) early in the project. The Concessionaire and Design-Builder can be more innovative and balance practicality with concept or theory. Again, focusing upon operational efficiency can create considerable savings over time. And the Concessionaire does not want to design or build projects with serious defects, as they are costly to maintain and can pose catastrophic risks of failure.

[5] Rapid Response on Design Issues

A P3 team can react fast and with clarity when design flaws are noted or ambiguities arise. In the traditional Design Bid Construction environment, the A/E's response to design flaws or ambiguities is often defensive and hostile. The P3 team must react immediately since it owns the problem and must therefore correct it immediately.

P3 also supports fast-track procedures which allow certain elements of construction to progress concurrently with the design process. This method allows work on one element of a project to proceed prior to the design for the structure being finalized. Fast- track procedures can overlap and compress the design and construction phases. Thus, the total time from conception to completion is greatly reduced.

For example, the foundation or structural steel work may be released for bids prior to the completion of the building design or before bids are solicited on the electrical, plumbing, or heating, ventilating and air conditioning (HVAC) work.

[B] Financing

Many in government see P3 as principally offering a wide range of financing options. By pushing payment into the future either through toll concessions or availability payments, government agencies take advantage of private equity to accomplish more than could be funded from the government's current budgets.

In the view of many Concessionaires, the ideal P3 project would not require the allocation of any government resources beyond the underlying land and would result in a profitable return of capital and those public resources at the end of the operations contract.

In the same way the public partner seeks to divest itself of project risk, the Concessionaire will not accept all of the project and financial risk. They are generally not interested in taking any risk that is largely or completely out of their control, such as the zoning, permitting or right-of-way risk.

[C] Quality of Design, Construction, and O & M

P3 contracts with operational components should focus the Concessionaire on measurable performance criteria and minimize the influence or disruption of the political winds.[52] The financial incentives for the Concessionaire to perform quality work can be substantial and come with reciprocal disincentives for failure to achieve benchmark operational criteria.

The standards for measuring the quality of services provided must be objective. These are service standards measurable with contractual metrics that are strongly correlated with the quality of the contractor's efforts.[53]

Transportation projects and water projects may be particularly well suited for P3s because of the ability to define such performance metrics, such as vehicle counts, passengers, treatment levels and volumetric throughputs of treatment facilities.

In contrast, P3 projects to supply teaching at schools or healthcare at hospitals poses more complex questions of measuring contract performance. Teaching quality is difficult to quantify, so objective measurements of inputs, like teacher-to-student ratio, may not correlate strongly to educational outcomes. Furthermore, even the criteria by which teaching results or health objectives are met can be controversial and can change over the course of time.

---

[52] *But see* Jim Steinberg, "American Water is out as operator for Rialto", San Jose Mercury News (July 10, 2012), (operations subcontractor removed under political pressure).

[53] Eduardo Engel, et. Al, "Public-Private Partnerships: When and How," §2.1, Department of Economics, Yale University, Department of Industrial Engineering, University of Chile, Discussion of characteristics of contractible services in P3 contracts.

[D] Allocation of Risks

A great advantage of a P3 contract is the ability to fine tune risk allocation.

The parties can allocate risk among them, ranging from design review to governmental approvals to accidents and injuries that may occur during the course of project use. This is true for the construction process as well. Although P3s are sometimes described as a "no claims" contracting method by which all risks are transferred to the Concessionaire, that approach is not the most efficient way to implement P3s. It is best to allocate that exposure to the party best able to control the risk.[54]

As Elyse Maltin writes in Harvard Business Review:

> "Received wisdom in P3 management is that ironclad contracts and tougher enforcement of them improves chances of success. But over the last three years, we conducted research interviews with 72 leaders from organizations that design, build, finance, provide legal advice, manage projects and advise North American P3 projects. Numerous interviewees told us that focusing on contract terms often set partners to act more like adversaries than allies. "Public clients prefer building iron-clad, oppressive contracts that are extremely one-sided and which start the relationship off on the wrong foot," said a leader of a semi-governmental Canadian agency. (HBR, January 8, 2019)

Changes in the labor market, schedule risks and construction cost overruns are examples of risks frequently assumed by Design-Builders. Such cost increases are typically built into the project contingency.

Transferring the public entity's entire development risk to a downstream party who does not have control over the risk in question

---

[54] Hartman, F. T., Snelgrove, P. and Ashrafi, R. "Appropriate Risk Allocation in Lump-Sum Contracts –Who Should Take the Risk?" Cost Engineering. Vol.40, No.7, pp.21-26 (1998).

(say permits or pre-existing environmental pollution) is similar to buying insurance.[55] It will be expensive to do so. Or, more typically, it will result in fewer or no bidders on a project. There is a definite trend of major contractors declining to bid on major Design-Build or P3 projects if the contractual risk is perceived to be too great.

During the bidding of the $1.3 Billion Gerald Desmond Bridge in Long Beach, California, one major contender declined to bid due to the public entity insisting on a broad environmental indemnity. (I was later selected as the Project Neutral for the Project, after the Design-Build project was awarded to another joint venture.)

During the summer of 2019, executives from both Granite Construction and Fluor called out P3 arrangements for having large negative impacts on their profitability.

Granite CEO James Roberts similarly told investors in August 2019 that the P3 process is no longer viable for his company, and that the firm's heavy civil division will no longer pursue megaprojects, though it had prior to that been active in transportation and infrastructure work ranging from aviation and roads to rail and mass transit.

One of the biggest problems with these arrangements, he said, is that they involve fixed-price agreements that lock contractors into a set fee and timetable. As things change on these jobs, additional costs are often incurred, leading to disputes between owner and contractor about who will pay for them.

Last fall, after taking a $100 million write-down on its P3 business, the company announced that it would no longer pursue major Design-Build transportation public-private partnerships in which it held an equity stake. Skanska also has said it will limit the type of P3s it takes on. (Construction Dive, October 25, 2019.)

The most specific expression of concern about bidding these projects came from Fluor. After substantial losses in the past two years, Fluor will avoid large, fixed-priced contracts with open-ended risks.

---

[55] Hartman, Francis T., "The Ten Commandments of Better Contracting: A Practical Guide to Adding Value to an Enterprise Through More Effective Smart Contracting," 210, ASCE Publications (2003).

CEO and Director Carlos Hernandez stated,

> "We have already enacted changes in our bid/no bid process so that our future backlog will be comprised of high-quality projects with a contract structure and execution approach that will generate improved risk-adjusted margins..."

To that end, Fluor will only bid on Infrastructure and Government projects that meet these following criteria:

- Infrastructure — Fluor will narrow its efforts to North America and extend its presence in states in which it has established track record and strong DOT relationships, including Texas, Arizona, California, Virginia and North Carolina.
- Government — Fluor will no longer pursue lump-sum projects unless there is an "appropriate allocation of risk between client and contractor."

Where the Concessionaire and Design-Builder are willing to insure any and all of the risks the agency wishes to allocate, it will adjust its pricing and availability charges upwards. The adjustment will typically assess the probability of the risk, the severity of the risk and the administrative and litigation costs of that risk. It will also include the costs of insuring the risk, if the risk is insurable. The P3 will then calculate the profit and overhead associated with assuming that risk. The public owner must appreciate that they will pay for any transfer of risk and that not all public agency risks are easily or cheaply transferable.

In some cases, the P3 proposer will ask for relief during the Request for Quotation (RFQ) process. If they do not get a reasonable amount of relief, especially for potentially catastrophic risks, they will simply decide to walk away from the project. That reduces the number of bidders who will then increase their prices or increase the pressure on the public entity to strike a deal with the selected P3 Concessionaire, as there may be fewer, or no proposers, waiting in line to sign a contract. So, reasonable contracts are key to the viability of P3 Projects.

If the public owner is better situated to undertake certain risks, it will be more efficient and cost effective for that owner to retain or assume those risks. An owner who selected the P3 format believing it is a means to "no claims" construction may find when it receives bids that it cannot fund the availability payments for a project in which it retains no environmental or permits responsibility or risk. Where the Concessionaire's profit opportunity has been substantially clawed back through legal language, the bidders will not be interested.

The responsibility for risk on a project should be managed by the party best able to manage that risk. Since a P3 contract can be tailored to a specific project risk matrix, it may be the best way to allocate those risks.

A contract with one-sided conditions that are potentially fatal to the Concessionaire, like obtaining complex permits from third parties, will result in far higher costs. Those costs are then passed on to the public through an increased bid amount, the claims process, poor performance during the operation and maintenance period, or other unexpected results.

The public owner is far better situated than a Concessionaire to retain risks like necessary permits with long lead times. For example, delays in permitting by a federal agency subject to the National Environmental Policy Act (NEPA) or state legislation and regulations that will require exhaustive environmental studies and public comment on the proposed project is likely a risk that cannot be reasonably insured or assumed by a contractor.[56]

That risk can be nearly cost-free for the owner. Therefore, the public owner typically has far greater leverage with sister agencies. And they may defray such risks by simply delaying the award of a P3 project until the operative permits are secured and in place.

It may also be prudent for the owner to retain the risk of catastrophic damages, particularly the loss of use, on large infrastructure projects. For example, a state agency may choose to retain the risks of earthquake,

---

[56] For example, the California Environmental Quality Act (CEQA) (Public Resources Code §§ 21000 *et seq.*) is the California analog to NEPA. CEQA requires government projects and government-approved projects to be planned to avoid significant adverse environmental effects.

flooding or terrorism that could result in a severe service interruption instead of paying increased bid prices for contractors to carry expensive insurance for such unpredictable risks.

The owner's risk management strategy should begin with identifying risks, valuing each risk and the probability of its occurrence, determining how to best allocate risks, and finally evaluating their impacts.[57] A fair allocation of risk on a specific project is a vital step towards project viability and success.

1.09   Who is the client?

This question can be the Achilles heel of a P3 Project. A misunderstanding as to who the critical stakeholders really are can be disruptive to the project, as well as result in grave financial hardships to all the parties. The real stakeholders may be a powerful group of internal staff who oppose the project. But, a more subtle concern are those third party agencies and institutions who have the power to impose further design criteria or withhold permits without the imposition of onerous conditions.

I was Project Counsel for the Design-Build JV's on three such projects:

Presidio Parkway Project (CalTrans)

The Presidio Parkway Project is a $1.3 billion P3 roadway and bridge project in San Francisco. The public agency contracting party was the California Department of Transportation (CalTrans). However, the project right-of-way goes through The Presidio, a National Park administered by the San Francisco-based Presidio Trust. Although the Trust had signed many agreements to enable CalTrans to upgrade of 1937 era

---

[57] For a detailed and instructive example of risk management analysis for a P3 bridge procurement, see Greater Vancouver Transportation Authority, Golden Ears Bridge Reference Case Report, Appendix K (2005), available at: www. translink.ca.

bridges, cloverleafs, and roadways, they blocked the Concessionaire and Joint Venture's efforts to proceed on the basis of a "dig permit."

Ostensibly, the Presidio's Dig Permit was for the purpose of assuring the contractors were not digging into locations of suspected military hazardous waste or old ordinance. However, the permits became a funding mechanism for project enhancements that benefited the Presidio Trust, even though they were not part of the original scope of the Concessionaire's scope or work.

CalTrans' position was the P3 agreement made permits the responsibility of the Concessionaire. And that the Concessionaire did not have the right to sue the Presidio Trust for imposing unreasonable permit conditions. The resulting costs and delays resulted in a formal claim and the filing of San Francisco Superior Court litigation against CalTrans for over $100 million in claims.

Oakland Connector Project (BART)

The Oakland Connector is a $500 million light rail Design-Build-operate project. The owner was the Bay Area Rapid Transit System (BART). The DBO contract included design, construction and twenty years of operation of a people mover connecting BART's Coliseum Station and the Oakland International Airport.

The 3.1 mile rail line passed over CalTrans freeways at two locations. Although BART was the project owner, CalTrans understandably insisted on substantial design scrutiny over the trusses used over the freeway crossings. The joint venture's design proposal was based upon the success of its subcontractor, with highly successful advanced truss designs in Europe. However, those designs were not incorporated into any U.S. design codes.

As a result, CalTrans required new design standards to be developed and approved for the highway crossings. Although the highway crossings admittedly presented special risks, BART desired rail and track consistency. It wanted an equally resilient and durable design for the rest of the trackway. So, CalTrans, a third-party to the contract, in reality exercised design approval over the entire 3.1 miles of elevated trackway for the project. The subcontractor made a large claim for the change.

Mid-Cities Exposition Project

The Mid-Cities Exposition ("Expo") light rail project extends from LA Live to Culver City. Its Design-Build contract, executed by a Fluor/Flatiron/Parsons Joint Venture (FFP), required the installation of 8.6 miles of dual tracks, new signalization at multiple locations and the relocation of hundreds of connections for gas, electric and communications utilities.

The Design-Builder was required to negotiate rights of way, relocation permissions and permits with dozens of third-party cities and public utilities. Its scope included coordinating utility relocation with investor-owned utilities. Finally, the railway, traction and control-system design needed the approval of LA Metro, the transit entity that would eventually operate the system.

In every case, the involved third parties had authority over design approval and permitting conditions, without their incurring any obligation to pay for work beyond the scope of the original DB contract.

In these type of situations, third parties such as permitting agencies, utilities and cities can impose substantial scope changes and quantity increases upon the Concessionaire or Design-Builder, without any risk of financial responsibility or consequence.

These projects were quite different from my experience as Project Counsel for building the John Wayne Airport in Santa Ana, California. In that instance, the County of Orange (OC) was the Airport's owner. As a major county agency, the Airport had substantial relationships with the OC Board of Supervisors, its sister agencies, the adjacent cities, Caltrans, the FAA, and the various water and air quality regulators. Generally, those aspects of the project went extremely well due to those long-term relationships. A private Concessionaire would likely not have found those regulatory tasks nearly as timely or as smooth.

One potential solution to this ongoing problem is having the involved third party agencies delegate their authority for design approval, utility relocation and permit conditions to the lead agency. This would be similar to the designation of a lead agency for NEPA or similar approvals. In many cases, legal or technical restrictions may limit that type of delegation.

Another mechanism might be a project teaming agreement between the owner and the third party agencies where those agencies may require items beyond the scope of the P3 project, but only if they pay for them. This would mean the third parties essentially "buy in" to the project scope document and technical requirements.

In any case, it is vitally important for the Concessionaire to ascertain who will be the actual client(s). And who will pay for major elements of required extra work. If that is not clear, then a substantial contingency or no-bid decision may be appropriate.

1.10 Enabling Legislation

[A] P3-Specific Enabling Legislation

Implementing a P3 generally relies upon explicit enabling legislation because typical state procurement statutes are generally inconsistent with P3 procurement.

Public Project enabling legislation classically requires "all purchases and contracts for supplies and services" to be advertised and competitively bid.[58] As applied to construction contracts, the legislation governing competitive bidding evolved to separate contracts for design services and low bid contracts for construction.[59] The procurement of construction services impliedly required approved plans and specifications before competitively bidding.[60] Although not intended to prevent P3 projects, statutes requiring approved plans and specifications prior to award of a construction contract typically restricted the consideration of P3 project delivery. But, it's now trending the other way. At present count, 38 states and one U.S. territory have enacted some form of P3 legislation.[61]

While federal construction contracts were classically awarded to the lowest responsive bidder, the Federal Brooks Act has long mandated selection of design professionals on the basis of superior qualifications, not solely price.[62] Similarly, many states have passed, so called "Mini-Brooks" acts.[63] A public entity's enabling legislation implied a request for bids could not combine design and construction services, because the criteria for award differed – design services awarded upon qualifications and construction contracts let to the low, responsible and responsive bidder.

The implementation of statutes permitting award of Design-Build projects based on best value proposals began to clear the path for P3 legislation.

A Best Value assessment of P3 proposals is especially appropriate because the variation of submittals in response to a P3 request (for proposals with performance specifications) can be so varied that a public entity needs to weigh the alternatives.

---

[58] 2 Stat. 535, 10 Cong. Ch 28 (1809).

[59] 28 Stat. 911, Act of March 2, 1895 (Authorizing Secretary of the Treasury to competitively bid architectural services).

[60] 23 U.S.C § 112(b), 72 Stat. 895 (1958) (Until amendments in 1998 permitting Design-Build).

[61] "State P3 Legislation" available at https://www.fhwa.dot.gov/ipd/p3/legislation/.

[62] Public Law 95-582, 40 U.S.C. §§541 *et seq.* (1972).

[63] 23 U.S.C § 112(b).; Public Law 92-582, 40 U.S.C. 541 et seq. (1972).; Public Law 92-582, 40 U.S.C. 541 et seq. (1972).

As one commentator wryly observed, "Thou Shalt Not Blindly Pick the Contractor who was Cheapest Because It may have Made the Biggest Mistake."[64]

Inconsistencies in legislation exist, even in states that have enabling legislation for P3 procurement. For example, a Developer who is primarily a financing entity is unlikely to hold a contractor's license or an engineering license. Thus, it may need to subcontract those services.

As the Best Value process is by its nature somewhat subjective, it is vital that the legislation and administration of the P3 process be vigilant to prevent any opportunities for fraud, corruption, undue influence or organizational conflict of interest. This can be accomplished by selecting a diverse, representative and respected selection committee.

[1] Constitutional Debt Limitations

In some states, the financing methods used in P3s may be incompatible with existing constitutional prohibitions or public debt legislation.[65] This is partially the result of constitutional debt limitations implemented as a reaction to ill-fated public investments in private companies in the early nineteenth century.[66] A public entity may be prohibited from allowing a contractor to borrow against the public entity's credit. It may violate statutes governing the approval of public debt. This may provide a sophisticated point of attack for the opposition to an otherwise favorable project.[67]

---

[64] Hartman, Francis T., The Ten Commandments of Better Contracting: A Practical Guide to Adding Value to an Enterprise Through More Effective Smart Contracting 133 (ASCE Publications 2003).

[65] See, e.g., FL. CONST. Art. 7, § 10 ("the State . . . shall [not] . . . lend or use its taxing power or credit to aid any corporation . . . .").

[66] See generally Clayton P. Gillette, Constitutional and Statutory Aspects of Municipal Debt Finance: Recent Developments, Practicing Law Institute, Tenth Annual Institute on Municipal Finance: Financing State and Local Governments in the 1990's, 377 PLI/REAL 9 (1991).

[67] See, e.g., Kitchell v. Franklin, 997 N.E.2d 1020 (Ind. 2013) (finding no grounds for challenge to RFP for proposals to replace an existing coal power plant with one powered by refuse-derived fuels).

Similarly, public investment in privately-owned facilities might be prohibited.[68] The Georgia Constitution prohibits joint ownership of the State "in or with any individual, company, association or corporation."[69] Other limitations include prohibitions on multi-year contracts that would obligate tax funds beyond the end of the fiscal year.[70]

As P3 legislation is enacted, it must be structured to avoid violating these constitutional debt limitations.[71] Investors should be reticent to invest in projects where these conflicts have not been resolved; an agreement is unenforceable if the acts to be performed would be illegal or would violate public policy. This is where capable bond and surety counsel earn their fees.

[2] Governmental Mandates

P3 contracts must also be sensitive to governmental mandates and ethical expectations. These include conflict of interest, local purchasing, local hiring, disadvantaged business enterprise (DBE), Disabled Veteran Enterprises (DVE), anti-discrimination rules, and open records compliance.

Any of these regulations can form the basis of litigation to prevent a P3 procurement. For example, traditional organizations (like public labor unions) may see a threat from the hiring of private employers by Concessionaires and challenge the project in court.[72] On the other hand, the construction trade unions are typically highly supportive of P3 projects as they may provide project private employment that might not otherwise be created.

---

[68] See *Montgomery Cnty. v. Virginia Dep't of Rail & Pub. Transp.*, 282 Va. 422, 719 S.E.2d 294 (2011).

[69] GA. CONST. Art. VII, § IV, ¶ VIII.

[70] See *Bauerband v. Jackson Cnty. Bd. of Comm'rs*, 278 Ga. 222 S.E.2d 444 (2004).

[71] See, *e.g., Kitchell v. Franklin* (Ind. 2013) (citing Ind. Code § 5-23-1-1 *et seq.*).

[72] See, *e.g., Prof'l Engineers v. Dep't of Transp.*, 15 Cal. 4th 543, 549-550 P.2d 473 (1997) (superceded by Proposition 35 in 2000).

However, outside contracting by public agencies is viewed favorably by the courts. In California, the legislature may not mandate that state employees be used for A/E assignments in every Design-Build project.[73]

Again, the use of highly capable public works, labor, environmental and bond counsel is critical to navigating the rocks and shoals of a large P3 project.

[B] Types of P3 Enabling Legislation

Enabling legislation for P3s tends to limit the types of eligible projects. A statute may allow P3 procurement by local, but not state government, allow or prohibit unsolicited proposals, set a maximum term, such as 50 years, allow specific project types, disfavor other project types (e.g. entertainment and sports arenas), allow exclusive concessions (remember the Charles River example), prohibit state highway projects, or, seeking the opposite, restrict P3 authority to only turnpike projects.[74] These limits are typically crafted by lobbyists.

In California, certain projects may be procured through a "competitive negotiation process."[75] However, a public agency cannot consider an unsolicited P3 proposal without seeking competitive proposals from other firms.[76] The California Infrastructure Financing Act authorizes local governments to pursue P3s for a range of "fee-producing infrastructure projects," excluding water projects.[77] Fee-producing infrastructure includes projects such as commuter and light rail systems, highways, bridges, tunnels, and energy production.

---

[73] *See Consulting Engineers & Land Surveyors of California v. California Dep't of Transp.*, 167 Cal. App. 4th 1457, 1462, 84 Cal. Rptr. 3d 900, 903 (2008) (The Constitution of the State of California unequivocally authorizes governmental entities to contract with qualified private entities for architectural and engineering services for all public works of improvement); Cal. Const. art. XXII, §1.

[74] CA GOVT § 5956, California Infrastructure Finance Act; VA ST §33.2-1808, Public-Private Transportation Act of 1995; MS ST § 65-43-3(3); AK ST. § 19.75.111; TX TRANSP § 371.103; CO ST § 43-3-202.5.

[75] CA GOVT § 5956.5

[76] CA GOVT § 5956.5; Cal. Sts. & High. Code § 143.

[77] CA GOVT §§ 5956-5956.10.

CalTrans and select regional transportation agencies are statutorily authorized to use one or more approaches for procuring P3 projects: 1) soliciting bid proposals, 2) prequalifying or "short listing" proposers before final evaluation of proposals, 3) final evaluation of proposals using either qualifications, best value, or a combination of the two, 4) negotiating with proposers, and 5) accepting unsolicited proposals while issuing requests for competing proposals.[78] Neither the Caltrans nor a regional transportation agency may award a contract to an unsolicited bidder without receiving at least one other responsible bid.

The highlights of the California Infrastructure Financing Act are as follows: (1) applies to limited types of infrastructure (*e.g.* no energy transmission); (2) a 35-year limit on term; (3) state financing is excluded; (4) there is no exemption from property taxes; (5) the prevailing wage requirement applies; and (5) private financing rates are generally higher due to tax effects.

[C] Federal Government Support

If there is one thing that Republicans and Democrats agree, it is the importance of infrastructure projects. Although the parties differ on their emphasis (Republicans favor highways and defense projects, Democrats, regional rail, public housing and mass transit), the funding of infrastructure has been a consistent theme for decades.

The parties have differed in their mutual embracement of the P3 approach. While Republicans favor private investment and operation of facilities, they disfavored subsidies of urban projects. Democrats have tended to view certain projects as privatization that may reduce public and unionized employment. Despite these differences, local finances have become so stretched, pension plans sufficiently jeopardized, the federal deficit so large, and roads and bridges so derelict that over the past twenty years, P3 has emerged as a viable option.

The federal government has also recognized its ability to assist P3 projects without raising taxes through loans and loan guarantees that in theory should not result in actual cash expenditures.

---

[78] Cal. Sts. & High. Code § 143.

In the Spring of 2014, Congress passed the Grow America Act, touting "a $302 billion, four-year transportation reauthorization proposal [that] provides increased and stable funding for our nation's highways, bridges, transit, and rail systems, ends the cycle of short-term manufactured funding crises and builds confidence in the public and private sector."[79]

On July 17, 2014, President Obama issued a Fact Sheet and a Presidential Memorandum regarding the use of public-private partnerships. [80] In recognition of the importance of revitalizing U.S. infrastructure, President Obama announced the Build America Investment Initiative, a government-wide initiative to increase investments in infrastructure and, specifically, to expand the P3 market.

The Presidential Memorandum announced that the Federal Government would encourage awareness and understanding of diverse opportunities for collaborative development, maintenance, upgrades, and financing of infrastructure. Additionally, an innovative transportation finance center was created at the Department of Transportation to serve as a central repository of expertise and resources for the various public and private infrastructure stakeholders. The Build America Transportation Investment Center at the Department of Transportation is designed as a one-stop shop "for state and local governments, public

---

[79] The White House Office of the Press Secretary, Fact Sheet: Building a 21st Century Infrastructure: Increasing Public and Private Collaboration with the Build America Investment Initiative (July 17, 2014), available at https://obamawhitehouse.archives.gov/the-press-office/2014/07/17/fact-sheet-building-21st-century-infrastructure-increasing-public-and-pr; The White House Office of the Press Secretary, Presidential Memorandum—Expanding Public-Private Collaboration on Infrastructure Development and Financing (July 17, 2014), available at http://www.whitehouse.gov/the-press-office/2014/07/17/presidential-memorandum-expanding-public-private-collaboration-infrastru

[80] Fact Sheet: Building a 21st Century Infrastructure (July 17, 2014), Presidential Memorandum—Expanding Public-Private Collaboration on Infrastructure Development and Financing (July 17, 2014), available at https://obamawhitehouse.archives.gov/the-press-office/2014/07/17/presidential-memorandum-expanding-public-private-collaboration-infrastru

and private Developers and investors seeking to utilize innovative financing strategies for transportation infrastructure projects."[81].

This Center helps to bridge gaps among both the public and private sectors in the development of mutually beneficial P3s.[82] President Obama described the federal government's role as that of "matchmaker" between private investors and the state and local governments that need funds to assist with infrastructure development. The DOT may develop a model enabling legislation for states to use P3 projects.

Former White House National Economic Council director Jeff Zients stated the Initiative aimed to "turbocharge private investment in our roads, rails, highways and bridges.[83]" Zients then stated, "A strong infrastructure is directly related to the strength of the United States in the global markets, but U.S. spending on surface-transportation infrastructure as a share of GDP has dropped about 50% in the last 50 years."[84]

In addition to the Initiative, the President's memorandum also created a new interagency working group chaired by then Treasury Secretary Jack Lew and DOT Secretary Anthony Foxx. With input from many federal agencies, the group focused on speeding up financing and completing major national projects, especially for projects involving multiple states. Water and energy infrastructure were also part of the scope of review for the task force. [85]

---

[81] The White House Office of the Press Secretary, Fact Sheet (2014), available at https://obamawhitehouse.archives.gov/the-press-office/2014/07/17/fact-sheet-building-21st-century-infrastructure-increasing-public-and-pr

[82] U.S. Dep't of Transportation, "Beyond Traffic 2045: Trends and Choices" available at https://www.transportation.gov/policy-initiatives/beyond-traffic-2045-final-report

[83] Tom Ichniowski, "Obama Seeks to Spark More Private Infrastructure Financing Publication" Engineering News-Record, July 7, 2014, available at https://www.enr.com/articles/7026-obama-seeks-to-spark-more-private-infrastructure-financing?v=preview

[84] *Id.*

[85] The White House Office of the Press Secretary, Presidential Memorandum (2014).

This working group analyzed how public-private collaborations could benefit the infrastructure sector.[86] It then issued recommendations as to how to most effectively promote awareness and understanding of innovative financing options for infrastructure.[87]

Although the Obama Administration neither allocated additional dollars to P3 projects nor created new enabling legislation, it did establish a strong priority to participate in innovative financing using P3 structures and formed a department to promote that program. Facing a huge lack in infrastructure spending, this program encourages and facilitates an increase in private sector financing in order to stretch federal dollars.

Despite who wins American elections, public infrastructure remains a pillar of the Federal Government's efforts to create jobs and improve the quality of life in US cities and towns.

---

[86] *Id.*

[87] *Id.*

CHAPTER 2

CONCEPTUAL PLANNING

2.01   Lead Agency

It is the responsibility of the lead, sponsoring agency to determine the viability of constructing a public infrastructure work using P3 concepts. The lead agency can select P3 financing only if so authorized by a legislative act.

In determining whether to use P3, the lead agency will compare the various costs associated with the traditional and the various P3 project delivery systems to ensure that the project is a suitable candidate for offloading risk to the private sector. It will identify project needs and goals, assess risk and fatal flaws, short and long-term costs and financing options, and balance priorities.

Studies completed in the planning stage can significantly improve the quality of proposals that are received during procurement. Concessionaires are particularly averse to the risks of scope creep (and leap) and aggressive permit conditions. They will add a steep financial premium for these contingencies.

A forecast of user demand is critical for evaluating needs and structuring the P3 contract. The forecast will define the size of the project, whether the facility should be designed with future expansion in mind, and total construction costs. It will also be relied upon by the future Concessionaire for operational purposes and planning of maintenance.

The Concessionaire may prepare the final project design and perhaps even revisit project assumptions, but the lead agency's obligations during conceptual planning are undiminished in P3 procurement.

At this point, parties should begin negotiating right-of-way, identifying utilities and easements, and performing site investigations. Such investigations in the development phase will allow for the preparation of a risk matrix. A risk matrix is followed by a risk analysis that will lead to appropriate risk allocation, value for money assessments, mitigation steps and updated cost and contingency estimates.

2.02   Governmental Stakeholders

Significant new public project construction inevitably impacts existing government agencies, programs and objectives. It will also require involvement of the existing regulatory structures maintained by other government agencies. For example, newly built highways may cross over existing highways, rail lines, and aqueducts. This may require temporary or permanent easements or permits over land owned by other entities.

The issues created by these interactions must be resolved by reinforcing the project vision with allied government entities impacted by the facility and by negotiating mitigation and terms for their fair treatment and full cooperation.

The early negotiation of comprehensive, realistic and binding cooperation and participation agreements is essential. These agreements may cover permanent or temporary land access, utility relocation, or other significant issues. They should emphasize that full cooperation is required from governmental stakeholders. The agreements should set forth each stakeholder's role in the project. If a stakeholder's assent and cooperation are crucial to the construction of the project, the terms under which that stakeholder can stop the project should be contractually established and fully disclosed. Obviously, if an agency has the power to critically impact a project by withdrawing its assent, it will be very difficult for the project to go forward.

The lead agency and stakeholders should agree on appropriate compensation to the stakeholders, technical standards, preliminary configurations, and a process for reviewing final designs. Also to be settled are a detailed process for utility relocation, scope and betterment limitations; dispute resolution, and whether the Developer has standing to enforce the agreement; and cost, indemnity, and insurance requirements. Agreements will ideally be executed and given to potential Concessionaires by the time the project is advertised.

Governmental stakeholders are sometimes brought together to make decisions in a joint advisory board. While this is an excellent tool during planning used to discuss and resolve concerns of multiple parties, it may not be ideal during the execution of a P3 contract. It is far better to have one lead agency that speaks for its sister and brother agencies.

The P3 contract is structured around granting the P3 Developer discretion to design, build, and operate the project within the standards set in the P3 contract. This enables the Developer to identify efficiencies and set its construction schedule. Governmental stakeholders need to set objective standards for the future P3 Developer; it is difficult for some stakeholders to comprehend that they have limited influence on the design process by the time the P3 Designer is in the midst of producing final designs and construction submittals.

After the contract has been awarded, third-party interference and delays that are contrary to the P3 contract may entitle the Concessionaire to additional compensation. The lead agency should manage the third party governmental stakeholders' expectations appropriately and employ in-house or outside contract administrators.

2.03   Community Stakeholders

Community organizations can have a strong voice in supporting or opposing P3 projects. Meeting with the community and identifying their concerns early in the development of a project concept is one of the critical tasks of the lead agency. These community organizations are varied and can include such varied groups as adjacent residents, Native American communities, military and cemetery historians, bicycle advocates, historic preservation groups, and labor locals.

Projects may be backed or attacked by many constituencies. This is part of the give-and-take of the political process. When the Developers or sponsors of a project feel sufficiently threatened by citizens expressing their views in a public forum, they may elect to bring a libel or slander suit—a tactic known as a Strategic Lawsuit Against Public Participation, or SLAPP. This is generally a very bad strategy. Courts may dismiss or stay SLAPP suits under Anti-SLAPP statutes as offending the constitutional rights of free speech, association and assembly.[88] And the press generally views such suits as defending a weak project.

In addition to challenging the adequacy of environmental impact reports, opponents may argue a project violates a provision of state or federal environmental law, such as endangered species, air and water quality, and other regulated areas.[89]

Project planners take these concerns seriously, engage the community, create formal outreach programs, embrace mitigation steps, and meet and confer with vocal opponents to negotiate or mediate environmental concerns.

2.04   Approving Jurisdictions

Federal and state statutes that regulate environmental issues have a major influence during the evolution of a P3 infrastructure project. Agencies with permit authority over projects may exercise "Go No- Go" authority. Thus, early engagement is essential to a successful P3 project.

Overturning an adverse agency decision is extremely difficult, as the courts often defer to the findings of specialized agencies and elected,

---

[88] Statements before a government body or official proceeding; or in connection with issue under consideration by government body; or in a place open to the public or public forum in connection with issue of public interest; or any other conduct in furtherance of petition/free speech in connection with issue of public interest, are protected. Cal. Civ. Proc. Code. § 425.16.

[89] *E.g.*, The California Endangered Species Act (CESA) (CA FISH & G §§ 2050, *et seq.*); The Safe Drinking Water Act (SDWA), 42 U.S.C.A. § 300f; The Clean Air Act (CAA), 42 U.S.C.A. § 7401, regulating all emissions into the air; and The Clean Water Act (CWA), 33 U.S.C.A. §1251-1387, which requires permits for all discharges into "the waters of the United States."

representative bodies. So the public owner and Concessionaire must make every attempt to meet the spirit and letter of the law. It is helpful for the project to develop attributes that "sell itself" to these agencies as a net positive environmental project. The public owner should push these approvals as far as possible before assigning the project to the Concessionaire. It will not get easier as the job progresses.

Under NEPA and similar state environmental policy statutes, public owners should generally complete their baseline environmental reviews and mitigation studies to achieve the required governmental approval before selecting the Concessionaire.

Even after the Concessionaire has been selected, certain technical permits might still be required for the project. If the Concessionaires are expected to obtain these permits, they may face non-cooperation from other stakeholders and regulatory agencies. Therefore, the public agency should manage the approval process in order to eliminate bureaucratic snafus or unrealistic demands from other agencies. Such demands may hold project permits hostage in a third party agency's effort to obtain other benefits from the project Developers.

2.05   Quality Assurance and Environmental Monitors

A public entity may feel like it has less control over a P3 project, including the design, construction operations, environmental compliance, and construction work, than it would over the same project were it structured as a Design-Bid-Build project.

The public entity can compensate for the perceived lack of control with independent design checkers, construction inspectors, and environmental monitors.

Independent third party inspectors can also be used to verify the Concessionaire's work product. Such inspectors can be granted the authority necessary to protect the public entities' interests, whether that requires rejecting design submittals or stopping work due to violation of procedures for environmental protection.

The public agency's outsourcing of these verifications has significant advantages. The consultants hired for verification are selected for their expertise in particular areas and offer a higher level of review of project components than could be provided by extremely busy, in-house staff. By outsourcing, agencies may also avoid the institutional bias that some public employees might still harbor against P3 projects.

Another advantage of the agency contracting for independent inspections is the ability to scale-up the numbers and specialties of the public entity's representatives. When those services are provided by contract, additional consultants can be sourced so that the public entity's ongoing operations do not become a bottleneck and impede the Developer's performance.

In order to guarantee that the public entity's quality assurance does not unreasonably interfere with the Concessionaire's execution of the work, the public entity must be held accountable for its decisions and for those of its authorized representatives.

A process for public entity to review and object to choices made by the Concessionaire must be set forth in the contract, including timelines for resolving comments and a prompt dispute resolution method. A Project Neutral or DRB can assist in this phase.

The public entity, either directly or through consultants retained for the purpose, must comply with the contractual timelines for reviewing the Concessionaire's work. The public entity's comments, once made, should be binding and not become a moving target.

If the public entity desires a change, they should dictate a revised approach with an agreement to pay for the change. Alternatively, the agency can express its concerns with the design approach as long as they are preferential and not a matter of life safety. They must also allow the Developer to proceed with the work with the understanding that it is proceeding at its own risk and that the party prevailing at dispute resolution of the issue will be entitled to compensation. And the Concessionaire is responsible for delivering a great project.

Another mechanism to manage compliance includes "noncompliance points," which result in a financial penalty to the Concessionaire. This is particularly used during the operations and maintenance period of a P3. Noncompliance points can be structured in various ways. One specific example is to deduct points for not fixing reported potholes within a specified period of time. Similar reductions can be made for not meeting water quality standards or throughput rates during operation of a water treatment plant.

Although more subtle, the Concessionaire's operations obligations are also likely to increase the Concessionaire's attention to design as the costs of future operations and maintenance will be affected by short sighted design decisions.

2.06   Right-of-way Agreements

The loss of cooperation from an underlying or adjacent landowner can stall a project indefinitely. Thus, unequivocal right-of-way agreements for site access and access routes are essential for timely completion of a project.

Public owners frequently negotiate right-of-way (ROW) and right of entry (ROE) agreements prior to forming the P3 contract. The public owner has the most leverage to negotiate right-of-way with adjacent landowners due to pre-existing relationships and political power so there may be sufficient lead time. Right-of-way agreements are best incorporated into the contract by reference with a high order of precedence. The P3 contract will typically obligate the Developer to perform, in all material respects, the right-of-way obligations of the owner under those agreements.

If the agreements grant the third-party landowners discretion, that discretion must be carefully restricted. Third-party landowners with discretion will have substantial leverage over the Developer to condition access upon the performance of extra work for their own benefit or, perhaps in good faith, simply try to impose their own view on the project.

The procedure for third-party review of Developer submittals can be strictly defined, including a clear timeframe and a standard of review based upon objective standards attached to the agreement.

A method of real time, semi-binding or truly binding dispute resolution should be incorporated, obligating the third-party to accept the dispute resolution provisions of the future P3 contract. At the minimum, either party should have the ability to enforce their contract rights during the course of project execution.

The P3 agreement may place the obligation of securing offsite fabrication and lay down sites for the project. This may vary depending on each contractor's approach to the job.

2.07 Third Party Permits

The issuance of permits has been the root cause of a great number of disputes.

Certain environmental processes, such as a California Environmental Quality Act Negative Declaration, are well understood based upon assumptions about the project and its likely environmental impacts.[90] The request for proposals would state that the Developer is either obligated to build the project within the constraints of the permitting assumptions and comply with the environmental mitigation measures or work with the public agency obtain an amended permit if requested by the public agency and be paid for that effort.

Regulatory agencies do not always have the same incentives as the parties to the P3 contract to process and approve necessary permits in the time needed. Pushing the risk of an unresponsive, obstructionist, or perhaps rule-violating regulatory agency onto the Concessionaire may raise bid prices too high.[91] Or result in substantial bidders dropping out of the competition.

A workable compromise is to provide that the Developer's inability to obtain permitting despite commercially reasonable attempts and mitigation efforts will constitute a compensable and excusable delay.

---

[90] A Negative Declaration shall be prepared for a project which the Department determines from an Initial Study will not have a significant effect. Or, a Mitigated Negative Declaration shall be prepared if the Initial Study identified potentially significant effects, but revisions in the project or mitigation measures to avoid or reduce the effects to a point where no significant effects would occur are agreed to by the Department before the negative declaration and initial study are released for public review (CEQA Guidelines, Section 15070).

[91] *See, e.g., Bell/Heery v. United States,* 106 Fed. Cl. 300 (2012) aff'd, 739 F.3d 1324 (Fed. Cir. 2014) (Denying federal contractor relief for unexpected interference from state regulatory agency).

CHAPTER 3

STRUCTURING FINANCING

3.01 Traditional Financing

Traditional project delivery requires significant up-front payments by the government. These include preliminary studies, site investigation, property acquisition, and design preparation. Then the government pays even more as construction work is completed. At project completion, the government pays public employees to service the facilities. Municipal Bond financing most commonly pays the construction costs.

Infrastructure planners must face stark political realities as to whether an agency can raise funds for infrastructure projects. In California, state bonds require a simple majority of voter approval to pass, while local bonds require fifty-five percent or a two-thirds "supermajority." (Other government funding mechanisms for infrastructure include municipal bonds, certificates of participation, traditional revenue bonds, sales tax allocations, grants, and redevelopment bonds).

3.02 P3 Financing

[A] Availability Payments

Availability Payments are a fixed compensation paid periodically to the Developer based on the availability of the completed infrastructure.

61

The "maximum" availability payment is subject to reductions based on penalties for performance deficiencies.

The use of availability payments in place of toll revenue may reduce the Concessionaire's risk and uncertainty of future revenue. This will assure the private investors of the smooth operation of the facility over the twenty or more years of operation. The owner can alternatively structure affordable payments, while toll road operators expect exclusivity if they shoulder demand risk.[92]

However, an availability payment is only as good as the public agency's ability to make the payments. While the US Government and its states are not allowed to declare bankruptcy, cities, special districts and counties may do so. So, the public agencies' creditworthiness should also be taken into account.

[B] Single Pay

Under Single Pay, a single payment is made from the government to the Developer that is tied to the long-term usage of the facility. This is rare, as it poses a risk of financial insolvency of the Concessionaire with no direct recourse by the public agency. A long-term surety bond will rarely be available for a twenty or thirty year term of the P3 agreement.

[C] User Fee/Tolls

In User Fee/Tolls approach, the Developer is granted an exclusive right to collect fees from the users of the facility or service. Traditional examples are water, wastewater, and toll roads. The facility returns to public control at the end of the contract period. P3 agreements include limitations on increasing toll rates. The Federal Highway Administration has collected sample escalation provisions in a guidance memo.[93]

---

[92] "A Guide for Hot Lane Development," § 7.2 Federal Highway Administration (March 2003) (Concessionaire of SR-91 threatened lawsuit when state proposed building additional adjacent lanes).

[93] "Public Policy Considerations in Public-Private Partnership (PPP) Arrangements," § 1 Federal Highway Administration (January 2009).

Airport fees under FAA's "Airport Privatization Pilot Program" are another type of user fee. Under this program, an airport can be sold or leased to a private entity and the private entity can collect the airport fees from carriers.[94]

The selection of User Fee/Tolls must take into account inflation and be flexible in early years where throughput may be lower. It also can mean the granting of exclusive concessions or non-competition clauses to limit the opportunity for new entrants to undercut the ability of the Concessionaire to recoup its investment and expected rate of investment return.

[D] Milestone Payments

Milestone Payments reward the Developer for the interim progress on the infrastructure project before it is operational and producing other types of revenue. Milestone Payments are tied to job progress or the opening of phases of the project. However, they are independent of time, unlike debt service. This may be a consideration in drafting private partner agreements and insurance.

[E] Public and Private Funding Sources

[1] (TIFIA)

Private entities can apply under the Transportation Infrastructure Finance and Innovation Act of 1998 (TIFIA) for credit assistance in the form of secured loans, loan guarantees, and standby lines of credit. The private entity will be the borrower for the loan. It is available for transportation projects eligible for grant assistance under chapter 53 of Title 49 of the United States Code.[95]The loan period can be as long as 35 years after substantial completion of the project.[96]

---

[94] Federal Aviation Administration Authorization Act of 1996, 49 U.S.C.A. § 47134.

[95] 49 U.S.C.A. § 53.

[96] 23 U.S.C.A. § 603(b)(5).

Lenders will have specific reserve account requirements based upon the risks of the particular project, like seismic risks or maintenance costs. Security for the loan may include project revenues like the Availability Payments. The amount of Federal credit assistance may not exceed 33 percent of total reasonably anticipated eligible project costs, so other sources of funding like equity should be applied first.[97]

[2] Private Activity Bonds (PABs)

Private Activity Bonds (PABs) are used to finance a variety of business projects, including public infrastructure. Eligible infrastructure projects, termed "exempt facilities," are airports, wharves, water supply, wastewater facilities, and transportation projects.

Governmental authorities must issue Private Activity Bonds. The authority sells the bond and provides the proceeds to the Concessionaire as a loan. Interest paid to bondholders is exempt from taxes and security for the loan can include the TIFIA loan and letters of credit.[98]

[3] Private Equity

Investments are typically made through special purpose investment vehicles. The investor provides equity in exchange for a percentage of future revenues.

[4] Contingency Fund

A liquid contingency fund is necessary to handle unexpected costs, like financing charges of an excused delay or construction cost overruns, without violating financing terms.

[5] Construction Loan

There are aspects of a P3 project that can be financed with traditional construction loans.

---

[97] 23 U.S.C.A. §604(b)(2).
[98] Internal Revenue Code, Exempt facility bond, 26 U.S.C.A. §142.

For example, the Developer may commit approximately a 20-percent equity into the land acquisition, design and construction costs. The construction loan is secured by the Developer's equity, underlying land, future revenue, and individual or corporate guarantees. After substantial completion, a lower-rate permanent loan pays off the construction loan and interest accumulated during construction. The liquidity of the construction loan can be a particularly vulnerable component of a P3.[99]

This situation is discussed in a court case describing a project in New York State. The City of Syracuse, New York, contributed $170 million to a P3 project for an 850,000 square foot shopping mall expansion that combined research, retail, entertainment, dining, hospitality and tourism.[100] The private partner, Destiny USA, contributed $40 million to initiate the project. Citigroup committed to loan $155 million.[101]

When the project was 90% complete, Citigroup—perhaps motivated by external market pressures in 2008—asserted that the loan was out of balance and stopped funding the construction draws.[102] Construction halted and the project was boarded up. The mall was completed after the courts sided with the contractor. The courts rejected Citigroup's claim that the contractor was in breach of the "Deficiency" provision, which required that completion costs did not exceed the amount of the loan yet to be advanced.[103] The court concluded that the Deficiency provision was a clearly defined formula and Citigroup's interpretation was unreasonable.[104] After the contractor posted a $15 million bond to the court, payments resumed and the project was successfully completed.[105]

[6] Other Federal Funding

There are numerous other sources of federal funding that can be found for the right project, like the federal "green bonds" intended for

---

[99] *Destiny USA Holdings, LLC v. Citigroup Global Markets Realty Corp.*, 69 A.D.3d 212, 889 N.Y.S.2d 793 (2009).

[100] *Id.* at 214.

[101] *Id.*

[102] *Id.* at 215.

[103] *Id.* at 220.

[104] *Id.* at 218.

[105] *Id.* at 224.

green building projects authorized by The American Jobs Creation Act of 2004, included in the IRS code with PABs discussed above.[106]

These funds tend to have regulatory strings attached; if a recipient of the green bonds fails to substantially comply with the Act, the recipient will lose their security and be forced to pay a higher interest rate to investors to pay the taxes on the now taxed bonds.

One Developer saw an opportunity to collaborate with a local government to seek federal disaster relief funding to re-purchase hillside land it had developed into residences that were destroyed in mudslides. However, the particular structure of the agreements with the property owners disqualified the city from disaster funding so the Developer was not reimbursed the 25% of the funding as it had anticipated.[107]

[7] Land Transfers to Concessionaire

A creative funding source that is used in dense urban areas is based on "land swaps." Public owners transfer land to the project Developer, likely with improved zoning, and the Developer is entitled to develop and sell to private buyers. The future sales act as security for, and ultimately fund, the public improvements.

A land swap has been carefully orchestrated to raise funds for the $2.7 billion San Francisco Transbay Terminal, the state-owned property that was largely nonproductive since a highway was dismantled after earthquake damage.[108] The State gave certain land parcels to the City, which sold the parcels to third-party Developers and will use the revenue to pay off the Terminal bonds.

Another example is in Lake Tahoe, where public recreational areas have been landlocked by dense private development. The Tahoe Regional Planning Agency has since transferred certain property rights

---

[106] Pub. L. No. 108-357, 118 Stat. 1418.
[107] *City of Laguna Niguel v. Fed. Emergency Mgmt. Agency*, No. SACV 09-0198 DOC MLG, 2009 WL 3122490, at *4 (C.D. Cal. Sept. 28, 2009).
[108] Eric Young, Land swap to clear way for $2.7B transit project, S.F. Business Times, June 1, 2003, available at: http://www.bizjournals.com/sanfrancisco/stories/2003/06/02/story7.html.

to a private Developer.[109] With the revenue from the public contribution, the Developer will construct a bike path through a residential area that will link landlocked recreation areas. The Developer will then dedicate other lands for public use. The partnership project was challenged and has been temporarily derailed by environmental litigation.[110]

The City of El Paso, Texas, funded a minor league ballpark with a public-private partnership. The city's contribution to the project included the land underneath city hall.

A former mayor, who led an attempt to stop the project with a ballot initiative and a corresponding lawsuit, protested the demolition of city hall.[111] The lawsuit was dismissed on procedural grounds and construction proceeded.

A variation on a land swap permitted a redevelopment project in Camden, New Jersey. In exchange for investing in a vast office park, Campbell's Soup was authorized to demolish a historic Sears building that was funded with public and private funds.[112] The project proceeded after a lawsuit regarding the building's historic status.

A P3 entity may be the recipient of a federal land transfer to grant the rights necessary to construct, operate and maintain a roadway crossing.[113] However, commentators have stated that the pace of arranging a federal land swap makes watching continental drift look like a NASCAR Race.

---

[109] Tahoe Regional Planning Agency Code of Ordinances, adopted by TRPA Governing Board December 12, 2012, amended effective February 15, 2015.

[110] *League to Save Lake Tahoe v. Tahoe Regional Planning Agency*, 2011 WL 3847185 (D.Nev., 2011) vacated and remanded, 497 Fed.Appx. 697, 2012 WL 4830462 (C.A.9 (Nev.), 2012).

[111] *Salazar v. City of El Paso, Tex.*, No. EP-12-CV-00403-DCG, 2012 WL 5986674, (W.D. Tex. Nov. 29, 2012.

[112] *In re Project Authorization Under New Jersey Register of Historic Places Act*, 408 N.J. Super. 540, 975 A.2d 941, 943 (App. Div. 2009).

[113] U.S. Dep't of Transp., Fed. Highway Admin., Manual for Federal Land Transfers for Federal–Aid Projects 1.0, (Feb. 27, 2009), available at https://www.fhwa.dot.gov/real_estate/uniform_act/acquisition/flt_manual/index.cfm.

[F] Cost-benefit analysis

The comparison of the overall cost of procurement between P3 procurement and Design Bid Build is called a "Value for Money Analysis" or a "Public Sector Comparator." The Federal Highway Administration published an introduction to the method in 2012.[114]

Some agencies have published their project-specific analyses, which can be very enlightening. The project outcomes are driven by assumptions about discount rates and equitable allocations of risk. [115] Public agencies often describe projects using just the "construction cost."

This is a very impractical way of thinking about true project costs. The so-called "soft" project expenses include very real expenditures such as agency administration, project management, design and engineering, inspection and testing, interest, software installation and maintenance, startup and performance testing and related expense. Soft costs can easily meet or exceed construction costs.

It is lamentably rare for a public agency to publicly disclose the long-term finance costs of a project (although that type of disclosure is imposed by law on every car dealership in California).[116]

In an era of an apparent lack of transparency and openness in government and the public markets it seems appropriate that the public be given a realistic estimate of the overall costs of major public decisions.

---

[114] Federal Highway Administration, Value for Money Assessment for Public-Private Partnerships: A Primer (December 2012). *See also* Industry Canada, The Public Sector Comparator: A Canadian Best Practices Guide (May 2003). *See also* Henry Kerali, Lead Transport Specialist,"Public Sector Comparator for Highway PPP Projects," World Bank. Retrieved February 10, 2015. The World Bank defines a Public Sector Comparator (PSC) as a tool used by a government to make decisions by testing whether a private investment proposal offers value for money in comparison with the most efficient form of public procurement.

[115] TransLink Golden Ears Bridge Team, Golden Ears Bridge: Value for Money Report (June 16, 2006); and Greater Vancouver Transportation Authority, Golden Ears Bridge Reference Case Report (November 4, 2005). *See also* Commonwealth of Virginia, Office of Transportation Public-Private Partnerships, PPTA Risk Analysis Guidance (September 2011) (also summarizing Value For Money studies for other projects).

[116] California Car Buyer's Bill of Rights FFVR 35 (July 2006).

Such public disclosure is vital when comparing the various types of project delivery systems.

[G] Financial Risk to Public Entity

The general principles of public accounting and overall standards of civic integrity require public entities to carefully arrange financing to pay for the publicly financed amounts and soft costs of the P3 (or at least the engineer's estimate).

Concessionaires should always verify the source and reliability of the funds (e.g. federal grants). A common failing with underground or complex urban projects is an unrealistically low contingency amount, which typically should be at least 10-15 percent of overall project cost and far larger amounts for particularly risky projects (e.g. the Oakland-San Francisco Bay Bridge Signature Span). Regardless of the contractual transfers of risk, both the public and private entities should have the means to pay contingency amounts.

Furthermore, bond rating agencies are extremely interested in whether a project is Non-Recourse (limited liability) or Recourse (unlimited liability). The latter is a type of financing that may subject the public entity's general fund to substantial financial risk. On the other hand, the investing community favors projects where the public agency makes a pledge of full faith and credit and where there is more generous financing and lower interest rates.

One of the major decisions that a public agency can make at the outset is whether to set up a special purpose agency, joint powers authority or other government entity that may limit agency liability, or, where the project is very large, such as a regional transportation system (e.g. the Los Angeles Metropolitan Transit Authority), spread the construction, operating and financing risk across many public entities.

Another critical aspect of any project-financing scheme is the risk management profile of the project. The nature of the project, the financial stability and strength of the public agency, the locale of the project, the quality and experience of the project participants, the risk of variations in future revenue and costs, and whether the technology and revenue concept is proven or experimental will strongly influence its "financeability."

P3 projects can involve numerous parties and have many moving parts. When the government's funding sources have conditions attached, it must consider whether it wants to remain obligated if the funding is declined.[117]

These factors include in-depth studies of the economics of the region and future projections, the expected revenues of the project and other various risk factors. This information often finds itself becoming part of the Official Statement (a bond industry term of art) for the issuance. Such studies can also provide substantial guidance regarding which of the various financing methods is right for the project.

[H] Financial Risks to Private Entity

Although contractors have traditionally been cautious about budgeting and financial matters, large projects envisioned by Concessionaires can overwhelm a contractor's traditional budgeting, revenue and profit rules of thumb. Speculative projects — which count on pie-in-the-sky revenue projections — should be avoided. An overly enthusiastic transfer of risk to the Concessionaire may leave the contractor with no administrative or legal relief.

Even the most conservative projections rely upon key assumptions that need to be carefully examined. What happens if the price of gasoline doubles, or fuel oil triples? Or, what if interest rates or commodity prices escalate out of control? How sensitive are the project's economics to those fluctuations (a so-called "sensitivity analysis")?

Starting with a Risk Matrix is as much a good starting place for the Concessionaire as it is for the public partner.[118] Once the risks are identified, a party is assigned to bear that risk.

---

[117] See *City of Laguna Niguel* (2009).

[118] See Virginia Office of Transportation Public-Private Partnerships, PPTA Risk Analysis Guidance, Appendix D (Sept. 2011).

It is recommended that language from the contract is placed directly into the risk matrix that allocates the risk.[119] The quantitative risk analysis can then be performed with the probability, cost and schedule impact of risks.

Third party design approvals, site access conditions, differing site conditions, and force majeure are risks that can be fatal to a project when allocated wholly to the Developer. Other sections of this book explain the evaluation of project risks in depth.

Even risks that are "shared" in a traditional sense can fall heavily on the Developer. The typical arrangement of "shared risks" with excusable but non-compensable delays may place a contractor and owner in a holding pattern. That this is a "shared risk" is of little comfort to the Concessionaire when it incurs financing charges every day before substantial completion.

P3 projects also present repayment risks. If there is a significant risk that up-front investment in a project may not be repaid, the reward for participation should be substantial. The famous Orange County, City of Vallejo, and City of Stockton, California bankruptcies are a reminder that Chapter 9 Federal Bankruptcy is a real threat and risk associated with public entity creditworthiness.[120]

Another source of repayment risk is the compensation of user fees. Although various P3 projects have a long history of success, toll-based P3 road projects in the United States have not shown consistent outcomes for investors.[121] The use of toll roads can depend on consumers' subjective feelings of paying for a service that is traditionally provided by the government at no cost. In some states, toll roads are rare (e.g. Georgia), while in others, they are very common (e.g. New Jersey). And

---

[119] Although prepared for another purpose, an example table with the necessary level of detail is the Golden Ears Bridge Schedule PA-31 Allocation of Obligations Under Certain Facility Lands Agreements and Encumbrances, p.1.

[120] Floyd Norris, *Orange County's Bankruptcy: The Overview; Orange County Crisis Jolts Bond Market*, The New York Times, Dec. 8, 1994, at http://www.nytimes.com/1994/12/08/business/orange-county-s-bankruptcy-the-overview-orange-county-crisis-jolts-bond-market.html.

[121] Cate Long, "Are private toll roads a losing idea?", Reuters, (January 19, 2013).

growing congestion favors the economics of HOV, FasTrak, similar "faster, better" alternative routes.

The future operational costs of a project also vary substantially depending on the volume of use.

[I] Contract Provisions

The P3 contract is the roadmap for the success of the project. It must be precise, understandable, and fair. The Concessionaire must be held to a fixed scope of the project, schedule and quality standards. But, the P3 contract can become lopsided in the other direction. In their desire to protect public agencies, their attorneys have devised increasingly sophisticated clauses and provisions that can cripple the Concessionaire and its Design-Build team. And in some states, there are already public contract codes that can prohibit, limit, and void many such one-sided clauses.

These statutes typically limit the public entity's ability to reallocate owner-caused delay and indemnity issues. They may also neglect basic issues of good faith and the importance of the government being a reliable contracting party.

However, the statutory protections for general contractors may be less applicable to P3 procurements. Project participants and their attorneys are strongly urged to review in detail not only the special provisions, but also the so-called boilerplate provisions of any contracts that do not contain pre-printed standardized general conditions that may have been subject to prior legal or commercial review. The fit with P3 contracts might not perfectly flange up.

A comprehensive commercial review by the Concessionaire includes an analysis of the business aspects of the project contract, including hidden risks, costs, and profit potential, as opposed to a mere review of the purely technical or legal risks.

As previously stated, where a Concessionaire or Design-Build team encounters clauses that pose unacceptably high risks and the public agency is unwilling to reconsider or modify those clauses, the P3 team may decide to make a "no bid" decision. The walk-away option is also understandable when a public entity fosters a reputation of unfairness or willingness to assert false claims allegations without significant justification.

Before the Concessionaire makes this business decision, it is generally appropriate to notify the public entity of the specific concern with the offending clause or management practice, perhaps through a bidder's inquiry, so there is an opportunity for change.

[J] Innovative and Risky Projects

There are a few types of projects that are recognized as exceptionally risky to design, build, and operate. Obviously, private facilities such as refineries, industrial plants, and oil and gas pipelines pose high risks of explosion and fire. Public airports and fuel farms can pose similar risks. However, the industry competence and established quality standards for such facilities are extremely high. Furthermore, these types of project risks are generally insurable by the owner and contractor.

If the facilities require new or complex technologies, or assigns the Concessionaire sole responsibility for permitting, design, construction, commissioning, and operation, it may be seen as a very risky endeavor. The complexity may also impact the number of qualified and interested bidders, thus affecting the competitiveness of proposals.

Generally, any structure open to the public poses the long-term risks of personal injury claims by individual members of the public. Airports, sports and entertainment complexes, retail and other similar facilities, and complex highways often remain open to the public during construction and generate a disproportionate number of such claims. In addition to the construction phase risks, they present long-term risks of slip and fall, public liability, and related claims.

Certain public projects may appear innocuous but can be extremely risky. Although the design and construction of water pipelines in the desert would appear to be a low risk venture, such a project led to a $146 million project failure and defect claim in Arizona.[122] Not only was the desert environment particularly corrosive to the pipeline system, the loss

---

[122] Central Arizona Water Project, http://www.cap-az.com/. Mr. Brown represented the contracting and pipe supply ventures in the US District Court (Arizona) and 9th Circuit case, resulting in a defense verdict for his clients.

ERNEST C. BROWN, ESQ., PE

of water flow to Phoenix and the threat of major flash floods was a risk the owner did not wish to accept. Loss of water supply or other critical needs during critical agricultural or manufacturing periods arguably would have generated vast consequential damages.

[K] Cash Flow Management

The Concessionaire's cash flow planning is crucial because revenue is not immediately collectible in long-term P3 construction projects. The Concessionaire invests money in the proposal and then makes an initial equity payment to either purchase land or as a condition of award. Once the project begins, the Designers and contractors incur expenses that must be financed. Milestone payments may partially offset these costs. Once the project is substantially complete and operational, the Concessionaire may be able to refinance the project on more favorable terms. The user fees or availability payments will then pay for the debt service.

An informative example in which the public entity overestimated toll revenue and is using general funds to make monthly payments is the Golden Ears Bridge in Metro Vancouver, Canada.[123] If the demand risk had been on the Concessionaire, the Concessionaire would have had to close the gap between revenue and expenses with equity. One explanation for slower-than-expected adoption of the commute route was construction of another bridge that provided an alternate route.[124] (This is now familiar to the reader.)

---

[123] Phil Melnychuk, "Golden Ears Bridge still 'underperforming,'" Maple Ridge News, (October 1, 2013), available at: http://www.mapleridgenews.com/news/226058811.html.
[124] TransLink, 2012 Year-End Financial and Performance Report 11 (2013), available at: http://www.translink.ca/~/media/documents/about_translink/governance_and_board/board_minutes_and_reports/2013/april/2012_yearend_financial_and_performance_report.ashx.

CHAPTER 4

PROCUREMENT

4.01   Prequalification of Bidders

As a policy, P3 contracts are typically let to the "best value" bidder, not the bidder who is most competitive on price alone. This provides reassurance for public entities that are not just handing over substantial control of their projects to a low bidder.

It is best to sort out those companies who have the appropriate skills and financial resources early in the process. As a result, a prequalification step is generally required prior to submitting a P3 proposal. Additionally, the prequalification process can result in Developers recruiting exceptional talent and expertise.

The prequalification process includes the next tiers of entities, including the Design-Build team and the O & M contractor. The last element is project finance and, as a result, the prequalification or evaluation of proposals is likely to evaluate these commercial criteria: the Maximum Availability Payment required by the proposal; the level of equity investment and financial support from lenders; and the coherence, robustness, and deliverability of the Financial Plan.[125]

---

[125] *See* California Department of Transportation, Presidio Parkway P3 Project PPR 35 (May 4, 2010).

4.02 Owner Preparation of Request for Proposals

There are three stages to drafting a P3 Request for Proposals. First, the nature of the project needs to be carefully described, including an agreed-upon set of "deal points" and the best estimate of the owner's and contractor's major risks. Second, a rough draft must be developed, often modeled on a contract for a project of similar scope and magnitude. Last, the final agreement must be completed, incorporating comments from various operating divisions and engineering professionals within the city or other public entity.

The final review of the P3 contract should be conducted by an experienced construction attorney, who will thoroughly assess: 1) a standard contract checklist; 2) required and prohibited statutory clauses; 3) a careful review for conformity with a) finance documents, and b) the local charter, municipal codes or ordinances; and 4) the binding legal conditions of any financing arrangements or the funding conditions for any federal, state, or local grants.

It should be apparent that extreme rigor is required in preparing public works contracts and bidding documents since contracts that: (1) result from improper bid processes, and/or (2) contain clauses that violate public policy or the grant documents may be found to be null and void.[126] At a minimum, bid protests may substantially delay a project or force re-bidding if all bids are rejected.

A determination of Best Value may include an evaluation of price, construction duration, technical quality of the design and construction and use of disadvantaged business enterprises.

[A] Financial Strategy

The owner's control over pricing is based on selecting an appropriate project concept, defining it with specifications that leave the Developer room to identify efficiencies, and allocating risks efficiently.

---

[126] *Valley Crest Landscape, Inc. v. City Council*, 41 Cal. App.4th 1432 (1996), which has been criticized by *Ghilotti Constr. Co. v. City of Richmond*, 45 Cal. App. 4th 897, 53 Cal. Rptr. 2d 389 (1996).

With respect to allocating risk, the owner should keep in mind that the P3 process neither requires nor benefits from the transfer of risks that are more efficiently retained by the owner.

[B] Project Scope

An owner may set explicit performance criteria, such as the number of square feet of warehouse space or the output of an electrical or steam co-generation plant. The details of the design and construction of the facility are left in the hands of the Design-Build Contractor or industrial vendor. This leaves discretion for the Concessionaire to identify cost savings. However, owners are sometimes ambivalent about the design concept or have specific preferences and combine performance specifications with specific criteria for the design.

In Design Bid Build contracts, the owner has liability for the sufficiency of the design provided to the contractor. This is known as *Spearin* liability.[127] To the extent that the contractor supplies the plans and specifications in a P3 contract, the contractor, not the owner, impliedly warrants their adequacy and sufficiency. Thus, an owner may assert that it is shielded from any *Spearin* liability when the design results in cost overruns or does not work. This is not a complete defense for the project owner, but it is a strong argument for P3.

A major error is attempting to writing an RFP that blends performance criteria with conflicting design specifications. For example, a Concessionaire bidding a parking garage could find itself subject to ventilation, fire safety, or accessibility requirements that are not based upon current codes and with no logical application to the proposal. Admittedly these problems can be difficult to anticipate, though they can be worked out through bidder's inquiries. An owner may be surprised by the expense and warranty liability it retains if it supplies design specifications to a P3 contractor.

In Design-Build and P3 contracts, even an owner's conceptual design in the Request for Proposals with a disclaimer that the provided design is "approximate" may be sufficient "control" over the design to

---

[127] *United States v. Spearin*, 248 U.S. 132, 39 S. Ct. 59, 63 L. Ed. 166 (1918).

assume liability for the failure of the design.[128] An attempt to transfer risk is less enforceable when the owner in actuality retains substantial control over the design.

Another distinction that determines whether the owner has liability is whether the specifications were labeled "design specifications" or merely "performance specifications." Government specifications will be deemed "design specifications" where (1) the government sets forth in precise detail the materials to be employed and the manner in which the work is to be performed and (2) the contractor is not privileged to deviate from those specifications.[129] Detailed measurements, tolerances, materials, and elaborate instructions on how to perform the contract are examples of design specifications. By contrast, performance specifications merely set forth an objective to be achieved, and the successful bidder is expected to exercise its ingenuity in selecting the means to achieve that objective.

In addition, for liability to attach to the owner, the contractor must comply with the design specifications. The contractor cannot just blindly follow what it knows are faulty specifications. But, if a contractor complies in good faith with the government's defective design specifications, the contractor should not be found liable for any ensuing loss arising from those defective specifications and should be able to recover damages equal to the amount expended in trying to comply with the defective specifications.[130]

[C] P3 Contract Components

Construction contracts generally contain a bundle of various documents commonly referred to jointly as the "Contract Documents." These documents may consist of bidding documents, the owner-contractor agreement, general conditions, supplementary conditions and/or special conditions, drawings and technical specifications, standard

---

[128] *Drennon Construction & Consulting, Inc. v. Dept. of the Interior*, 13 BCA P 35213, CBCA 2391, 2013 WL 996042 (Civilian B.C.A., 2013).

[129] *J.L. Simmons Co v. United States*, 412 F.2d 1360, 1362 (Ct. Cl. 1969).

[130] *Martin Constr., Inc. v. U.nited States.*, 102 Fed. Cl. 562, 575-76 (2011), quoting *United States v. Spearin*, 248 U.S. 132, 136, 39 S.Ct. 59, 63 L.Ed. 166 (1918).

specifications, reference specifications, addenda, and modifications. These individual documents cross-reference each other in order to form the contract. A common issue is whether the language of these documents are intended to be guidelines, starting points for judgment and interpretation or are mandated requirements. They are often also phrased as requiring the most stringent requirements, when those may not be cost effective or safe in a particular instance.

[D] Insurance Coverage and Performance Bonds

Owners on P3 projects frequently select an Owner Controlled Insurance Program (OCIP), also known as a "wrap-up." It creates a single point of contact with respect to insurance claims. These types of owner policies do not always provide adequate coverage for design, catastrophic loss, loss of use or the property of the private parties.[131]

[E] Termination Provisions

P3s are unique because of the private equity invested. A termination provision framed after a Design Bid Build or Design-Build contract may make the project unfinanceable.[132]

Termination is the remedy available to the non-breaching party when the other party has breached a material obligation of the contract. Traditionally, the owner's obligation is to pay and the contractor's obligation is to follow the specifications. The standard owner's remedy is to take control of the project, subject to surety step-in rights.

This may be appropriate where the owner has predominately invested its own equity in the project to-date but can result in unjust enrichment for the government in a P3. Investors in a P3 need some

---

[131] Associated General Contractors of America, "Look Before You Leap! A Contractor's Guide to Owner Controlled Insurance Programs," (May 10, 2001). This material is AGC's prepared explanation of the limitations of OCIPs from the contractor's perspective.

[132] European PPP Expertise Centre, "Termination and Force Majeure Provisions in PPP Contracts: Review of Current European practice and guidance," (March 2013). The European PPP Expertise Centre offers an extensive whitepaper on this important topic, although focused on European nations.

rights of redress and compensation if there has been a major failure by the Concessionaire. Accordingly, the P3 contract should grant cure rights to an identified agent for the investors as well as to the performance bond surety. Similarly, the termination for owner's default should provide predictable compensation to investors, accounting for equity and some return on the investment.

[F] Competitive Bidding and Selection

The P3 solicitation will often "cut and paste" competitive bidding requirements. This may include the submittal of sealed bids by all bidders on a specific date and to a specific place prior to an ironclad time deadline. The bids are then opened and a contractor is selected according to previously published "best value" criteria, as discussed elsewhere.

In California a competitive negotiation process is provided by the enabling legislation for P3s, the Infrastructure Financing Act. Competitive negotiation must utilize the demonstrated competence and qualifications of the contractor for the studying, planning, design, development, financing, construction, maintenance, rebuilding, improvement, repair, or operation, or any combination thereof, of the facility as the primary selection criteria.

The bid selection criteria must ensure that the infrastructure facility is operated at fair and reasonable prices to the user of the facility's services. The competitive negotiation process cannot require competitive bidding.

Competitive bidding statutes are state-specific and their application can be quite nuanced. For instance, in Maryland, a P3 conducted entirely on state-owned land is not a "procurement," so it is not subject to the otherwise applicable competitive bidding and small business preference regulations.[133] A committee appointed by the public owner reviews the proposals or packages and costs.

The criteria for selecting the best P3 proposal varies from state to state and from statute to statute, but generally includes successful performance

---

[133] *Host Intern., Inc. v. Maryland Transp Authority,* (Md.Cir.Ct.) 2012 WL 6677791.

of prior projects, résumés of project executives, qualifications of the Designers, financial strength, and whether the Design-Build team has worked together previously.

The National Society of Professional Engineers (NSPE) has advocated developing criteria for a two-step selection process.[134] In the first step, the involved agency would select at least five offerors on the basis of their qualifications. In the second step, each of the offerors would be required to submit detailed proposals, including cost information. A single offeror would then be selected. This process greatly reduces the cost of proposal preparation by the initial candidates. However, it is clear that four companies will spend a great deal of money and only one will get the job. In some cases, it might make more sense to ask for three proposals, where the parties have a better chance of success.

---

[134] National Society of Professional Engineers, "Taking Action: 39 Stories from 2013 That Show NSPE, State Societies, and Members Working for the Profession," p.22-23 (2013). Under current federal law, there are two Design-Build selection processes—the two-step/two-phase process and the turn-key selection process. The two-step process, which follows the guidance laid out in the Federal Acquisition Reform Act as well as the Brooks Architect-Engineers Act of 1972, is preferred by the U.S. Army Corps of Engineers and is NSPE's preferred method for Design-Build procurements. NSPE in July requested lawmakers require the two-step/two-phase Design-Build selection process on all military construction projects. In a July 9 letter to House Appropriations Committee Chairman Hal Rogers (R-KY) and Ranking Member Nita Lowey (D-NY), NSPE's 2012–13 President Dan Wittliff, P.E.. NSPE, urged the committee to carefully review, amend, and clarify ambiguous language in the House Report 113-90 on the Military Construction, Veterans Affairs, and Related Agencies Appropriations Act of 2014 (H.R. 2216). The bill does not address specific project delivery methods defined under current law, nor does it describe the strengths or weaknesses of either of the situations under which one may be preferable to the other. —NSPE believes the two-step/two-phase selection process ensures that competent and qualified design professionals are initially involved in the procurement process so that quality-based design considerations are incorporated into the drawings, plans, and specifications consistent with the interests of the public health and safety. Available at https://www.nspe.org/resources/press-room/press-releases/nspe-urges-house-committee-support-two-step-dDesign-Build

[G] Evaluation of Proposals

A "responsive" bid is one that is in strict and full accordance with all material terms of the bid package.[135] For example, the bidder has used the correct bid forms, has fully completed all questionnaires, has submitted all requisite enclosures, and has provided a proper bid bond when security is required.

Any material variations place the bidder at risk of being rejected by the public entity as non-responsive.[136]

The definition of material terms include: (1) terms that could affect price, quantity, quality, or delivery; and (2) terms that are clearly identified by the public entity and that must be complied with at the risk of bid rejection. For example, failing to fill in all of the blanks or failing to submit all required attachments might be the basis for characterizing the bid as non-responsive.

Often, one test can be used to determine whether a bid fails to materially comply with the bidding documents. This test considers whether the failure to comply gives the bidder a substantial economic advantage or benefit not enjoyed by other bidders.[137]

The concept of "responsiveness" may be a source of bid protests when proposers are granted the discretion to provide innovative solutions in responding to a request for proposals. The procuring agency may want to clearly define "responsiveness" for evaluating proposals and state

---

[135] *Menefee v. County of Fresno*, 163 Cal. App. 3d 1175, 210 Cal. Rptr. 99 (1985) illustrates the application of the rules governing bid responsiveness for public works contracts.

[136] See *Great W. Contractors, Inc. v. Irvine Unified Sch. Dist.*, 187 Cal. App. 4th 1425, 1428, 115 Cal. Rptr. 3d 378, 380 (2010), as modified (Sept. 30, 2010), opinion supplemented on denial of reh'g, No. G041688, 2010 WL 3789323 (Cal. Ct. App. Sept. 30, 2010). This case presents the problem of how to distinguish a "nonresponsive" bid from a de facto determination that the bidder is not a "responsible" bidder. This case also illustrates the necessity of following the rule that a public agency cannot reject the bid of the lowest bidder on a public works project on the theory that the *bid* is "nonresponsive" to the agency's request for bids when, *in substance*, the real reason for the rejection is that the agency thinks the lowest *bidder* is "not responsible."

[137] See *Leo Michuda & Son Co. v. Metro. Sanitary Dist. of Greater Chicago*, 97 Ill. App. 3d 340, 422 N.E.2d 1078 (1981).

which technical criteria will result in a non-responsive proposal if not satisfied.

P3 project assessment by the government can be fairly subjective and not based on a low-bidder scheme.[138] However, a Puerto Rican court found that without accompanying justifications, it may be abuse of discretion for the government agency to choose the highest bidder.[139]

P3-enabling statutes sometimes permit unsolicited proposals. The competitive aspect of bidding is typically resolved through soliciting other bids on relatively short notice and competitive negotiations with all parties after a government entity's receipt of all of the "unsolicited" proposals.

[H] Attacks on procurement by third parties

[1] Constitutional Challenges

There can be a variety of potential constitutional challenges to the award of a P3 Project. In Connecticut, an operations contract was awarded to the second-low bidder under a point system for evaluating proposals.[140]

The low bidder argued that the procurement system was invalid because it was subject to favoritism. Despite the fact that the point system contained some subjective elements, the court held that the government made a good faith interpretation of the bidding requirements and applied them in a consistent fashion.[141] The existence of subjective elements did not make the procurement invalid due to favoritism and, as a result, the protest was dismissed.[142]

A long-time lessee of port berths at the Port of Oakland alleged a breach of its lease by the Port awarding a public-private partnership to

---

[138] *Good Earth Tree Care, Inc. v. Town of Fairfield*, No. CV126028878S, 2013 WL 1189304, (Conn. Super. Ct. Feb. 19, 2013)

[139] *PG Engineering Solutions, Inc. v. Autoridad de Carreteras y Transportacion*, 2013 WL 601666 (TCA) (Jan. 17, 2013).

[140] *Good Earth Tree Care, Inc., supra.*

[141] *Id.*

[142] *Id.*

a private investor to develop and operate adjacent berths.[143] The P3 will have exclusive control of six berths for fifty years.

The challenger argued that the award violated the "most favored nation" clause of its lease agreement and the Shipping Act of 1984 because the lease rates for the new operator were more competitive.[144] A federal judge denied the Port's request to dismiss the suit.[145] The Port reached a settlement with the challenger extending its lease at current rates.[146]

A constitutional law challenge was made to a Virginia Department of Rail and Public Transportation partnership with a private railroad.[147] The challenger argued that the Department's interest in a privately owned and operated terminal would violate the internal improvements clause, which states "nor shall the Commonwealth become a party to or become interested in any work of internal improvement, except public roads and public parks, or engage in carrying on any such work," as well as the credit clause.[148]

The Supreme Court of Virginia held that the railroad terminal is directly related to roads, so the internal improvements clause was not violated.[149] They added that the grant was not an extension of the Commonwealth's credit to the company in violation of the credit clause.[150]

Another unsuccessful state constitutional debt limitation challenge to a P3 was brought in Indiana on the basis that a city issued a Request for Proposals (RFP) for a P3 before adopting Indiana's Public-Private Agreements statute.[151] The agreement was to replace a coal burning power plant with an alternatively fueled plant. The Supreme Court of

---

[143] *City of Oakland ex rel. Board of Port Com'rs v. SSA Terminals, LLC*, No. 11-CV-01446-YGR, 2012 WL 2501101, 1 (N.D. Cal. June 27, 2012).

[144] *Id.*

[145] *Id.*

[146] Eric Young, Oakland port ends lawsuit, creates 'mega-terminal' with SSA, San Francisco Business Times, July 23, 2013.

[147] *Montgomery Cnty. v. Virginia Dep't of Rail & Pub. Transp.* 282 Va. 422 (2011).

[148] *Id.* at 436, quoting Va. Const. art. X, § 10

[149] *Id.* at 442.

[150] *Id.*

[151] *Kitchell v. Franklin, supra.*

Indiana explained that "creative mechanisms" have been structured to permit P3s that do not run afoul of the constitutional limitations.[152] The court held that the City needed to adopt the enabling legislation before entering into the agreement, but not before issuing the RFP.[153]

In California, a public-interest partnership was formed between the Department of Fish and Game and a charitable foundation to pay for the costs of the Department implementing the Marine Life Protection Act by funding a comprehensive plan to manage marine habitats.[154]

A challenger argued that the agreement was an unconstitutional appropriation of money, violated constitutional separation of powers, and was an unlawful private "gift" to the state.[155] The court found the agreement valid and dismissed the challenge.[156]

[2] Environmental Statute Challenges

The often-used challenge of insufficient Environmental Impact Review failed to halt a California State University development of a sports complex P3 project.[157] The challenge questioned whether changes to the project design were extensive enough to require a full environmental impact report or whether a supplement to the prior EIR would be sufficient.[158] The privately funded complex on University property features soccer and tennis stadiums, a velodrome, a track and field complex, baseball and softball fields, and parking.[159] The University also guaranteed a percentage of ticket and parking sales.

---

[152] *Id.* at 1022

[153] *Id.* at 1025.

[154] *Coastside Fishing Club v. California Res. Agency,* 158 Cal. App. 4th 1183, 71 Cal. Rptr. 3d 87 (2008)

[155] *Id.* at 1189.

[156] *Id.* at 1212.

[157] *Carson Harbor Vill., Ltd. v. Bd. of Trustees of California State Univ.,* No. B193879, 2008 WL 1704400, (Cal. Ct. App. Apr. 14, 2008) (unpublished/noncitable).

[158] *Id.* at 6.

[159] *Id.* at 2.

Another environmental-statute-based challenge was unsuccessful in stopping a P3 redevelopment project in New York.[160] The state redevelopment agency issued an RFP to develop a historic armory building under a P3.[161] The P3 was a 99-year term lease to a nonprofit organization of neighborhood residents and art enthusiasts to begin a $120 million renovation to operate the property as a cultural center.[162] The sufficiency of the Negative Declaration prepared by the agency was disputed.[163] The court found that the various challengers either did not have standing or that the agency's determinations would not be overturned, and the challenge was dismissed.[164]

[3] Union Challenges

While trade unions generally support P3 projects, that is not the case for public unions. A union of public employee engineers working for the California Department of Transportation argued that procurement of the Presidio Parkway Project under the state's enabling legislation for P3 projects on state highways, Streets and Highways Code Section 143, violated the statute.[165] The highway rehabilitation project would be designed, constructed, and operated by a private entity; payment to the private entity would be through availability payments, not toll revenue.[166] The union claimed that the statute required the Department to perform the design with its own employees and that the project funding must be solely by tolls.[167] The court rejected all of the union's arguments, allowing the project to continue.[168]

---

[160] *Chu v. New York State Urban Dev. Corp.*, 13 Misc. 3d 1229(A), 831 N.Y.S.2d 352 (Sup. Ct. 2006) aff'd sub nom. In re Chu, 47 A.D.3d 542, 850 N.Y.S.2d 82 (2008)

[161] *Id.*

[162] *Id.*

[163] *Id.*

[164] *Id.*

[165] *Prof'l Engineers in California Gov't v. Dep't of Transp.*, 198 Cal. App. 4th 17, 23, 129 Cal. Rptr. 3d 255, 259 (2011), *citing* CA STR & HWY § 143.

[166] *Id.* at 26.

[167] *Id.* at 27.

[168] *Id.* at 28.

A teachers' union in California similarly opposed privatizing certain after-school programs.[169] The union opposed the "at-will," rather than permanent employment positions, and argued that the agreement violated the state's Education Employment Relations Act.[170]

The court conceded that the allegations may have had merit, but it dismissed the case for the union's failure to comply with administrative remedies, and the privatized after-school program continued.[171]

[I] Governmental Duties by Private Entity

[1] Public Records Acts and Transparency

There is an ongoing debate whether the records of a P3 Concessionaire should be considered public records under the so called "Sunshine Act" or similar public access statutes.

Under the Federal Freedom of Information Act (FOIA), records exchanged as part of a partnership between the Army and a corporation qualifies for the Exemption 5 "inter-agency relationship" to FOIA, despite the fact that one party was not a government agency.[172] State public records acts and FOIA generally increase the level of transparency that is required of P3 contractors, but court cases and state statutes have gone both directions.

In New Jersey, an advocate for open government argued that the records of a tourism marketing entity formed with some public assistance, but funded privately and composed of private corporations, should be disclosed.[173] The entity was found not subject to its state's Open Public Records Act.[174]

---

[169] *California Sch. Employees Ass'n v. Santa Ana Unified Sch. Dist.*, No. G047078, 2013 WL 2338430, (Cal. Ct. App. May 29, 2013) (unpublished/noncitable).

[170] *Id.*

[171] *Id.*

[172] *Am. Mgmt. Servs., LLC v. Dep't of the Army*, 703 F.3d 724, (4th Cir.) cert. denied sub nom. *Am. Mgmt. Servs., LLC v. Dep't of Army*, 134 S. Ct. 62, 187 L. Ed. 2d 27 (2013).

[173] *Paff v. Atl. City Alliance, Inc.*, No. A-1123-12T4, 2013 WL 4515915, (N.J. Super. Ct. App. Div. Aug. 27, 2013).

[174] *Id.*

A union brought an action against the Governor of Rhode Island to release records relating to state-agency-privatization contracts regarding services formerly performed by public employees.[175] State legislation in 2006 expanded the obligation of the government to release such information.[176] The court held that the statute acted retroactively and that the requested information should be released.[177]

In *San Gabriel Tribune v. Superior Court*, a California newspaper sought access to withheld data regarding rate increases by a waste disposal company acting under a long term contract with the City of West Covina.[178] The court mandated disclosure, explaining that the private company had injected itself into the public sphere by entering a contract to provide public services under public oversight.[179] As a result, the information was not confidential and it was a matter of public interest as it pertained to the rates paid by residents for service.[180]

In *Justice v. King*, Petitioner sought to compel production of documents pursuant to New York State's Freedom of Information Law (FOIL) by the executive director of an organization that owned and operated residences for previously incarcerated men and had contracts with the state to receive parolees upon their release from incarceration.[181] New York's test for disclosing records pertaining to a contractor performing governmental services is particularly strict and essentially requires that the contractor be embedded with the public agency.

New York law weighs whether the entity is required to disclose its annual budget, maintains offices in a public building, is subject to a governmental entity's authority over hiring or firing personnel, has a board comprised primarily of governmental officials, was created exclusively by a governmental entity, or describes itself as an agent of a governmental entity.

---

[175] *Downey v. Carcieri*, 996 A.2d 1144 (R.I. 2010).

[176] *Id* 1145.

[177] *Id*. at 1148

[178] *San Gabriel Tribune v. Superior Court*, 143 Cal. App. 3d 762, 192 Cal. Rptr. 415 (Ct. App. 1983).

[179] *Id*. at 781.

[180] *Id*.

[181] *Justice v. King*, 60 A.D.3d 1452, 876 N.Y.S.2d 301 (2009).

Although the company at issue in *Justice v. King* was supervising parolees on behalf of the Division of Parole, it was found to be acting as a private contractor and was not subject to the New York public records statute.[182]

[2] Public Access

P3 agreements appear unlikely to change the status of a project regarding public access for free speech or other purposes; public versus private ownership of the underlying property is typically not part of public forum analysis. In Seattle, a public easement was granted within a shopping center to provide public access to a monorail station.[183] Anti-war protestors brought a free speech challenge against the shopping center when the shopping center restricted their protest activities.[184] The private shopping center was found to not be a public forum subject to free speech protections, despite the public easement.[185]

A contrasting scenario occurred when private funding contributed to the redevelopment of a large promenade in Las Vegas. The "Fremont Street Experience" maintains a pedestrian route for that is open at all times.[186] Again, the source of funding for the project was of limited importance.

[3] Prevailing wage

The applicability of prevailing wage to a project is generally determined by whether the project falls within the definition of "public works" under the applicable state labor law. Projects on public land will likely remain public works projects regardless of the percentage of private funding. Oregon revised its statutory definition of "public works," apparently to subject projects on private property with public

---

[182] *Id.* at 303.

[183] *Sanders v. City of Seattle*, 160 Wash. 2d 198, 156 P.3d 874 (2007).

[184] *Id.* at 203.

[185] *Id.* at 225.

[186] *Am. Civil Liberties Union of Nevada v. City of Las Vegas*, 333 F.3d 1092 (9th Cir. 2003).

investment to prevailing wages.[187] California also has an expansive definition of "public works" for the purposes of requiring prevailing wages under the Labor Code 1720 and 1720.2 that encompass most P3 projects.

Practice Note: Many states have a different definition of "public works" in their public contracting codes for competitive bidding laws and under their labor codes for prevailing wage laws. Typically, the labor code definition is broader.

[4] Property Taxes

Property and other tax laws applicable to P3 Projects remains a complicated, federal and state-specific topic.

A bed and breakfast operated within a state park remained subject to taxation, as it was not necessary to the public purpose of the park.[188]

Comparatively, a contractor in a partnership with the Navy to develop military housing units on federal land was not subject to the taxing authority of the surrounding counties under the Federal Enclave Clause, despite the fact that it received a 50-year lease.[189]

[5] Governmental Immunity

Governmental entities are frequently immune from personal injury claims when the injury was caused by an allegedly defective roadway so long as the design was approved by the governmental entity.

It remains an issue whether such governmental immunity will protect a Concessionaire who is responsible for the design, construction, and operation of a public facility.

California Government Code § 830.6 provides neither a public entity nor a public employee is liable for an injury caused by the plan or design of the construction of (or an improvement to) public property

---

[187] O.R.S §279C.800(6)(a) (requiring prevailing wage when public financial investment in a project on private land exceeds 15 percent).

[188] *Willowdale LLC v. Bd. of Assessors of Topsfield*, 78 Mass. App. Ct. 767, 942 N.E.2d 993 (2011).

[189] *Atl. Marine Corps Communities, LLC v. Onslow Cnty., N. Carolina*, 497 F. Supp. 2d 743 (E.D.N.C. 2007).

when such a plan or design has been approved in advance by the legislative body of the public entity, other body, or employee exercising discretional authority to give such approval. This also applies when such a plan or design is prepared in conformity with previously approved standards.[190]

The trial or appellate court can decide there is substantial evidence upon which a reasonable public employee could have adopted the plan or design or the standards therefore.[191] Alternatively, a reasonable legislative body or other body could have approved the plan or design or the standards therefore.[192]

In order for the State to establish design immunity as a defense, a state must typically show: (1) a causal relationship between the plan and the accident; (2) discretionary approval of the plan prior to construction; and (3) substantial evidence supporting the reasonableness of the design.[193] On the other hand, plaintiffs often argue a dangerous condition was allowed to exist, or that poor operation and maintenance of the approved highway or bridge caused the accident.

In California, the opinion of a civil engineer as to the reasonableness of a design ordinarily constitutes substantial evidence sufficient to support a design immunity defense.[194] However, by force of its very terms, the statutory design immunity is limited to a design-caused accident.[195] It does not immunize the government from liability caused by negligence independent of design, even though the independent negligence is only a concurring, proximate cause of the accident.[196]

In some cases, public entities have appointed a private engineer as the Assistant City Traffic Engineer or similar title to attempt to avail the individual of the government's design immunity.

---

[190] CA GOVT § 830.6.

[191] *Id.*

[192] *Id.*

[193] *Hefner v. Cnty. of Sacramento*, 197 Cal. App. 3d 1007, 243 Cal. Rptr. 291 (Ct. App. 1988) abrogated by *Cornette v. Dep't of Transp.*, 26 Cal. 4th 63, 26 P.3d 332 (2001).

[194] *Id.* at 1015. *See also* CA GOVT § 830.6

[195] CA GOVT § 830.6

[196] *Hefner, supra* at 1017.

Practice Point: There is no reason this Assistant City Engineer appointment could not be done for the P3 Concessionaire or the Design-Builder's Engineer of Record (EOR).

A government contractor cannot assert immunity against state tort law claims when it exercises significant discretion over the work on a federal project. For example, a contractor who built levees in New Orleans before Hurricane Katrina was not free of potential liability when its negligence may have caused levees to fail.[197]

On the other hand, a "Task Force" established between the California Department of Fish and Game and a nonprofit to provide additional resources for preparation of environmental studies was found not to have independent legal liability.[198]

Similarly, an advertising company performing the governmental function of mailing auto registration renewal reminders to Florida drivers, alongside targeted advertising in the envelope, was found to be acting on behalf of the state and not liable for violations of the state's Driver Privacy Protection Act.[199]

An operations contractor performing maintenance for the City in New York's Central Park was found to be insulated by the city's immunity from liability for a personal injury tort claim arising from a hole in a cobblestone path that about which the city did not have notice.[200]

The issue of immunity is important to explore on a case-by-case basis and appropriate insurance should be custom-tailored to the risks anticipated during the P3 project.

---

[197] *In re Katrina Canal Breach Litigation*, 620 F.3d 455 (5th Cir. 2010).

[198] *Gurney v. Marine Life Prot. Act Initiative*, No. A132856, 2012 WL 1004764, (Cal. Ct. App. Mar. 26, 2012), unpublished/noncitable.

[199] *In re Imagitas, Inc., Drivers' Privacy Prot. Act Litig.*, No. 3:06-CV-690-J-32HTS, 2008 WL 977333, (M.D. Fla. Apr. 9, 2008) aff'd sub nom. *Rine v. Imagitas, Inc.*, 590 F.3d 1215 (11th Cir. 2009).

[200] *Haxhaj ex rel. Haxhaj v. City of New York*, 19 Misc. 3d 1135(A), 862 N.Y.S.2d 814 (Sup. Ct. 2008) aff'd sub nom. *Haxhaj v. City of New York*, 68 A.D.3d 612, 892 N.Y.S.2d 341 (2009).

CHAPTER 5

CONCESSIONAIRE'S PROPOSAL AND TEAM

5.01   Assembling the P3 team

The Concessionaire typically assigns the responsibilities for design and construction to a Design-Build partnership or independent entity. The chosen Design-Builder will either contain a Designer partner, or independently secure a Designer. This creates a single source for both the design and construction, which leaves the Concessionaire with a fixed price for design and construction. The Concessionaire will generally hire a separate O & M Contractor to perform the long-term operation and maintenance of the Project.

[A] Prepare for the Prequalification Submittal

Similar project experience is a major component of the scoring of a response to a Request for Qualifications. Experience will be evaluated based upon the P3 Partners, the individual managers identified, and the subcontractors and suppliers. Ideally, the assembled team has experience with construction management on similarly-sized projects, the local regulatory agencies, public relations, access to the local labor pool, compliance with government contracts submittals, sufficient equity, and skill in the primary technology needed for the project.

[B] Partnership Agreements

The Design-Build entity is frequently formed through a partnership for a single project commonly called a joint venture (JV) or Limited Liability company (LLC). The Partnership or Member Agreement will define the management of the JV, each party's percentage share, how project costs are allocated, what role each party will perform, and dispute resolution provisions.

JVs can be formed prior to submitting a proposal. The parties may alternatively proceed with the proposal under a simpler agreement called a Teaming Agreement. Either type of agreement will contain provisions regarding preparation of the proposal and sometimes success fees for a party that contributes more to the proposal preparation.[201]

5.02 Concessionaire Issues

[A] Pass Through Provisions

The Concessionaire is typically a special purpose entity that largely assembles the team and arranges the financing. The Concessionaire generally does not expect to retain substantial contractual risk.

In fact, the Design-Builder often becomes the de facto manager of the Concessionaire's P3 Agreement with the Owner Agency.

This often is a surprise to novice Design-Builders who assume they are only brought into the project to provide design and construction services. These other services are often passed down to the Design-Builder in flow down clauses that appear harmless on their face. The Design-Builder then finds itself in the role of a Developer – a role that their strategic leadership and technical staff may be ill-equipped to accomplish. In such case, they need to bolster their teams with development professionals who are more familiar with dealing with

---

[201] *E.g.* ConsensusDocs 299 Joint Venture LLC Agreement. *See* Carrie Ciliberto, *ConsensusDocs Releases a New Joint Venture LLC Agreement: Contract is First of its Kind for the Design and Construction Industry*, ConsensusDocs (Feb. 7, 2013), available at https://www.consensusdocs.org/consensusdocs-releases-a-new-joint-venture-llc-agreement/.

public relations, cutting through "red tape" and negotiating through political stalemates.

[B] Insurance portfolio for the P3 Concessionaire

A complete treatment of the coverages, exclusions, ISO forms, manuscript policies and insurance coverage disputes for P3's is beyond the scope of this guide. However, the Concessionaire will often benefit from an Owner Controlled Insurance Program (OCIP) or Contractor Controlled Insurance Program (CCIP) that creates a single point of contact for the management of first party and third party claims.

5.03   Design-Builder Issues

The Concessionaire typically assigns the design and construction work to a contractor with extensive Design-Build experience. The Concessionaire will then provide oversight as the Design-Builder proceeds.

A Design-Build contract in a P3 can differ from the typical experience, as it may include field exploration, permitting, right-of-way acquisition and other project development activities. Liquidated damages may also be higher because they could include the Concessionaire's financing expenses and the public entities loss of use. (Bridge Projects have been known to have liquidated damages of more than $250,000 per hour).

The Design-Builder works with the Designer, provides expertise on constructability, administers construction subcontracts, manages relationships with funding and oversight agencies, and provides a system of communications, public information, emergency response, and policy advice for the owner. The Construction Manager (CM) also manages the independent design checkers, cost estimators, and testing firms working for the public entity.

The most apparent risk for the contractor is possible inflation of scope and quality of a project and the resultant impacts on cost and schedule. In a typical construction contract, the contractor is usually entitled to a change order when there has been a change to the scope of work, a shift in conditions, or errors or omissions in the plans and/ or specifications. However, in a P3 contract, unexpected permitting conditions, or obstructed site access can severely disrupt scheduling.

Once the Design-Builder assumes responsibility for the design, it also assumes responsibility for the accuracy of the drawings and specifications. However, a general contractor who has contracted for the design services may bring an E/O claim against its design firm, partner or consultant, depending on the contract (see below).

Insurance and disclaimers of liability are key issues that must be addressed in the Design-Build context. A Designer may be hesitant to participate in a Design-Build project because of the increased liability exposure. Such exposure includes the presence of guaranty/warranty clauses in Design-Build contracts. Guaranty/warranty and insurance provisions must be specially drafted to fit the situation or P3 project type.

5.04   Designer Issues

[A] Team Partner or Consultant?

Architecture and engineering firms do not generally have the equity to contribute substantially to the construction of a P3 project or to share in losses. Designers are more often selected as Consultants and are paid for their work on the proposal, sometimes with a bonus if the proposal and the project are successful.

[B] Engineer of Record

The Engineer of Record (EOR) is a licensed professional who takes independent responsibility for the adequacy of the design. State law typically makes the EOR legally responsible for errors and omissions in each construction plan they sign. Some states require the EOR to stamp all project drawings, even those prepared by other design teams and outside of the EOR's licensed specialty. Care must be exercised to express in writing the limits of such a stamping exercise, if the designs were prepared by others.

[C] Designer Proposal & Quantity Estimates

In keeping with the policy to assign risk to the party best positioned to manage it, Designers may take responsibility for quantity overruns when their preliminary designs are used in bid preparation. This is a contractually assumed risk. The Designer may agree to be liable to the Concessionaire regardless of the extent of their negligence. The contract with the Designer may also require it to prepare an estimate of operational costs that will be relied upon by the Concessionaire in preparing its proposal.

Designer's traditional errors and omissions insurance will not provide coverage for certain warranties, guarantees, contractual liability, fines, penalties, or punitive damages. Instead, it provides only limited coverage for errors and omissions and may not cover construction estimates or environmental impairment.

[D] Key Clauses in Design Agreements

When negotiating the Design Agreement for a P3, keep in mind these issues:

[1] Project Description and Scope of Work

The project description should provide the main elements and limits of the project, (i.e. purpose of structure, the budget, square feet, number of floors, exterior skin). It should specifically exclude any elements (such as landscaping or lighting) that are not included in the project or services.

Although P3 contracts ostensibly give discretion to the Designer, design submittals inevitably go through additional iterations, perhaps even showing the owner alternatives. A separate payment provision may be appropriate for this type of additional work.

[2] Standard of Care

The Architect/Engineer (A/E) will be subject to the professional standard of care for negligence unless the contract provides for a higher standard.[202] The owner or Concessionaire may want to require a higher standard.

An owner typically will craft a standard of care for a Designer in a P3 project that may read like this:

> Standard of Care means the exercise of the degree of skill, diligence, prudence and foresight which would reasonably and ordinarily be expected from time to time from a skilled and experienced designer, engineer, constructor, operator or Developer seeking in good faith to comply with its contractual obligations, complying with all applicable Laws and Governmental Approvals, and engaged in the same type of undertaking under similar circumstances and conditions."[203]

However, there is tension between the Designer's standard of care and the design specifications and other performance specifications:

> In the event of a conflict between or among provisions in Contract Documents having the same order of precedence, the provisions that establish the higher quality, manner or method of performing the Work, exceed [Designer's Standard of Care], or use more stringent standards will prevail.[204]

A P3 contract may have further elaboration on the Designer's obligations in the contract's technical provisions:

> Developer shall design and construct the drainage systems in accordance with the relevant requirements of the standards. If there is any conflict in standards,

---

[202] *Gagne v. Bertran*, 43 Cal. 2d 481, 275 P.2d 15 (1954).

[203] California Department of Transportation, Presidio Parkway Project Public-Private Partnership Agreement, Appendix 1, definition of Best Management Practice.

[204] California Department of Transportation, Presidio Parkway Project Public-Private Partnership Agreement, § 1.2.4.

Developer shall adhere to the standard with the highest priority. If Developer's Proposal has a higher standard than any of the listed standards, adhere to the Proposal standard. If there is any ambiguity in standards, it is Developer's responsibility to obtain clarification from Department before proceeding with design and/or construction. [The contract then listed the specific published standards with respect to the design issue.][205]

The Designer's standard of care on a P3 that incorporates extensive design specifications can transform the design process into an intractable labyrinth. The Designer is often asked to identify the highest theoretical standard and then comply with it.[206]

In *Gee & Jenson Engineers, Architects and Planners v. U.S.*, the Designers argued that they were not responsible for water damage because their design complied with the local building code and the standard of care.[207] Additionally, the Designers contended the various referenced design guides were contradictory or ambiguous on the issue.[208] The court made it clear that when the government contract requires a higher standard of performance than the local building code, as in this case, the requirements of the Contract, not the local building code, controls.[209]

Further, the government's approval of design submittals did not waive the contract control requirement. Under typical contract provisions the government's review, approval, acceptance, or payment does not operate as a waiver of any rights under the contract. The approval in *Gee v. U.S.* did not function as a change in the contract requirements. The court explained that only the Designer specifically requesting authorization from the Navy's Engineer in Charge, in order to omit the flashing and

[205] California Department of Transportation, Presidio Parkway Project Public-Private Partnership Agreement, Division II, p. 28.
[206] *Gee & Jenson Engineers, Architects & Planners v. United States*, No. 05-457C, 2008 WL 4997488, (Fed. Cl. Nov. 7, 2008).
[207] *Id.*
[208] *Id.*
[209] *Id.*

receiving specific authorization from the Engineer in Charge, could alter the contract's design requirement.[210] The government was awarded damages for the cost of correcting the work.[211]

The Concessionaire may also set a higher standard of care for the Designer. Under the basic Designer's standard of care, the Designer only has liability when its design is negligent with respect to industry practice. However, the Concessionaire may incur direct expenses due to Designer mistakes that are not "negligent" by this definition. For example, the Designer's non-negligent choices or mistakes may result in higher construction costs.

So, the Concessionaire might have included a contract provision as follows:

> Designer will be liable to Concessionaire for cost overruns caused by increases in actual quantities above quantities estimated by Designer in the Proposal.

Expansion of the standard of care by the Public Owner or Concessionaire may be uninsurable under typical A/E liability insurance, which only covers professional negligence, rather than adherence to elaborate warranties or "highest and best" standards. A typical professional liability insurance policy excludes damages for the insured Designer's alleged liability "under any contract or agreement . . . except to the extent that the Insured would have been liable in the absence of such contract or agreement."[212]

The Concessionaire may also have trouble making a claim against its own Designer, even for professional negligence, depending on the definition of "insured" in the policy and the exclusions pertaining to the relationship between the insured and the claimant.

In most cases, expert testimony is required to establish the standard of care.[213] The defendant-engineer may be overly defensive and therefore

---

[210] *Id.*

[211] *Id.*

[212] Travelers, "Miscellaneous Professional Liability, Exclusions," A.14.

[213] *Huber, Hunt & Nichols, Inc. v. Moore*, 67 Cal. App. 3d 278, 136 Cal. Rptr. 603 (1977), *Allied Properties v. John A. Blume & Associates*, 25 Cal. App. 3d 848, 102

an ineffectual witness. And their testimony might not even be allowed.[214] Moreover, a specific type of consultant may be needed as a testifying expert.[215]

As parties are busy drafting the contract language defining the standard of care, they are wise to bear in mind where they will be able to find an expert able to testify about that specific standard of care.

A contract that obligates the A/E to design a plant or equipment that will meet specific performance criteria will be generally be enforced as an express warranty of the design.[216] For an experimental or innovative design assignment, the Designer might negotiate the standard to be stated as "best efforts" or the design liability can be disclaimed entirely.

[3] Schedule of Performance

Traditionally, A/Es do not have binding schedules in their professional services agreements. Where no time is specified for performance of a contract, a reasonable time is usually implied.[217]

A P3 contract, however, needs to be coordinated to minimize the time to substantial completion as financing charges accrue every day of the project. Where the contract states that "time is of the essence," any delay in the performance of the contract may constitute a material breach if it causes prejudice or harm to the Concessionaire or Design-Builder. The A/E will often be contractually bound to the milestones

---

Cal. Rptr. 259 (1972), and California Evidence Code §801, *et seq.*

[214] The requirement for expert testimony to establish the standard of professional care for an architect is not satisfied by the testimony of the defendant-architect even where the claimant relied on the testimony *Garaman, Inc. v. Williams*, 912 P.2d 1121 (Wyo. 1996).

[215] Property owner's failure to offer expert testimony regarding the standard of care owed by environmental cleanup consultant precluded recovery on a breach of contract claim, since standard of care was not within the common knowledge and experience of the jury. *Delta Envtl. Consultants of N. Carolina, Inc. v. Wysong & Miles Co.*, 132 N.C. App. 160, 510 S.E.2d 690 (1999)

[216] *Arkansas Rice Growers Co-op. Ass'n v. Alchemy Indus., Inc.*, 797 F.2d 565 (8th Cir. 1986) (applying California law).

[217] CA Civ. Code §1657.

and times set forth in the Concessionaire or Design Build Agreement, due to flow down clauses in the design agreement.

[4] Construction Site Visits and Observation

The role of a design professional at a site has been subject to vigorous debate regarding the extent of the inspection of the contractor's work, the purpose of the inspection, and any resulting liability for defective work. This is an even more important issue in P3 Projects.

The general rule is that where the A/E's contract imposes a duty to inspect the work or the A/E undertakes such a responsibility by its actions, the A/Es will be liable to the Concessionaire and Design Builder and potentially third parties for negligence in performing that work.[218] By statute, architects do not have a duty to observe the construction of works for which they provide plans and specifications, but they may, by contract, agree to provide such services. Under the California Architect's Practice Act, those services are defined as "periodic observation of completed work to determine general compliance with the plans, specifications, reports, or other contract documents."[219]

The P3 project poses additional risk, as the Designer is part of the integrated Design Build team with greater day to day involvement in construction activities. They may be performing construction engineering, as well as overall project design.

Further, the Designer does not share worker compensation immunity with the Contractor or Subcontractors. As such, they are vulnerable to third party worker lawsuits for construction accidents and failures. This is again a subject to be addressed in the design of the OCIP or CCIP insurance program.

[5] Indemnification

Indemnification is the contractual allocation of future risk. The stronger party who drafts the contract often shifts risks onto the weaker

---

[218] *U.S. for Use & Benefit of Los Angeles Testing Lab. v. Rogers & Rogers*, 161 F. Supp.132 (S.D. Cal. 1958).
[219] CA Bus. & Prof. Code § 5536.25(c).

party (who wants the work). Generally, the indemnification clause will require one party to defend the stronger negotiation party and pay the resulting loss. Indemnification is a legal area that requires special expertise.

An example is California Civil Code § 2782, which places limits on the extent to which construction participants can shift the risk of loss to others, particularly where the indemnified party is solely at fault or supplies defective designs. Overly aggressive indemnity clauses present great risks to Concessionaires, Design-Builders, and subcontractors. If they are too overbearing, there may be few bidders.

[6] Insurance

A typical contract requires the A/E to maintain certain types of insurance coverage with specified limits, deductibles and coverage features. It is important that the requirements can be fulfilled by the A/E in the commercial insurance marketplace. In general, the A/E's insurance coverage for a large P3 should be at least $20 million or 20 percent of the project value, whichever is greater. This may be incorporated into the OCIP or CCIP insurance program.

[7] Suspension or Termination of A/E

If no contract clause governs the parties' rights to terminate the Design Agreement, the common law requires the examination of many factors to determine whether it is fair to allow termination.[220]

These factors include the reason for termination (breach of conduct), its impact on the non-breaching party, the likelihood of further breaches, whether the breach can be compensated by economic damages, the effect on the breaching party and the likelihood of losses or forfeitures on it, the likelihood that the breach can be cured, and the reason for the breach.[221] It is common to include both a termination for default and a

---

[220] Restatement (Second) of Contracts §§ 251 and 252 (1981).
[221] *Id* §251.

termination for convenience clause in the design agreement, so that a "no fault" termination may be made.[222]

Since termination disputes are resolved on a case-by-case basis, different facts lead to different outcomes. In a typical case, for example, the party breached a contract by failing to make payment and the court held that the other party could rescind and recover the reasonable value of the work done.[223]

[8] Claims against the Designer

The Concessionaire and Design-Builder will rely on the Designer's preliminary designs to prepare a cost estimate and scheduling for bidding. Public Owner or third-party driven changes in criteria between the preliminary design plans to the stamped construction plans may increase the project cost. If those costs cannot be recovered from the Owner or third parties, the Designer may be responsible for the cost overruns due to those design changes.

Practice Pointer: It is important for the Designer to keep track of changes in design criteria and alert the Design-Builder and concessionaire of such events. There are typically time limits for asserting claims based upon design changes and the passage of time may prejudice the Design Builder's ability to recover from the Concessionaire or Public Owner. This is often culturally difficult for Designers who are used to satisfying all stakeholders and typically do not have financial responsibility for those costs.

This is particularly important to keep in mind, as the Designer's contractual liability may be absolute and not limited to cost overruns

---

[222] Mark J. Linderman and Aaron P. Silberman, *Construction Subcontracting: A Comprehensive Practical and Legal Guide*, Forum on the Construction Industry (Mar. 26, 2014), citing 48 C.F.R. 52.239-1 (1984); 48 C.F.R. 52.249-2, Alternative I (2012).

[223] *Barris v. Atlas Rock Co.*, 118 Cal. App. 606, 610,5P.2d 670 (Cal. Ct. App. 1931).

resulting from their negligence.[224] This type of liability may not be covered by traditional errors and omissions coverage.[225]

Other types of claims are regularly made against Designers regarding errors, omissions, lack of constructability, lack of timely responses to submissions, and related A/E services issues.

In most states, the statute of limitations generally begins running against A/Es from the completion of the Plans and Specifications, not the project itself. In a P3 project, the statute of limitations may be tolled during the course of the design and construction process, so long as the Designer is providing ongoing engineering or architectural services.

5.05   General Contractor Issues

[A] Contractor Liability

[1] Assumed risks

The Design-Build team on a P3 takes on considerable responsibility. They are responsible for, among other matters, project cost, liquidated damages, and performance of the completed facility. For the most part, these are tasks uninsurable and the contractor must manage the risks by identifying and tracking them, in addition to taking steps to make them less probable or to limit the consequences of adverse outcomes. (The comments on coverage insurance that follow are generalities and may not track the manuscript or industry policies at issue in any specific P3 Project).

[2] Exclusion for Professional Liability

Commercial general liability policies typically exclude professional services performed by a general contractor. Professional services may

---

[224] Tracy Alan Saxe, David G. Jordan, John S. Sandberg, Caroline W. Spangenberg, and Julie A. Lierly, *Construction Insurance A Guide for Attorneys and Other Professionals Chapter 6:Professional Liability Insurance Coverage*, 195-196, American Bar Association (2011).

[225] *Id.*

be defined as supervisory, inspection, architectural, or engineering activities. General Contractors can obtain limited professional liability policies at additional expense.

[3] Builder's Risk Insurance

Builder's Risk insurance covers the structure under construction plus machinery, supplies, and scaffolding. It can be held by the Public Owner, Design-Builder or General Contractor.

[4] Rectification Coverage

Rectification coverage consists of first-party coverage for the contractor for expenses arising from losses such as cost overruns, schedule delays, and rework due to the negligence of a subcontracted design professional. (This is also known as "mitigation of loss" coverage.) These policies may be broader than the architect or engineer's underlying professional policies.

Practice Pointer: This is not coverage for the Designer; on the contrary, it may lead to a subrogation claim against the Designer.

[5] "Faulty Workmanship" Errors and Omissions Coverage

"Faulty Workmanship" errors and omission coverage covers faulty workmanship or defective materials incorporated into the work. (This is usually an excluded risk under the Workmanship exclusion from most CGL policies.)

[B] Subcontractor Issues

[1] Project Labor Agreements

Many P3 Projects have a Project Labor Agreement (PLA), that applies to project participants, whether their employees belong to a union or not. It is strongly recommended that specialized review of such an agreement be conducted by non-union contractors to determine whether its provisions place them at a disadvantage in future labor-organizing activities or disputes. The PLA is designed to resolve labor disputes quickly. (I have been named in the past as a "rapid project neutral" for PLA's for BART Extension Projects.)

[2] Pass-through Agreements

Pass-through agreements are intended to allow a Concessionaire or Design Builder to pass along a lower tier claim (say, a subcontractor or supplier), assist in its preparation and share in its analysis, while preserving joint attorney-client privilege and protect the general contractor against independent liability beyond the pass through amounts. These agreements vary in impact and enforceability by federal agency and state.

5.06   Operation and Maintenance Contractor

The Operation and Maintenance (O & M) contractor's risks include the costs of labor, benefits, consultants, electricity, insurance, chemicals, and a myriad of other expenses.

For a long period of time, O & M contractors have been in the business of maintaining buildings, roads and treatment plants, keeping excellent cost records, and knowing how to hedge future costs. It is important to have this type of expertise on any P3 Team from early in the proposal process. The biggest risk to an O & M Contractor in a P3 arrangement is a cost commitment that may last 20, 30 or even 50 years. The careful and skilled hedging of those cost risks is a vital part of the O & M's pricing strategy.

5.07   Preparing the Proposal

[A] Contract Provisions

An Owner's P3 contract that is one sided can create large project risks. It is tempting to grade the fairness of such project contracts on a one-to-ten scale. There are numerous agencies that regularly issue unfair and unconscionable contracts. On the other hand, some publicly-issued contracts are too lenient or vague to be effectively administered or enforced.

The presence of lengthy disclaimer statements, indemnities, or outrageous insurance provisions may be a tip-off towards the type of attitude and approach to contracts administration that the public agency intends for the project. Often, such clauses are met by a flurry of inquiries and comments during the bidding period or by a dearth of bids on the appointed day of submission itself.

A solitary and stratospheric bid on a major civic project can be both an embarrassment and an economic hardship for a public agency.

It is critical for the parties to carefully review every unfamiliar style of contract. Parties are especially warned to beware of typewritten contracts that sound like they follow Standard AIA, Engineers Joint Contract Documents Committee (EJCDC) or ConsensusDoc formats, but are substantially re-written and may contain unexpected and incredibly oppressive terms.

[B] Financial Investment in Proposal

Preparing a proposal is a significant investment of time and finances, particularly for a losing bidder or even for a winning bidder when the project does not proceed. Developers who invest significant effort into potential projects that the government ultimately does not award sometimes attempt to seek compensation in court.[226] Such claims can be expensive.

In one case, the San Francisco International Airport saw the value in utilizing a P3 to develop air cargo facilities when it had reached its bonding capacity on other projects.[227] The Airport held competitive selection and chose a private partner for the Exclusive Negotiation

---

[226] *See, e.g., Bldg. 11 Investors LLC v. City of Seattle*, 912 F. Supp. 2d 972 (W.D. Wash. 2012) (lawsuit filed by Developer after negotiations for building lease deteriorated, including alleged breach of good faith and fair dealing).

[227] *Airis SFO, LLC v. City & Cnty. of San Francisco*, No. A121855, 2010 WL 3687508, (Cal. Ct. App. Sept. 22, 2010), as modified on denial of reh'g (Oct. 20, 2010) (unpublished/noncitable).

Agreement to finalize the project concept. However, the project never got off the ground because, behind closed doors, the Airport was not viewed as sufficiently promoting the project to obtain the necessary Board of Supervisors votes.[228]

A court found that the Airport breached the duty of good faith and fair dealing in order to undermine the project it had initiated by withholding information, refusing to correct misinformation, and working behind the scenes to ensure that the City took a course contrary to the project for which it was ostensibly seeking approval.[229] The winning bidder (who was unable to proceed with the project) was awarded damages by a jury and the decision was upheld on appeal.[230]

It is generally difficult for a Developer to demonstrate that it reasonably relied on the promises of government employees because government employees are known to have very limited authority to promise specific outcomes.

A Developer made it over those initial hurdles in Philadelphia. The Developer had worked with city support to obtain a special development status from the state for its property and the surrounding city-owned property.[231] The Developer then formed a nonprofit P3 with a regional development authority and pushed the project further in reliance on zoning changes promised by the city.[232] After expiration of the city's 20-year written commitment, the city imposed a height limit on the Developer's property inconsistent with the Developer's plans.[233] The frustrated Developer sought damages from the city on the doctrine of promissory estoppel.[234] The district court initially found that the city's extensive involvement over a long period of time permitted an inference of reasonable reliance.[235]

---

[228] *Id.* at 6.

[229] *Id.* at 13.

[230] *Id.* at 17.

[231] *CMR D.N. Corp. v. City of Philadelphia,* No. CIV.A. 07-1045, 2008 WL 4055823 (E.D. Pa. Aug. 28, 2008)

[232] *Id.* at 3.

[233] *Id.* at 2.

[234] *Id.*

[235] *Id.*

However, the Court of Appeals fundamentally disagreed, explaining that any "encouragement" by local officials cannot reasonably be interpreted as "a promise of perpetual support for the Project," and therefore was not actionable.[236]

Real estate Developers making unsolicited P3 proposals appear particularly unlikely to prevail on these types of claims.[237] They have no reasonable expectation of success.

[C] Budget and Scheduling

[1] Revenue and profitability

The private partner in a P3 contract will make significant initial investments in infrastructure and will assume responsibility for long-term operations, yet risks like land acquisition or permitting can threaten project completion. Pricing a P3 must take into account the risks unique to bundled contracts. There is a body of literature and scholarship on estimating true and complete project costs and benefits that would fill a library.

During the course of certain projects, it may be appropriate to evaluate the potential gains that might be generated from certain activities versus their expenses and financial risks. For example, a company may wish to design and build certain types of water treatment facilities but refrain from operating them due to the different set of risks and insurance programs associated with such ventures.

Or, a company may be willing to take on a Design-Build Operate water treatment project over thirty years but is not willing to absorb the risk of the fluctuating cost of electricity, changes in environmental laws, or union labor rate changes. It might, on the other hand, be willing to accept the risk of variable interest rates on borrowed funds.

---

[236] *CMR D.N. Corp. v. City of Philadelphia*, 703 F.3d 612 (3d Cir. 2013).
[237] *Warren v. New Castle Cnty.*, No. CIV. 07-725-SLR-LPS, 2008 WL 2566947 (D. Del. June 26, 2008); *Condemnation by Cnty. of Berks*, In re, 914 A.2d 962 (Pa. Commw. Ct. 2007).

The literature on P3 projects sometimes refers to one advantage of P3 procurement as preventing "white elephant" projects.[238] The government may be using private investors' willingness to invest as an indicator that the project has merit and, as a result, no assumptions about the project should be taken for granted. A proposer may need to commission its own demand forecasts, or at least reevaluate the government data with skepticism, to determine the magnitude of demand risks.

[2] Exclusive Concessions

When the Concessionaire's future revenue is primarily based upon user demand, the Concessionaire should carefully evaluate whether the business model will work without an exclusivity agreement. At least one government entity appears to have undercut its own bridge toll revenue by constructing an alternate route – the Port Mann Bridge.[239]

[3] Competition Analysis

There is concern that a Concessionaire team may go through an extensive vetting process for a project, engage in time-consuming and costly negotiations with an eligible agency, and then find itself without the contract. The public partner may sometimes reserve the right to use the design or elements of the design from a rejected P3 proposal. Many states allow unsolicited bids but require advertisement and solicitation of bids based on the substance of the unsolicited project proposal. In that case, the unsolicited proposer may find that its new competitors are free to use its concepts, designs and business model, despite the original proposer having developed its intellectual property after considerable thought and great expense.

---

[238] *See, e.g.,* Vickram Cuttaree, Benefits and Risks of PPP (The World Bank February 2011).
[239] *See* TransLink, 2012 Year-End Financial and Performance Report 11 (2013).

CHAPTER 6

DESIGN AND CONSTRUCTION

6.01   Project Development

[A] Flow-down to Design-Build Contractor

A flow-down clause binds the Design-Builder to the terms of the contract in the same manner as the Concessionaire, similar to traditional contractor/ subcontractor relationships.[240] The Concessionaire often will assign all investigation, permitting, design and construction responsibilities to one entity, typically the Design-Build contractor. That Design-Build contractor is, perhaps to its surprise, responsible for project development activities through the flow-down provision.[241] This may include environmental permitting, which is commonly outside of a Design-Builder's purview.

[B] Permits

Owners are traditionally limited in their ability to pass unreasonable risks onto a contractor despite contractual disclaimers and some allocation of design responsibility, particularly when the disclaimer is an

---

[240] *See, generally* E. Sanderson Hoe et al., *Flow-Down Clauses in Subcontracts,* Briefing Paper No. 85-5 (1985).
[241] *See* American Institute of Architects, *AIA Document A401, Article 2.1* (2007).

excuse for the owner's inadequate planning.[242] However, these legislative protections are not usually applicable to the Design-Build context and is even less likely to occur on P3 projects.

In *Bell/Heery v. U.S.*, the contractor was designing and building a prison for the Federal Bureau of Prisons. [243] The contract required the contractor to obtain permits from the state of New Hampshire. It read, "[t]he Contractor shall, without additional expense to the Government, be responsible for obtaining any necessary licenses and permits . . ."[244] The contractor received a permit in time for construction from the New Hampshire Department of Environmental Services, but the Department's subsequent administration of the permit was inconsistent with the original permit, contrary to generally accepted industry practice, and the piecemeal authorization of work resulted in extremely inefficient performance.[245]

The prison contractor sought assistance from the Bureau to no avail and felt compelled to accede to the Department's unreasonable demands.[246] The contractor sought compensation from the Bureau for the delays and particularly for the Bureau's failure to intercede as the Bureau was obligated to "consult" with a permitting agency at the request of the contractor.[247]

The contractual transfer of risk for permits onto the contractor was upheld. The court explained, "How risk is allocated is ultimately up to the parties themselves."[248] This can be squared with the traditional approach referenced above by evaluating the level of control retained by the owner. In a case where the transfer of risk was not enforced, the government's suggestion to "tweak" the design was contradicted by the government's extensive control over the design requirements and the

---

[242] *Drennon Constr. & Consulting, Inc.* (Jan. 4, 2013) 13-1 B.C.A. (CCH) ¶ 35213 (including disclaimer of design furnished by government did not transfer risk of inadequate design onto contractor).

[243] *Bell/Heery v. United States*, 106 Fed. Cl. 300, 305 (2012) aff'd, 739 F.3d 1324 (Fed. Cir. 2014)

[244] *Id.* at 305.

[245] *Id.* at 306.

[246] *Id.*

[247] *Id.* at 309.

[248] *Id.* at 304.

impossibility of correcting the government's defective design within its constraints.[249]

In contrast, the P3 contractor is more likely to be handed a blank slate. Along with the contractor's discretion to plan and design the project comes an enforceable transfer of risk for those activities.

Reading these cases closely, the obstruction encountered by contractors is frequently from an overzealous or coercive third party, usually staff-level employee who may be acting outside of their authority. A lawsuit by the contractor against the regulatory agency to compel the agency to follow its own regulations is the last source of relief available to the contractor.

The question left for the Concessionaire is what probability to assign this risk in its risk management spreadsheet to determine the contingency. The questions for a future project sponsor are whether it can afford to transfer this risk and, if so, whether all bidders will be bidding on the same basis.

[C] Right-of-way

As with permitting, the risk of loss of right-of-way due to an obstructionist third party is not typically transferred to a general contractor.[250] Courts

<hr />

[249] *Drennon Constr., supra* ("the Design-Build portion of the retaining walls was rather a bit of a subset of the rest of the contract" which set strict confines).
[250] *See generally Appeals of J.E. Mcamis, Inc.*, ASBCA No. 54455, 10-2 B.C.A. (CCH) ¶ 34607 (Nov. 18, 2010), (concluding that the P & R clause did not bar recovery where a contract identified certain "haul routes" for transporting materials and county officials later passed an ordinance restricting use of such routes); *Appeal of Odebrecht Contractors of California, Inc.*, ENGBCA No. 6372, 2000 WL 975128 (July 6, 2000) (concluding that "the boiler plate 'Permits and Responsibilities clause'" did not preclude an equitable adjustment where a contract provided for unrestricted access to certain wells and the local regulatory authority later denied the contractor access to those wells); *Appeal of Dravo Corp.*, ENGBCA No. 3800, 79-1 B.C.A. (CCH) ¶ 13575 (Nov. 30, 1978) (concluding that the P & R clause did not preclude recovery where a contract specifically designated certain areas as "work/storage areas" and local officials subsequently denied a contractor access to those areas); *Appeal of ABC Demolition Corp.*, GSBCA No. 2288, 32, 869-70 68-2 B.C.A. (CCH) ¶ 7096 (June 20, 1968) (concluding that risk of National Park Service Superintendent refusing truck permits was not assumed

generally find that the owner explicitly or implicitly warrants site access, or sometimes, a particular route.

The trend for public owners sponsoring P3 projects to negotiate most site access prior to advertising the project. The risk of a property owner not complying with the negotiated agreement and unexpected third-party interference remain. Any greater transfer of risk is likely to be ineffectual due to the lack of eminent domain rights by the Concessionaire.

6.02 Design Phase

[A] Design Approvals by Owner

The Concessionaire is rarely fully responsible for design, as the owner generally retains the ability to influence design choices and approve the final plans. After the P3 is signed, the question is whether the Concessionaire's design satisfies the project specifications. Particularly with performance specifications, the issue of design adequacy and safety becomes the whether the design meets the standard of care and the letter of the P3 Agreement.

The always owner retains the right to review the submittals for conformance with the specifications. If the owner wants to financially benefit from the P3 approach, it must allocate real discretion to the Concessionaire along with the responsibility and risk.

When the Developer is responsible for design, the contract must fairly apportion the owner some responsibility for unreasonable delays in the approval of submittals.

The contract must also provide a mechanism to resolve disputes over the interpretation of design criteria that preserves the Developer's right to design and construct the project as bid.

---

by contractor); *Appeal of Carl W. Linder Co.,* ENGBCA No. 3526, 78-1 B.C.A. (CCH) ¶ 13114 (Feb. 14, 1978) (concluding that government identification of access to bidders constituted a warranty of access breached by third-party interference).

The design phase of a project element is distinct from construction and typical dispute resolution procedures are not well suited to their resolution. One dispute resolution approach specific to the design phase is the Interpretative Engineering Decision.

If the Developer is out of time to negotiate a resolution regarding whether a design meets the technical requirements, the Developer can request an Interpretative Engineering Decision from the owner. The owner's stated position becomes binding for the owner and preserves the Developer's right to additional compensation if it proceeds at the owner's direction and can later demonstrate that the owner's interpretation of technical requirements was incorrect.

The Interpretative Engineering Decision provision may resolve the situation where an owner is reticent to reject a design concept outright and instead repeatedly supplies "comments" to the Designer providing non-binding suggestions or requesting additional design justification. While the result may be the same as an IED, the death by a thousand lashes approach consumes far more time.

At a minimum, the owner should not be entitled to reject the Designer's design unless the submittal or subject provision thereof fails to comply, or is inconsistent, with an applicable covenant, condition, requirement, term or provision of the contract documents. For certain submittals, such as colors and signage, the owner might specify that it has a higher level of discretion, including sole or absolute authority. However, that type of exercise of discretion should be coupled with a cost provision or allowance that requires the public agency to pay for costs above those reasonably inferable from the specifications.

Other solutions may include a third party design checker with binding (but eventually appealable) authority to approve designs, a clearly designated type of engineering analysis that will be sufficient evidence of adequacy of the design if performed correctly (e.g. "3D finite element models with soil/structure interaction must be supplied at request of the owner") or strict timeframes for the owner to state that a design does not conform to technical requirements.

[B] Design Approvals by Stakeholders

Large projects may fall within the purview of many sister regulatory agencies. Pipelines or rails that cross highways may require structural reviews not only by the owner of the project, but by the regulatory agency for the highway. These other entities are sometimes called Third-Party Stakeholders or Authorities Having Jurisdiction ("AHJ"). Project owners frequently negotiate the right-of-way agreements with the adjacent jurisdictions themselves because the owners have long term relationships with the AHJ and thus have more leverage to negotiate. The owner is better suited to sustain project delays during the early planning stages. The right-of-way agreements invariably grant a right of review to the AHJ.

However, the right of entry agreements signed by the AHJ rarely set forth the mechanism for their review or set standards for the review. The AHJ is likely to passionately advance their concept of the project, or their own technical provisions, without regard to what the Concessionaire agreed to in the P3 contract. These are unusually dangerous provisions for the Concessionaire.

The submittal process in the P3 contract and the right-of-way agreements with AHJ's need to address the limited leverage that the Developer has to demand prompt comments from government entities with which the Developer is not in contract.

These agreements must incorporate clear scope, standards, time limits, and a rapid binding dispute resolution process of design issues with the AHJ. Otherwise the Developer will be sustaining delays and liquidated damages while the AHJ is unapologetically uncooperative.

One solution is to define AHJ delays as a Relief Event and excuse those delays that are out of the Developer's control. Another solution is to grant the Developer the right to enforce the right-of-way agreement against the AHJ in court (perhaps by identifying the Developer as a third-party beneficiary) or with the dispute resolution procedures of the prime contract.

The risks of AHJ's who are seeking their own advantages cannot be understated. One analyst who conducted a survey on P3 projects explained that "by far the most frequently reported cause of distress affecting P3 construction works relates to the inexperience, lack of commitment, lack of engagement, bureaucracy, and interference of public-sector project participants; and associated scope changes and enforced delays."[251]

[C] Permits and Governmental Approvals

P3 contracts may involve a higher level of Developer responsibility for permitting. In addition to the risk and cost of obtaining the permits, the contractors are likely obligated to perform the mitigation required by the various Governmental Approvals. Owners may transfer this risk by using this language: "Developer shall be solely responsible for compliance with the requirements of the Governmental Approvals."

The scope of design and construction responsibility associated with the governmental approvals may be less than crystal clear. The owner may be able to better communicate its understanding of the obligations by annotating the approval.[252] Non-typical items of work that are expected should be specifically listed in the scope of work (instead of obliquely referring to "fulfill permit obligations"). If the owner is unable to definitively define the mitigation work, it may also limit the Concessionaire's maximum exposure (to rein in proposal costs) by setting forth a cost sharing mechanism. For example, where the Concessionaire bears the first $1 million of mitigation expenses measured by force account and additional expenses will be split 50/50 with the Public Owner.

[D] Cost of Redesign

On traditional projects, the owner impliedly warrants the quality of plans and specifications that they provide to contractors. Under the common law rule, a contractor is not responsible for the consequences of problems with the design and is not responsible to correct the design.[253]

---

[251] Robert Bain, The Anatomy of Construction Risk: Lessons from a Millennium of PPP Experience 2 (Standard & Poor's April 5, 2007).

[252] *See, e.g.,* Golden Ears Bridge Schedule PA-31 Allocation of Obligations Under Certain Facility Lands Agreements and Encumbrances.

[253] *United States v. Spearin,* 248 U.S. 132, 133, 39 S. Ct. 59, 60, 63 L. Ed. 166 (1918)

This widely followed rule was established by the U.S. Supreme Court decision *United States v. Spearin* and is known as the *Spearin* Doctrine.[254] The principle argument of the agency was that the contractors had a full and adequate opportunity to judge the plans and specifications with regard to completeness and accuracy.[255] The contractors replied that they were neither licensed nor capable of designing these projects and that they had reasonable expectations of completeness and accuracy. Furthermore, they continued, if they were to check every possible aspect of every design they bid on, there would not have been any time to actually build anything. The *Spearin* doctrine is less likely to offer protection to the Concessionaire or Design-Builder in a P3 project.

The Concessionaire should expect to be largely responsible for any redesign costs and impacts for design erroneous work reasonably under its control. The public owner should bear the degree of responsibility associated with instances where the owner supplies designs, directs changes or insists on certain aspects of the design elements.

When the Concessionaire is entirely running the planning and design from the early stages of the project, it will have little recourse except against its own Designer. If there is any exception to the inapplicability of *Spearin*, it may revolve around detailed preliminary drawings furnished by the owner, the baseline geotechnical conditions, the governmental approvals and permits, rights of way, or detailed technical specifications imposed by the owner.

6.03 Construction Phase

[A] Unexpected Challenges

More construction risks may be transferred to the Concessionaire and then to the Design-Builder than in traditional contracting. Courts will try to enforce the intent of the parties when a risk transfer is clear in the contract. The primary exception is when the risk transfer is superficial mentioned in the Contract, but the owner continues to

---

[254] *Id.*

[255] *Id.* at 137.

control the contractor's means and methods. Even if a claim is valid, the Concessionaire and Design-Builder must have sufficient reserves to continue with the project and to pay debt service during delays; as reimbursement by the owner may be years away.

[1] Project Location

Urban, suburban and rural projects each have inherent and peculiar risks. Does the responsible Designer and contractor have the experience, familiarity, and professional exposure in the region to fairly evaluate and effectively mitigate those local risks?

I have seen an inordinate number of claims where the participants have chosen: 1) local Designers with limited experience with the type of project (*e.g.* their first major hospital); and/or 2) highly experienced project architects from another state with limited local experience in the region (*e.g.* a Southern California architect designing ski condos in the Sierras).

Remote jobs pose another set of risks. The availability of materials and labor productivity may be a significant risk. A Design-Builder may be assuming far more risk than they expect, as illustrated by Fluor Intercontinental, Inc. v. Department of State, the Civilian Board of Contract Appeals (CBCA). [256]

The contract set forth a fixed-price government Design-Build contract for the construction of an embassy in Astana, Kazakhstan. DOS ultimately awarded the project to Fluor for $63,057,022.

As of February 2004, there were no paved roads, public water, or permanent power services. Fluor claimed these services were implied by the contract scope and bidding materials.

The Court summarized the positions of the parties as follows:

> Fluor asserts that DOS had formal and actual notice of the project delays. Fluor claims that, despite this knowledge, DOS failed to grant contract extensions when requested, causing it to accelerate the schedule to compensate for the delays. In its reply brief, Fluor

---

[256] CBCA 670, 2007 WL 3055018 (October 4, 2007).

clarifies its claim of constructive acceleration, stating that DOS's "threat of liquidated damages, and instruction to Fluor to meet the original project schedule constitute a constructive change to the contract.

DOS contends that Fluor is responsible for its delays, none of the delays are excusable, and, accordingly, Fluor is not entitled to any additional costs resulting from its efforts to compensate for the delays. In addition, DOS contends that Fluor failed to submit a request for a schedule extension supported by a time impact analysis, as required by the contract. Finally, DOS states that the Government never ordered Fluor to accelerate performance, and that Fluor has not established entitlement to damages on a constructive acceleration theory.

The CBCA further quoted the contract for the Design-Builder's obligations as including: "complete all work to design and construct the [embassy complex]"; "[t]he Contractor remains solely responsible and liable for design sufficiency and should not depend on reports provided by the [Government] as part of the contract documents"; "[d]rawings are included for the sole purpose of illustrating the design intent of the owner"; "Design-Build Contractor shall gather the required data during the site visit and design phase"; and each offeror was responsible for "ascertaining the availability of all materials and equipment necessary to produce the work required by the proposed Contract Documents, of sufficient skilled labor to perform the work, and of the availability of transportation to the site."

The CBCA then compared these risk shifting provisions of the contract to the trial testimony and rejected over $24 million in Fluor's claims.

[2] Site Risks

Many site risks not within the control of either party are commonly shared between the Public Owner and Concessionaire by providing a time extension, but no compensation, for difficulties that arise. A Concessionaire should be wary of accepting a contract that does not grant time extensions, and perhaps be entitled to assistance with debt service, for events that are out of its control. That is because the structure of a P3 generally starts payment only when the project is completed or in beneficial use. Thus, the impact of delays can have a severe impact on the financial model of the project.

The physical risk to a project from natural disasters during construction is commonly insurable through reasonably priced Builders Risk Policies. Similarly, property insurance can insure the facilities after completion. Although owners frequently require that they are listed as the "loss payee" on the policy, it may be more appropriate to list the party bearing the financial risk of natural disasters.

Other physical risks, like differing site conditions, are typically not insurable. The transfer of such risk onto the Concessionaire is probably enforceable. Unforeseen conditions are the most likely type of claim to be encountered on large civil, highway or marine projects. They can cause millions of dollars in changes and years of delay to major projects.

Difficulties like easements, site access, or ownership rights may be insurmountable hurdles for a Concessionaire. The Concessionaire cannot invoke some of the tools that are only available to the government, like eminent domain. A contract provision merely requiring the cooperation of the owner in resolving such issues is an insufficient remedy because "cooperation" is difficult to measure.

[3] Differing Site Conditions

In most public works construction contracts, differing subsurface conditions result in excusable delay and additional costs to the contractor. The contractor prevails on a differing site conditions claim by proving that the subsurface soil conditions encountered by the contractor differed from the conditions indicated in the bid documents (Type I) or are unusual for the vicinity (Type II).

A differing site conditions dispute on a Design-Build contract was litigated in *Metcalf Constr. Co. v. United States*.[257] The bid documents

---

[257] *Metcalf Const. Co. v. United States*, 742 F.3d 984 (Fed. Cir. 2014)

contained geotechnical investigations but included a disclaimer that the information was "preliminary information only."[258] The differing site conditions provision was as follows:

> (a) The Contractor shall promptly, and before the conditions are disturbed, give a written notice to the Contracting Officer of—
>
> > (1) Subsurface or latent physical conditions at the site which differ materially from those indicated in this contract; or
> > (2) Unknown physical conditions at the site, of an unusual nature, which differ materially from those ordinarily encountered and generally recognized as inhering in work of the character provided for in the contract.
>
> (b) The Contracting Officer shall investigate the site conditions promptly after receiving the notice. If the conditions do materially so differ and cause an increase or decrease in the Contractor's cost of, or the time required for, performing any part of the work under this contract, whether or not changed as a result of the conditions, an equitable adjustment shall be made under this clause and the contract modified in writing accordingly.[259]

In *Metcalf*, the government argued that because the information provided to bidders was only "preliminary," it could not provide the basis for a claim. The Federal Circuit disagreed, explaining that "[t]he natural meaning of the representations was that, while Metcalf would investigate conditions once the work began, it did not bear the risk of significant errors in the pre-contract assertions by the government about the subsurface site conditions."[260]

---

[258] *Id.,* at 996.

[259] *Id.* at 995.

[260] *Id.* at 996.

Many states also have statutes that require public agencies to pay valid differing site conditions claims. This is an effective long-term strategy so the agency only pays an increased cost when the disruption occurs; otherwise the contractors will build a contingency into their bids and the agency will pay the premium on every project regardless of actual impacts. The loss aversion cognitive bias may make the strategy difficult for some owners to appreciate.

The structure of a P3 may allow public agencies to evade the risk sharing required by state statutes by not performing any subsurface investigations prior to award. This would be a novel legal issue and the agency could be required to pay for the differing site conditions twice: once when they pay for the Concessionaire's bid contingency and a second time when they lose the differing site conditions lawsuit.

Assigning risk allocation layers between the agency and Concessionaire may be an enforceable risk allocation (i.e. in which the Concessionaire pays the first $5 million of differing site condition costs and the agency the second). Alternatively, compensation to the Concessionaire may be adjusted through an extension of the operations period.

Differing site conditions are not generally categorized as a Designer error. They are unlikely to be covered by insurance policies. Whether the agency, Concessionaire, or Design-Builder retains the risk, they need to carefully evaluate the enforceability of the risk allocations and set aside an appropriate contingency. If the private partners are unable to absorb cost overruns, the entire financing equity may be at risk.

[4] Impossibility of Performance

Impossible and impractical specifications are often encountered, especially in contracts governed by state contract law and in federal defense and energy contracts where the government is constantly pushing for state-of-the-art technology.

California law provides for an excuse of performance due to impracticality or impossibility of performance.[261] In fact, modern cases in California provide for an excuse from performance even when

---

[261] *See Witkin*, Contracts § 831.

performance is impractical because of excessive and unreasonable difficulty or expense.[262]

In federal construction law, the excuse of performance principle has been established in cases such as *Foster Wheeler Corp. v. United States.*[263] The case considered a contract in which a required 19 – 24 month research and development period was clearly longer than the entire 13 month contractually allocated performance period. *Dynalectron Corp. (Pacific Div.) v. United States* presented a scenario in which no contractor could manufacture certain antennas within the specified tolerances without significant waivers of the specification requirements.[264]

Lastly, *Hol-Gar Mfg. Corp. v. United States* identified a contract in which no engine of the specified design could meet the performance requirements.[265]

The difficulty of prevailing on an impracticability excuse on a construction project is illustrated in *Nippo Corp. /International Bridge Corp. v. AMEC Earth & Environmental, Inc.*[266] The contractor had agreed to construct a runway in Guam according to U.S. Air Force standards but its performance was hindered by an ability to meet strict hot mix asphalt specifications.[267] All parties appeared to agree that the hot mix asphalt specifications could not be satisfied with locally available materials.

Nevertheless, the court found that use of local materials or waiver of the specification was a fundamental assumption of the contract and held that the contractor bore the risk of importing other materials should local materials prove inadequate or were the specifications not waived.[268] The court said that the contractor failed to prove that importation was genuinely impracticable.[269] Some relief was found for the contractor;

---

[262] *See Witkin*, Contracts § 842.

[263] *Foster Wheeler Corp. v. U.S.* 206 Ct. Cl. 533, 513 F.2d 588 (1975).

[264] *Dynalectron Corp. (Pac. Div.) v. United States*, 207 Ct. Cl. 349, 518 F.2d 594 (Ct. Cl. 1975)

[265] *Hol-Gar Mfg. Corp. v. United States*, 360 F.2d 634 (Ct. Cl. 1966).

[266] *Nippo Corp./Int'l Bridge Corp. v. AMEC Earth & Envtl., Inc.*, No. CIV.A. 09-0956, 2013 WL 1311094, (E.D. Pa. Apr. 1, 2013).

[267] *Id.* at 23.

[268] *Id.* at 22.

[269] *Id.*

the court agreed that delays in approval of the mix design, where the final approved mix was substantially similar to the contractor's initial proposal, was a breach of the duty of good faith and fair dealing.[270]

[B] Public Owner's Contract Administration

[1] Relationship with the Public Owner

Success of a project depends on the objectives, commitment, engagement, experience, and sophistication of the public-sector partner or partners.[271]

The most direct methods of checking out a potential party to a public works contract include: 1) checking their references; 2) reviewing their bidding materials carefully; 3) surveying the social media, and 4) talking to agencies and firms familiar with their project management performance.

With the advent of the Internet, there is very little information about a public entity, contractor, or individual that is not in the public record, private research databases or blogosphere commentaries. The issues to investigate include current and past projects, litigation history, licensing status, disciplinary record, bankruptcy, tax liens, credit history, and numerous other factors are available immediately over the Internet.

The parties' financial rating according to Dunn and Bradstreet, Standard and Poor's, and others can be obtained. These are generally available through a preliminary title search, a public records search, and news clipping services, at little cost. In addition, ENR.com, Construction.com, Lexis/Nexis, and Google.com are excellent sources on firms and individuals in the construction industry. This applies equally to Public Owners and their personnel.

[2] Change Orders

---

[270] *Id.*

[271] Robert Bain, The Anatomy of Construction Risk: Lessons from a Millennium of PPP Experience 4 (Standard & Poor's April 5, 2007).

Shifting responsibility for the design onto the Concessionaire eliminates the source of many change orders. The Concessionaire will be responsible for the vast majority of design-related change orders from contractors, subcontractors, and suppliers. By offloading project development to the Concessionaire, the owner eliminates a huge and costly source of risk and litigation in the form of subsequent change orders.

Professional management of the contract by the owner is still required. Interference with the project development and design, whether through directed extra work or inefficient approval of submittals, revives the owner's liability.[272]

[3] Oversight and Monitoring

Prequalification of proposers, the assignment of long-term operations to the Concessionaire, and the hand-back reserve account may increase the owner's confidence in the quality of the project when completed. Self-reporting by the Concessionaire can provide increased transparency. Nonetheless, the public agency remains responsible for protecting the public interest and needs to engage professional oversight at a level appropriate for the public's investment in the project.

[4] Payment

In a traditional infrastructure project, the public entity or government owner frequently assigns the design professional to track, review, and approve progress payments. In a P3 project, where the design professional is typically one with the Concessionaire, the public entity's independent contract administrator should instead make progress payments to the Concessionaire. Due to the fact that the public entity may not be comfortable without power of oversight it may seek, as discussed above, to include in the P3 contract language mandating Concessionaire cooperation with a Construction Managers' review of financing payments and revenue collection.

---

[272] See *Nippo Corp./Int'l Bridge Corp. v. AMEC Earth & Envtl., Inc* (2013).

[C] Changes and Modifications

P3 contracts retain the standard "change order" clause. The Concessionaire is advised to evaluate the design and construction impacts of the change, but also any long-lasting effects on operations.

The change order provision assigns the owner's representative the right to unilaterally make moderate changes to the project scope and provide compensation. Typically, all changes must be in writing.[273]

In addition to change orders, "extras" play a large role in contractors' performance on public works construction projects. Extra work provisions may be inserted in the contract by the public entity.[274] If the work to be performed is extraneous and not related to the original bid or contract, the contractor may have the right to refuse to perform, as the work is beyond the scope of the contract.

If the contractor chooses to perform extra work, it will, of course, seek extra compensation. While public works contracts generally provide for payment for extra work, a P3 may not be as generous. Such a provision typically requires a contractor to obtain a written extra work order that specifies the amount to be paid for the extra work and it must be signed by a public agency representative.[275] A contractor need not prove an affirmative fraudulent intent to conceal the need for the extra work, for the contractor to recover additional compensation as relief for a public authority's failure to disclose information in its possession that materially affects the cost of performance on a public contract.[276]

There are limits to the amount of changes that may be made under various California Statutes.[277]

---

[273] *See* AIA Form A201.

[274] *See e.g.,* CA PUB CONT § 10251.

[275] *See e.g., Bares v. City of Portola,* 124 Cal. App. 2d 813, 269 P.2d 239 (1954); *Thomas Kelly & Sons, Inc. v. City of Los Angeles,* 6 Cal. App. 2d 539, 45 P.2d 223 (1935).

[276] *See e.g. Los Angeles Unified Sch. Dist. v. Great Am. Ins. Co.,* 49 Cal. 4th 739, 234 P.3d 490 (2010)

[277] *E.g.,* Public Contract Code § 20455, limiting changes to $25,000, plus 5 percent of the contract amount above $250,000, not to exceed an aggregate of $150,000 for projects under the Improvement Act of 1911.

[1] Relief Events and Delay

In traditional contracts, the contractor is entitled to additional payment for extra work, which is defined as work not covered by any bid items.[278] The contractor is only responsible for the work it reasonably expected from the bid documents. The owner takes responsibility for everything that is outside of the "extra work" definition.

A P3 contract may attempt to limit its exposure through using a "Relief Event" clause. This approach attempts to flips the traditional construction risk allocation. The owner specifies the unexpected events it will bear risk for, and the Developer takes responsibility for everything outside of that realm. A list of "acceptable" relief events may include:

- Force Majeure Event
- Change in Law
- Owner Breach of Contract
- Discovery of hazardous materials
- Discovery of endangered animals within ROW
- Owner-Caused Delay
- Unreasonable delays by permitting entities
- Owner Change
- Differing Site Conditions[279]

These are events that are either within the owner's control or outside of the Concessionaire's control. The cost of the Concessionaire assuming the risk for these events would prohibitively increase the price of the Developer's proposal.

Any event that is not on the relief event list is not excusable from the public agencies' view. For example, a coercive and obstructionist utility company with utilities in a key location that refused to negotiate utility line relocation without an outrageous fee might not be grounds for relief in the view of some P3 owners. Generally, public utilities are

---

[278] California DOT 2006 Standard Specifications § 4-1.03D Extra Work.

[279] Texas Department of Transportation Public-Private Partnership Agreement IH 35E Toll Road Project, Term Sheet, Relief Event Categories.

restricted on their charges and fees to the public and those charges must be commensurate with the service provided.

An excusable delay in typical construction contracts is more lenient. It is one that is unforeseeable, beyond the contractor's control, and not the fault of either party. Examples of excusable delays are Acts of God, strikes, unusually severe weather, and the inability of the contractor to obtain construction materials or fuel (as in the energy crises in 1973 and 1979). Excusable delays allow the contractor to obtain a time extension to complete the contract without being penalized. This type of a delay normally does not entitle the contractor to any overhead damages caused by the delay. However, contractors often claim additional expenses when the delay pushes them into a "wet" season or otherwise unbuildable weather.

Delays due to Relief Events are typically excusable. In the event of a Relief Event, the contractor should be excused from performance of the obligations it is prevented from performing and granted an appropriate extension of time to perform that obligation.

To prevent ambiguity, the Relief Event contract provision should state that the time extension, if the time extension affects any task on the critical path, will apply both to the Completion Target Date and the intermediate milestones.[280]

A compensable delay is generally one that is caused by the owner or its agents, such as the architect or engineer, but a concurrent contractor delay may negate the owner-caused delay.

Usually, the contractor will be entitled to an extension of time and has the right to recover damages due to the owner-caused delay. However, contracts vary in their approach to compensable delays, generally attempting to limit the recovery of the contractor, except in extreme circumstances. As previously stated, public entities are limited in their ability to insert no damage for delay clauses in their contracts.

In the P3 context, it is extremely important to evaluate whether the Relief Event will give an extension of time, compensation for the delay, or an adjustment of the start of Owner payments, as these will substantially affect the financial model and risk for the Project. If

---

[280] *See, e.g.,* Golden Ears Bridge Project Agreement, § 10.11(b)(ii).

the event is non-compensable, the Developer may will usually not be reimbursed for the delay impacts on the debt service payments.

[2] Notice Provisions

A notice of claim must be provided to the public entity by the entity that is filing the claim. While many contractors feel notice clauses are just an attempt to place one more hurdle in the path of valid claims, the intent of such clauses is to provide the public agency an opportunity to address the potential claim by eliminating the cause of the claim, deleting troublesome scope of work items, or reducing the impact of delays. Notice clauses also allow the agency to begin to build a record in order to defend itself from the claim.

In those instances where the contractor has not given the required notice of potential delay and claims, the courts have often denied the contractor the relief to which it would otherwise be entitled.

In the P3 context, the Concessionaire is admonished to strictly adhere to the claim notice requirements to prevent a waiver of its claim rights. A careful reading of all notice provisions at the outset of the claim review process will reveal all applicable noticeable events.

There is a spit in the courts regarding the enforceability of notice clauses. Certain courts have strictly construed such notice of delay clauses, barring entire claims for time extensions or delay damages to contractors who fail to give timely notice. However, in the view of more liberal courts, failure to comply with notice clauses should not cause a forfeiture of the claim if the public agency is not prejudiced. The determination of prejudice may turn on whether the public agency did, in fact, have notice of the claim, and it could minimize the impact on the contractor and begin to collect data on the claimed increase in costs.

Many contracts require the contractor to provide immediate notice when any unanticipated or concealed condition is encountered during the course of the work. These clauses allow the public agency to inspect concealed conditions and, in certain cases, issue design modifications or change orders that may tend to minimize project disruption.

Disputed work is often the heart of a claim. Standard specifications generally require daily reports to the engineer on all labor, materials and equipment involved for any extra work claimed by the contractor. In these situations, at least the extent of the financial impact can be documented, even though entitlement may be disputed.

A notice of termination for default (or convenience) may be required by the terms of the contract documents, as well. In extremely difficult situations where the contractor is in material default on the contract or where the public agency is unable to perform, the affected party may be forced to give notice of termination for default. Events that may call for a notice of termination include an agency's inability to provide job site access, an agency's failure to make the agreed upon progress payments, or a contractor's failure to maintain the required contractor's license.

In fact, termination clauses typically require a series of termination notices, allowing a grace period during which the noticed party can cure the default. It cannot be emphasized enough that initiating termination for default is a serious matter. Improper compliance with the notice provisions for termination could result in the public agency becoming the defaulting party. The notice should also comply with the notice and termination procedures of the project bonding or letter of credit agreements. Failure to give proper notice and an opportunity to cure can waive the entire bond entitlement.

Lastly, the arbitration clause of a contract may require some type of notice. The procedures for triggering arbitration are normally contained in the arbitration clause.

[D] Scheduling & Delay Claims

Scheduling is an important aspect of any type of public works project, particularly critical when the Concessionaire is financing the project. The contract and resultant milestones and schedules provide expected completion dates. The contract also serves as the basis for coordination of the various subcontractors and trades involved. The series of approved and modified schedules, including as-bid, as-impacted, and as-built, is often utilized as the key documentation with regard to disputes over timely performance.

Two types of scheduling methods are used in the construction industry: the critical path method (CPM) and bar charts.

The CPM method depicts the flow of time and work. It identifies the critical activities of the project and the duration of each activity, along with critical deadline dates.

Bar charts are the more dated form of scheduling. The chart identifies the start and completion dates of particular activities, providing visual clarity. These charts are often prepared for presentation purposes, but are not as useful as the CPM.

Various construction phases and activities are identified and organized into these detailed schedules, which are updated as a project progresses, reflecting the contractor's equipment purchases, and completion or various phases of construction.

One of the oddities of P3 projects is the general absence of liquidated damages clauses. The reason is that the Public Owner is not responsible for any payments until the project is complete. They argue they should not need to make an availability payment if the project is not "available" for their use. As a practical matter, the delay in a one month payment means that payment will occur twenty or thirty years in the future. In view of the time value of money, those funds are essentially worthless. So, the delay of an availability payment can be seen as a *de facto* liquidated damage assessment.

[E] Suspension of Work

In typical construction projects, a standard provision would be inserted to allow the suspension of work by an owner. Such a clause is set forth in the AIA General Conditions. The provision states that the owner may suspend work in whole or in part for any duration of time.[281] An adjustment will be made in the contract amount for any increases in costs caused by the suspension. In a typical project, a general contractor has been paid progress payments for the work in place, so the suspension generally affects only future work and payments.

In a P3, a suspension bears a far greater risk. Since the Concessionaire may have put tens or millions of dollars into the job, the delay in moving toward completion and the start of payments of availability payments

---

[281] AIA General Conditions Form A201, Article 14.3.

is far more severe. This is even more of a problem for an indefinite suspension that might lead to the termination of the P3 Project.

The following are a few examples of situations that may amount to a suspension of work:

- The failure of the city to proceed under a contract provision giving it the power to suspend work for an indefinite period amounted to a suspension of work[282]
- The City's failure to provide required construction permits, easements, or rights-of-way required for construction to proceed in an orderly manner was determined to be a suspension of work[283]
- The failure to act upon a contractor's request for information that was critical to the contractor's performance also amounted to a suspension of work[284]

---

[282] *Hensler v. Los Angeles*, 124 Cal. App. 2d 71, 268 P.2d 12 (1954).
[283] *COAC, Inc. v. Kennedy Engineers*, 67 Cal. App. 3d 916, 136 Cal. Rptr. 890 (Ct. App.1977).
[284] *Coleman Eng'g Co. v. N. Am. Aviation, Inc.*, 65 Cal. 2d 396, 420 P.2d 713 (1966), decision criticized in *Earhart v. William Low Co.*, 25 Cal. 3d 503, 600 P.2d 1344 (1979).

CHAPTER 7

LONG TERM OPERATIONS AND MAINTENANCE

7.01 Why Include Operations & Maintenance?

The pricing of a P3 project includes operations and maintenance for a reason. It's like a car warranty. If the car is poorly designed and manufactured, the auto company will have to bear the costs of repair and replacement of parts. So with P3s, there is a strong incentive to build quality projects that are operationally reliable, easy to maintain and energy efficient.

Aligning the interests of design, construction, operations, and revenue collection has the effect of fine tuning the design and materials to save significant costs over the duration of the project's life.

7.02 Estimates of Future Use

When user fees are a significant component of the private partner's compensation package, the private partner holds the risk of low demand and low revenue. Demand forecasting is the major component of revenue projections. The second component is the mechanism for setting prices during the duration of the project. While the first is largely an economic projection, the later has both political and regulatory aspects.

The rapid development of Gig Apps, Ridesharing, & Autonomous Vehicles may also affect user usage and demand risk.

7.03   Lifecycle Costs

[A] Long-term risks

This is a partial list of longer-term technical and operational issues that may significant affect the long-term costs of operations and maintenance:

- Corrosion
- Subsidence
- Welding Failures
- Stress Failures
- Concrete Failure
- Derailment
- Railroad Crossings
- Intersection Collisions
- Technical & Economic Obsolescence
- Structural Collapse
- Foundation and Masonry Failures
- Site Contamination & Mold
- Chemical Release
- Alternate Routes
- Changes in Commuting Patterns
- Ride Sharing
- Bus Service
- Gig App Services
- Autonomous Vehicles

[B] Sustainability

The design and construction must be highly sensitive to the sustainability and energy efficiency of the facility through the entire life cycle of the P3 Project. This goal is strongly supported by the

Concessionaire and O & M contractor having long- term responsibility for care, operation and costs of the Project.

[C] Liability of O&M Contractor

An O&M Contractor typically has the duty to maintain the facility with ordinary care.[285] However, the P3 structure may insulate the Concessionaire from tort claims by carefully structuring the contractual relationships to capture the sponsor agency's immunities.[286]

7.04   Measuring Quality of Service

[A] Noncompliance Points

When the expertise and quality of Developer-provided services corresponds directly to Concessionaire tasks, the service may be appropriate for privatization through a P3. An easy example is the design, construction and operation of a parking lot. A monetary incentive (or disincentive) can be structured to foster the public entities' intended outcomes.

A simple example of this is the Developer's response to repairing potholes in a P3. A fast response time to perform repairs with quality materials guarantees a quality road surface. Water quality treatment plants are another example where there is a strong correlation between the quality of service and the operator's performance. A contrary example might be painting a mural; the quality of the art is neither tied to the amount of money spent on paint nor the time spent. It is also a highly subjective type of performance to create a metric or enforce.

---

[285] *Henson v. Terminal R. R. Ass'n of St. Louis,* 414 S.W.2d 791 (Mo. Ct. App. 1967) (finding that toll bridge operator exercised due care and was not liable for injured motorist); *Gerhard v. Terminal R. Ass'n of St. Louis,* 299 S.W.2d 866 (Mo. 1957) (toll bridge operator not liable where motorist did not exercise due care).

[286] *Haxhaj ex rel. Haxhaj v. City of New York* (N.Y. Sup. Ct. 2008) 19 Misc.3d 1135(A) aff'd sub nom. *Haxhaj v. City of New York* (N.Y. App. Div. 2009) 68 A.D.3d 612.

The Concessionaire is incentivized to perform the tasks that are correlated to quality with Noncompliance Points. The contract will contain a rating system that penalizes the Concessionaire for failing to meet performance metrics. As Noncompliance Points accumulate, the Developer suffers monetary fines that are deducted from the Concessionaire's toll revenue or from availability payments.

7.05 Regulatory Challenges

[A] Adjustments in Toll Revenue or Zoning

Toll rates are generally subject to approval by a regulatory agency specified in the contract. A change in toll rates by the regulatory agency could affect a regulatory taking if the toll pricing did not maximize revenue.[287]

An argument could be made that when circumstances change and a P3 ceases to be profitable, the public agency may be imposing a regulatory taking if it refuses to allow alternative uses of the property.[288]

[B] Grant of Exclusivity

The value of the concession is impacted by whether or not the public owner retains the right to build a competing project or improve existing facilities. The breadth and term of any exclusive rights should be clearly stated in the contract to prevent ambiguity. Courts may evaluate breaches of exclusive rights as a breach of contract versus a constitutional taking.[289]

---

[287] *See Dimino v. Sec'y of Com.*, 427 Mass. 704, 695 N.E.2d 659 (1998) (holding that eliminating tolls entirely would constitute a taking).

[288] *See Wensmann Realty, Inc. v. City of Eagan*, 734 N.W.2d 623 (Minn. 2007) (zoning of a private public-access golf course exclusively for that purpose constitutes taking if not profitable and no reasonable use remains).

[289] *Bldg. 11 Investors, supra.*

[C] Vested Rights

Projects may require zoning changes or other land use exemptions. Vested rights may be formed by a private owner's investment that protects it from subsequent changes.[290]

---

[290] *See, e.g., Norfolk 102, LLC v. City of Norfolk*, 285 Va. 340, 738 S.E.2d 895 (2013) (holding that restaurants in P3 commercial development did not have vested rights to serve alcoholic beverages); *Tyler v. City of Coll. Park*, 415 Md. 475, 3 A.3d 421 (2010) (holding that new rent control ordinance was not impermissibly confiscatory of rights of landowners).

CHAPTER 8

INSURANCE

Many risks are inherent in the construction of new public works projects. To the extent possible, those risks should be covered through a comprehensive program of liability and property insurance coverage. However, it is critical to observe that many construction project risks are not insurable or must be specially negotiated as part of the project's insurance program.

Types of insurance for consideration on a P3 project include:

[1] Design Errors and Omissions
[2] Warranties and Guarantees
[3] Faulty Workmanship
[4] Damage to Contractor's Own Property
[5] Third Party Property Damage
[6] Bodily Injury and Death
[7] Auto Policies
[8] Equipment Floaters
[9] Contractual Liability
[10] Fire and Natural Calamities
[11] Owner Controlled Insurance Program
[12] Contractor Controlled Insurance Program
[13] Rectification Coverage

8.01   Coverage Issues

The P3 project poses many aspects of risk and insurance coverage that depart from traditional projects. The following is a brief overview of the various types of coverage and policies generally available for P3 Projects. It is important to note that the highly-complex fabric of construction insurance policies and exclusions — along with insurance company marketing and claims practices, the impact of case law, and the dynamics of the litigation process — often does not meet the coverage expectations of design professionals, contractors and public agency owners. As such, getting expert insurance broker and legal advice is important.

The major coverages for construction projects are divided into liability policies and property policies. Liability policies protect the insured against legal liability and defense costs for claims asserted by third parties for negligent injury to persons or property. Generally, there must be an occurrence — often thought of as an accident or unexpected consequence — that leads to actual damage.

The principal liability coverages are set forth in Commercial General Liability (CGL) Policies carried by virtually all parties to the construction process. There are many written exclusions in these policies, and whether they extend to products liability, completed operations, explosion and underground liability, environmental impairment, contractual liability, professional liability, workmanship, subsidence, ultra-hazardous activities (such as blasting), and other potential losses, depends on the policy language and manner of issuance. As some contract insurance requirements are at minimal limits, most construction firms also carry umbrella coverage ranging from $1 million to $250 million and beyond.

There are two substantial dangers in professional liability and environmental impairment policies. These policies are typically written on a claims-made basis. Thus, if a claim is not made during a specific policy year, the policy will not cover the loss, even if the loss or negligent acts occurred during the policy year. Also, these policies may contain "wasting aggregate" provisions. In other words, as defense funds are expended, the policy limits decrease by the amount of defense funds.

An important form of liability coverage are Workers' Compensation and Employers Liability policies. Workers' Compensation is really no fault insurance. The policy will cover specified loss amounts for injuries to workers that are incurred within the scope of their employment. Generally, Workers' Compensation also serves as a bar against suing the employer in typical employee injury claims. Employer's Liability insurance covers more esoteric claims by employers under various state statutes and theories of liability. Workers' Compensation is required for contractors operating in California.

The typical property policy covers loss, destruction or damage to property owned by the insured. There are also policies for equipment floaters, auto coverage, goods in transit, etc.

A major form of policy carried by most owners is the Builder's Risk Policy. A list of insurance policies provided by general contractors and subcontractors on traditional projects are set forth in the AIA General Conditions.[291]

Each of the participants in a public works project has its own set of coverages and exclusions. In fact, it is not uncommon for 50 to 100 policies to be involved in a major public works construction accident or dispute. Due to inconsistency among insurance policies, conflicts often arise between subcontractors' insurance provisions which eventually affect the owner. Therefore, an Owner Controlled Insurance Program (OCIP) is a common provision of large P3 projects. Alternatively, the Concessionaire may require a Contractor Controlled Insurance Program (CCIP).

It is critical to evaluate the insurance program and the resulting covered and retained risks with regard to these additional criteria: limits and deductibles, named insured status, additional insured status, waivers of subrogation, written indemnity agreements, and the quality and financial strength of the respective carriers, and self-insurance programs.

There are several types of insurance policies that contain traps for the unwary. For example, the so-called "self-consuming, or "wasting aggregate" policies may be worth far less than their face policy amounts. In these types of policies, the amounts expended by the carriers for

---

[291] Article 11 of the AIA A201.

defense costs reduce the available coverage amounts. Thus, a hard fought case may leave no policy funds for an adverse verdict. On rare occasions, insurance companies will attempt to issue policies to general contractors or others with these provisions, which should be highly discouraged.

There is a tremendous distinction between a certificate of insurance, which states generally the type of policy that has been issued, and the policy itself. Only a review of the insurance policy, with its policy limits, deductibles, insurance declarations, named and additional insured parties, and exclusions will yield the true nature of coverages afforded by the policy. Finally, it is much easier to forge or alter a certificate of insurance than to create an entire fraudulent policy form. Certificate forgery is a common problem in the industry. A certificate is typically not legal proof of insurance coverage.

8.02   Insurance Coverage Litigation

The litigation of insurance coverage claims is extremely complex, as it involves highly technical policies and ever-changing case law. Extrinsic evidence of what is intended to be covered by a policy can include discovery of the insurance company's claim adjustment manuals and other internal documents.

In the *Glenfed* case, after an insured real estate developer's excess insurance carrier denied coverage of the insured's claims, the insured brought an action for declaratory relief and reformation, as well as damages for breach of contract and breach of the implied covenant of good faith and fair dealing.[292] Reformation means the court interprets the contract using reformed or modified terms intended to affect the original intent of the parties. During discovery, the Trial Court denied the insured's motion to compel production of the insurer's claims manual, finding that the insured had failed to show good cause for its production.[293]

---

[292] *Glenfed Dev. Corp. v. Superior Court,* 53 Cal. App. 4th 1113, 62 Cal. Rptr. 2d 195 (1997).
[293] *Id.*

The Court of Appeals ordered the Trial Court to: (1) void its order denying the insured's motion to compel production of the insurer's claims manual; and (2) enter a new order granting the motion.[294] Although a party who seeks to compel production of documents must show "good cause" where there is no privilege issue or claim of attorney work product, that burden is met simply by showing relevance.[295] Since claims manuals are admissible in coverage dispute litigation, it follows that they are discoverable. As for this manual's relevancy, the Insurance Code requires insurers to maintain guidelines for processing claims and these guidelines are maintained in claims manuals.[296]

Since virtually all policies detail the manner in which claims must be presented, the instruction manual for the insurer's employees was very likely to address such policy terms. Also, in this type of litigation, extrinsic evidence as to reasonable expectations of the insured may be admissible at trial. Even if it was inadmissible at trial, the claims manual could lead to the discovery of other, relevant evidence that was admissible.[297]

[294] *Id.* at 1120.
[295] Code Civ. Proc. § 2031.
[296] Cal. Ins. Code § 790.03.
[297] Opinion by Vogel (Miriam A.), J., with Ortega, Acting P.J., and Masterson, J., concurring. [*Glenfed Development Corp. v. Superior Court*, 53 Cal. App. 4th 1113, (1997).]

CHAPTER 9

DISPUTE RESOLUTION

The resolution of P3 disputes is unique because there are more participants, more stakeholders, and more complex contractual relationships. The scope of the Concessionaire's discretion is usually broad but the boundaries of that decision-making power may be unclear. The impact of minor decisions can affect the Concessionaire for 20 years or longer. Relief Events do not cover all unmanageable risks, delays increase debt service costs; and the costs of extra, disputed, or contingency work must be agreed upon and settled.

The goal is real-time dispute resolution. Arguing over ongoing disputes distracts from the work. Safety may neglected. The unaddressed costs of disputed work continue to snowball. All parties and as many stakeholders as possible should be bound to the P3 contract dispute resolution provisions. These should include the third parties who have control over right-of-way and permits, so a single process can serve the project as a whole.

A Dispute Review Board (DRB) or Project Neutral can provide the parties a non-binding opinion based upon an experienced understanding of P3 contracts and deep technical knowledge. Such a "deep keel" mentor can assist senior leadership in facilitating an early resolution. Early attempts at settlement can be shielded by the mediation privilege. A more formal dispute resolution process can be conducted as formal hearings and their non-binding outcomes can be agreed in advance to be admissible evidence in a future arbitration or litigation.

In considering the dispute resolution process, the P3 Team should be careful to review any contractual limitation on remedies or commercial damages—restricting extra payment to the occurrence of Relief Events when proper notice was given. These clauses may be used to stop a dispute resolution process before it begins. Courts will be reluctant to overturn these contract provisions. Doing so will require demonstrating very significant, such as the owner did not uphold their material obligations (such as a breach of the implied duty of good faith and fair dealing), a major flaw in the owner's disclosures, or that the work was commercially impracticable.[298]

I have recently participated as a DRB panel member for the UC Merced P3 expansion ($1.3 Billion), as well as several large design-build endeavors, including major highways, the largest bridge project in California, a railroad electrification project and several university medical research buildings. In each of these cases, the DRB, Project Neutral and Mediator roles acted to facilitate the negotiation and resolution of disputes.

Some third-party disputes and claims may need to be resolved outside of the P3 contract mechanism. Methods may include a lawsuit seeking declaratory relief, a court injunction, a lawsuit alleging "arbitrary and capricious" administrative action by a permitting agency, a Sunshine Act, Public Records Act, or Freedom of Information Act request to involved public agencies, media attention or public petitions to the Concessionaire or stakeholders.

It is often the case that P3 contracts defer the civil litigation of claims until completion of the construction or termination of the contact. During the operational period, there is no need for a similar deferment of the resolution of disputes.

In any case, the P3 contract should incorporate early resolution of claims to keep the project going.

---

[298] See *Nippo Corp./Int'l Bridge Corp. v. AMEC Earth & Envtl., Inc., supra.*

9.01 Early Claim Resolution

Design Builders often do a poor job of explaining in writing the factual basis of their claims to public agency staff and their outside consultants who are often tasked with analyzing the claims. The contractors may adopt an aggressive negotiation approach that may work with the subcontractors, but not with an experienced concessionaire. And certainly not a public agency who may think P3's never have disputes or claims. The General Contractor must be prepared to submit a well written and fully-supported claim, then come to the table ready for a true "give and take" negotiation.

"See you in court," is not a negotiation strategy. In fact, a trial is a failed negoation.

A contractor's lack of effectiveness in attempting to resolve a claim should not prevent the Concessionaire or public agency from taking the initiative to determine the fair value of the claim, the amount owed to the contractor, and the costs to be subtracted from the amount owed. The contractor will most likely wish to reach an early settlement to ensure the company's cash flow.

The administrative and budgetary constraints in an action by a public agency may be difficult for a contractor to understand. It is the goal of the agency to conserve and protect public funds, achieve the stated project quality objectives, and the project time schedule. It is the public agency's mandate to establish a clear written record to support all change orders and requests for extension. Because of these factors, an early well-documented approach by the public agency in evaluating the contractor's claims for cost increases and extensions of time is suggested. Successful claim negotiation can occur only in a business environment where facts are discussed.

One major advantage of a P3 contract is the adjustment of the Availability Payment. If the Public Agency sees value in a change in scope, the Availability Payment can be adjusted. This has the effect of financing a change in scope over 20 or more years.

If a claim or dispute cannot be resolved, then some form of litigation may be necessary, as outlined below.

9.02 Litigation

Most everyone would agree it is in the best interest of all the parties involved in a public works contract dispute to settle their differences through negotiation and compromise in order to avoid unnecessary costs and staff time of litigation.

However, if litigation is necessary, documentary evidence is very important. The key documents generated during a project are contracts, plans, specifications, revisions, bids, progress payment requests, detailed job costs reports, change order forms, schedules, daily reports, correspondence, photographs, videos, time lapse sequences, weather data, and testing reports. Due to the complicated nature of construction, it is essential to present the claim in a manner that both the court and the jury can understand.

Construction litigation over a P3 dispute involves the same familiar stages as any other type of litigation: pleadings, discovery, pretrial motions, trial, post-trial motions and appeal.

In cases of such complexity, the appointment of a Special Master may be helpful.

9.03 Arbitration

A P3 contract may provide an arbitration clause, whereby the parties agree to resolve potential disputes by means of an arbitrator. California Public Contract Code § 10240 provides that all claims under the State Contract Act are subject to arbitration.[299] However, Caltrans and other state agencies have opted for civil litigation in certain P3 projects, such as the Presidio Parkway Project.

Many form agreements require arbitration according to the American Arbitration Association guidelines (some require mediation, see below). An agreement to arbitrate may be made either in advance of a dispute (e.g., in the contract) or after the dispute has arisen.[300]

---

[299] Public Contract Code § 22300.
[300] Code of Civil Procedure § 1281.

The California Arbitration Act and the Federal Arbitration Act enforce arbitration provisions in contracts. California courts and public policy favor the resolution of commercial disputes through arbitration "to promote judicial economy, and to settle disputes quickly and fairly."[301] Thus, courts will generally enforce such contractual provisions between businesses and government.[302] (This is not always true for employment agreements with staff personnel, where a recent California statute, being challenged in State and Federal courts, would prohibit the arbitration of employment disputes.)

Construction disputes are extremely complex. And because arbitration involves many of the same challenges as litigation, it may not be the best alternative. For example, arbitration involving a three-person panel can be slow and quite expensive. It may be difficult to schedule three arbitrators and the rates of experienced arbitrators have escalated in recent years. But there may be other significant efficiencies, in part because the panel members may be subject matter experts in different areas, scorched earth discovery rules do not apply, proceedings are informal and private, and it is not necessary to follow formal rules of evidence.[303]

A major source of guidance in the resolution of disputes is the American Arbitration Association's *Construction Industry Arbitration Rules and Mediation Procedures (Including Procedures for Large and Complex Construction Disputes).*[304] The following is a summary of the 2015 Edition of the Regular Track Procedures for Construction Arbitration:

The rules contain Regular Track Procedures that are applied to the administration of all arbitration cases, unless they conflict with any portion of the Fast Track Procedures or the Procedures for Large,

---

[301] California Arbitration Act; Federal Arbitration Act, Code of Civil Procedure § 1283.05, *et seq.; Garden Grove Cmty. Church v. Pittsburgh-Des Moines Steel Co.,* 140 Cal. App. 3d 251, 191 Cal. Rptr. 15 (Ct. App. 1983).

[302] *Jones v. Kvistad,* 19 Cal. App. 3d 836, 97 Cal. Rptr. 100 (1971).

[303] *See Lesser Towers, Inc. v. Roscoe-Ajax Const. Co.,* 271 Cal. App. 2d 675, 77 Cal. Rptr. 100 (Ct. App. 1969) (19 months of arbitration costing $400,000 in arbitration expenditures, exclusive of attorneys' fees.)

[304] American Arbitration Association Rules.

Complex Construction Cases whenever these apply. In the event of a conflict, either the Fast Track procedures or the Large, Complex Construction Case procedures apply.[305]

The highlights of the Regular Track Procedures are:

- Opportunities for an administrative conference to help structure the dispute resolution process from the starting point;
- Party input into the AAA's preparation of lists of proposed arbitrators;
- Checklists for parties and arbitrators to organize the management hearing to address the needs associated with each dispute;
- Express arbitrator authority to control the discovery process; Broad arbitrator authority to control the hearing;
- Award format choices; and
- A demand form and an answer form, both of which seek more information from the parties to assist the AAA in better serving the parties.[306]

A significant consideration to keep in mind is whether any specific proceeding will be affected by the arbitrator's expertise and/or possible bias. Certain cases are stronger on the equities of the claim, rather than the law. They may thus have greater appeal to the arbitrator's sense of fairness, resulting in a more favorable decision than in a judicial setting.

The major strategic concerns in arbitration are the selection of the arbitrators, dealing with the lack of comprehensive discovery, and the significant barriers to "appealability." On the other hand, arbitration is generally faster, less expensive and, rather than relying upon a sole judge or lay jury, employs a specialized panel of experts with considerable industry understanding and knowledge.

The preparation for arbitration is similar to that of a jury trial, including extensive use of graphics, photographs, videos, drawings, timelines, and factual summaries. Often, the arbitration panel will read a great deal of the exhibits and other materials before the case begins, streamlining the overall presentation. Further, preliminary issues,

---

[305] *Id.*
[306] *Id.*

such as the nature of a construction process, the delineation of design and construction responsibilities and other matters are generally well understood by the panel that can then focus upon the specific project contracts and events that make up the instant controversy.

Generally, arbitration panels must render a decision within a set period (i.e. 30 days after the close of hearings). This is often a major source of delay in bench trials where the judge may delay ruling for months or even years. Although the relief that may be granted by arbitration panels can be quite broad, such thorny issues as disqualification of counsel, continuing injunctions, the existence of valid contractor licenses, and punitive damages are normally subject to review by Trial Courts.

In *Eternity Investments, Inc. v. Brown*, the California Court of Appeals held that if one wishes to have an arbitration award vacated or corrected, he or she must act within one-hundred days of service of the award or be precluded from attacking the award.[307] In *Coordinated Construction, Inc. v. Canoga Big "A," Inc.*, the owners did not serve a petition or response to correct or vacate the award before the 100-day period expired.[308] Accordingly, the Court of Appeals affirmed the Trial Court's decision that established the AAA award in favor of *Eternity*. (This was true in that case even though the owner was asserting the lack of a license by the contractor.)

At present, the most likely route to overturning an arbitration award, especially under the state court and legislative requirements, is the lack of full disclosure of any material facts or relationship by one of the arbitrators that may have created bias or unfairness in the arbitration proceeding.

9.04 Mediation

Parties often turn to mediation in an effort to avoid the high cost of litigation or arbitration. The parties agree to employ a private mediator

---

[307] 151 Cal. App. 4th 739, 742, 60 Cal. Rptr. 3d 134, 135 (2007), as modified (June 20, 2007) citing the California Arbitration Act (CAA) (Code Civ. Proc. §§ 1280–1294.2).
[308] 238 Cal. App. 2d 313, 320, 47 Cal. Rptr. 749, 753 (Ct. App. 1965).

who assists and facilitates negotiations or settlement of a dispute in an informal manner. The mediator typically identifies the strengths and weaknesses in each party's case and helps resolve the dispute.

There are two often cited rules regarding construction mediation: it is voluntary and the settlement discussions are confidential.[309] It is usually successful, even at the early stages of a dispute. Mediation can offer substantial savings over the discovery and trial process. It satisfies the desire to end disputes with a handshake (and a signed settlement agreement that has language that specifically makes it admissible). It turns adversaries into future clients and bidders.

There are several major impediments to a successful mediation. The most significant is that everyone assumes that the parties will be prepared and that the necessary people, knowledge, and documents will be readily available during the proceeding.

Unfortunately, during the course of mediation the parties and/or their legal counsel often realize that an essential party, representative (read: insurance claim person), vital document, or other piece of key information is not present. It can leave a gaping hole in the settlement process and keep the parties from reaching agreement. In that case, a great deal of time and effort is expended in rescheduling. Even then the parties may discover a new missing party, document or item of information. Mediation can be great, but it can become an expensive waste of time if the parties are not fully prepared to wholeheartedly participate.

9.05   Judicial Arbitration

Judicial arbitration is a mechanism available in many states. It is different from the contractual arbitration discussed above. Judicial

---

[309] California Rules of Court, MEDIATOR ETHICAL STANDARDS, PART 1. Rules of Conduct for Mediators in Court-Connected Mediation Programs for Civil Cases, Title V, Special Rules for Trial Courts — Division III, Alternative Dispute Resolution Rules for Civil Cases — Chapter 4, General Rules Relating to Mediation of Civil Cases — Part 1, Rules of Conduct for Mediators in Court-Connected Mediation Programs for Civil Cases, first adopted effective January 1, 2003

arbitration is governed by state codes, such as the California Code of Civil Procedure, which provides that a case may be required to go to arbitration before it can proceed to trial.[310] Mandatory submission applies to many construction dispute of under $375,000 and to all at-issue civil cases in a superior court with more than 18 judges if, in the opinion of the court, the amount in controversy will not exceed $50,000 for each plaintiff.[311]

9.06   Dispute Review Boards (DRB)

A growing trend among public agencies engaging in P3 projects is the use of a Dispute Review Board (DRB). These boards typically consist of or public works professionals with broad experience in the type of work being undertaken. The DRB meets regularly, often once a quarter, keeps abreast of the course of the project, and issues advisory decisions on any trends, controversies, or claims that may arise.

Depending on the contract language, the Dispute Review Board's recommendations may or may not be admissible in later proceedings, such as arbitration or court proceedings. It is expected that due to the expertise of the DRB panel and their significant involvement during the course of the project, DRB findings may be given significant weight in any later arbitration or judicial proceedings.

9.07   Fact Finding

A relatively recent development is the appointment of neutrals or teams devoted to neutral fact finding, such as the American Arbitration Association Rules for Fact-Finding (2002). This involves an appointed individual or group of team members that carry out an independent investigation and report their findings to all concerned parties.

Fact-finding can assist the parties in establishing common ground or likely results if the matter is litigated, as well as a factual basis for

---

[310] §§ 1141.10 – 1141.31.
[311] *Id*, § 1141.11.

settlement. It is faster than the normal discovery or court process, as the fact finders are generally expected to have full and complete access to the parties, witnesses, documents, physical evidence, job site, party- selected expert witnesses, and other records. Their investigations and reports can be generally be kept confidential and covered by the mediation or joint attorney work product privilege if well drafted engagement letters are utilized by the parties.

CHAPTER 10

PAYMENT, BONDS & WAGES

10.01 Statutory Issues Unique to P3's

When a contractor, subcontractor or supplier remain unpaid on a typical construction project, public or private, there are a variety of statutory remedies that are available for the collection of the debt.

The nature of a P3 concession may severely affect these rights in several ways. First, the land, and perhaps the facility itself, is typically public property, and public property is generally not subject to mechanics liens rights. Second, the Concessionaire is not a public owner, so many of the remedies traditionally available to public works contractors, such as a public agency stop notice, may not be effective.

Fourth, he creation of the P3 Concessionaire slides in another layer to the "wedding cake," so eligible claimants may be further removed from the public entity and not have traditional public works protection. Fifth, the public agency might not require a labor and materials payment bond at all, relying upon letters of credit that may serve the public agencies' need for security, but not protect the interests of the project subcontractors, suppliers and laborers.

10.02 Surety Bonds and Letters of Credit

The purpose of a typical surety bond is simple. If the contractor defaults or does not pay its subcontractors, suppliers, or laborers, then the surety will be responsible for those debts. The bonding company will then seek repayment by the contractor under the General Indemnity Agreement (GIA) from the collateral or assets pledged by the contractor in securing the issuance of the bond.

In some instances, the surety may assist or step into the contractor's shoes and pursue claims against the owner for project issues that may have been responsible for the default. In other situations, the surety may simply preside over the liquidation of the contractor's assets.

A Letter of Credit may be required by a public agency. If there is a perceived default, the Public Entity may have the right to draw down the funds without any further due process.

However, the use of bonds and Letters of Credit in P3 projects are more complex.

An attorney fees provision cited by a subcontractor recovering against a public works payment bond was found not to be applicable to a contract for the construction of a toll road by a private Concessionaire, despite the road being public property.[312] The determinative factor was whether a public entity contracted for the construction.[313]

At the outset, it is important to know who is being asked to post letters of credit or a surety bond. These may be required of the Concessionaire, the Design Builder, major subcontractors, or the O & M Contractor. And, whether the required bonds assure performance, payment or both.

There are two types of surety bonds: 1) those that guarantee the payment of the general contractor's subcontractors (the so-called

---

[312] *Best W. Paving, Inc. v. Granite Const., Inc.*, No. G022890, 2002 WL 31682370, 18 (Cal. Ct. App. Nov. 27, 2002), unpublished/noncitable.

[313] *Id.*; *see also Progress Glass Co. v. Am. Ins. Co.*, 100 Cal. App. 3d 720, 729, 161 Cal. Rptr. 243 (Ct. App. 1980) (although land was owned by the county, the county was not a party to the contract so it was a private project).

payment and materials bond); [314] and 2) those that guarantee the actual performance of the general contractor (performance bond).[315] In many cases, they are issued as a unified bond document. Unlike insurance policies, the bonding companies are not assuming the contractor's risk of non-payment or performance, which remains with the contractor. They are only taking on the role of guarantor of those obligations.

In the event of insolvency or the contractor's failure of performance, the bonding company is obligated to complete the project and pay the subcontractors and materialmen. It may seem that the surety takes the largest risks on the project, but that exposure is tempered by several factors. Admittedly, the surety writes a bond for the entire contract amount, a daunting amount. At any moment in the project, the actual exposure of the surety is far less than the penal amount of the guarantee. At the beginning of the project, the contractor is still owed the entire revenue of the project, so the risk is that the project has been bid too low.

At the end of the project, the surety is responsible for completion costs, but that amount may only represent a small percentage of the overall project cost. The surety's greatest risk lies in the "fog of war" during the project, when the owner's payments should be keeping track with and applied to the contractor's progress and payments to its labor, materialmen, and subcontractors. As such, sureties closely watch the progress of major projects, as well as the balance sheets and income statements of their contractor clients.

Dealing with contractor's bond sureties, the Second District Court of Appeals in *Federal Ins. Co. v. Superior Court* found that a subcontractor's claim on a payment bond should be stayed by the court, along with the subcontractor's claim against the general contractor, pending the outcome of the general contractor/subcontractor arbitration proceeding

---

[314] Miller Act, 40 U.S.C.A. §§ 3131-3134 (the "Miller Act") governs payment bonds on federal government construction projects. *See also* 40 U.S.C.A. *See also* AIA A201 §11.4.1 (2007 ed.) and AIA A201 §11.5.1 (1997 ed); ConsensusDocs 200, Subsection 10.7.1; EJCDC C-700 ¶6.01 (2013).

[315] *See* 40 U.S.C.A. §§3131 (requiring performance bonds on federal projects); ConsensusDocs 200, §10.7 (making performance bond optional); AIA A201, §11.4 (2007 ed.) (Owner may require performance bond).

and pursuant to the arbitration provisions found in the subcontractor/contractor contract.[316]

Surety bonds also differ from insurance policies when a bonding company becomes insolvent. When an admitted insurance carrier becomes insolvent, the State of California Insurance Guarantee Fund provides certain financial protections to policyholders. However, there is no State of California guarantee fund for sureties or bonding companies.

Bonds also differ from insurance in that the claimant on the bond does not have the right to sue the surety for bad faith, as set forth by the California Supreme Court in *Cates Construction, Inc. v. Talbot Partners*:

> *This case presents issues relating to the contract and tort liability of a commercial surety to a real estate developer under a bond guaranteeing the contract performance of a general contractor on a multimillion dollar condominium construction project. For the reasons set forth below, we conclude that the bond at issue contractually obligates the surety to pay damages attributable to the general contractor's failure to perform, promptly and faithfully, its contract obligations by the agreed date.*
>
> *We further conclude that, as a matter of law, the developer may not recover in tort for the surety's breach of the covenant of good faith and fair dealing implied in the performance bond. In light of these conclusions, we reverse the judgment of the Court of Appeal insofar as it affirmed the underlying award of tort damages for breach of the implied covenant and permitted an award of punitive damages.*[317]

As a result of cases like *Cates Construction*, bonding companies responding to claims against their principals may simply reiterate back the claim and contract positions of the contractor, indicating the surety's

---

[316] *Fed. Ins. Co. v. Superior Court (Mackey)*, 60 Cal. App. 4th 1370, 71 Cal. Rptr. 2d 164 (1998).
[317] 21 Cal. 4th 28, 34-35, 980 P.2d 407 (1999).

belief that their principal is not in breach or that monies are not owed.[318] This can mean the bond becomes little more than a guarantee of any ultimate judgment against the contractor for non-performance or non-payment. Still, the surety is obligated to perform a prompt review of the claim and take a position on whether or not the surety is obligated to perform or pay funds on behalf of the contractor.

The track record of sureties taking over projects for defaulting contractors varies greatly. They have a statutory obligation to investigate, but often seem to take inordinate amounts of time to make a decision as to whether to proceed with the job or back the contractor in its claims and allegations of material breach by the owner. When a surety does take over a job, it will often incur substantial consulting and legal services that it will eventually seek to recover from the contractor, its principal, under its indemnity and collateral agreements.

Thus, investigating the quality, reputation, efficiency, and financial strength of the bonding company is a critical issue for owners, subcontractors and material vendors.

10.03 Prompt Payment Statutes

A public works contract typically contains provisions regarding the payment of progress and final payments. In addition, several statutory provisions apply to payments in the context of a public works project. There is considerable controversy over whether these provisions apply to either the Concessionaire or the Design-Builder in a P3 project.

For example under California Public Contract Code, retention payments withheld from payment by a public entity must be made to the original contractor within 60 days after completion of the project and by an original contractor to a subcontractor thereafter (10 days after receipt of funds by the original contractor to a subcontractor).[319] Failure to release such payments will result in a penalty assessed at the rate of 2 percent per month and reasonable attorneys' fees.[320]

---

[318] *Id.*

[319] CA PUB CONT §7107.

[320] *Id.*

Public Contract Code further establishes a 10-day period for progress payments to subcontractors after receipt of funds by the general contractor.[321] The Code further regulates payments made to contractors and subcontractors by a state agency.[322]

Public Contract Code § 10261, referred to as the "prompt pay statute," specifies that a state agency shall pay interest to a contractor at the rate of 10 percent per annum if the agency fails to make a progress payment within 30 days after receipt of the contractor's payment request.[323]

Public Contract Code § 10262.5, also a "prompt pay statute," provides that any prime contractor that fails to make a progress payment to a subcontractor within 10 days from receipt of funds by the contractor must pay a penalty at the rate of 2 percent per month, interest, reasonable attorney's fees and costs.

California Public Contract Code § 20104.50 sets forth strict requirements for prompt payment to local public entities, including up to 30 days for payment of undisputed and properly submitted requests for payment.

10.04 Prevailing Wages

Bid invitations generally state that prevailing wages must be paid by general contractors and subcontractors on most public works projects.[324] These wages are calculated and published by the Division of Labor Statistics and Research.

If a contractor fails to pay these wages, it is liable to the public entity and the workers for repayment and fines whether or not the contractor is a union contractor.

---

[321] § 7108.5

[322] § 10258 (payment where control is terminated or work abandoned), § 10261 (payments upon contracts, progress payments), § 10262 (payment to subcontractors), § 10262.3 (notice of progress payments to contractor), and § 10264 (partial payment for mobilization costs)

[323] Public Contract Code § 20104.50 is the local agency prompt payment statue, which is identical to the requirements of Public Contract Code § 10261.5.

[324] *See for example*, California Labor Code § 1775.

As of June 2012, the enforcement procedure for the Division of Labor Standards Enforcement (DLSE) for civil wage and penalty assessments was substantially overhauled.[325]

Penalties for violating the act remain high at up to $50.00 per employee per day. Strict adherence to the prevailing wage laws is an absolute issue of survival for contractors.

A recent law in California, codified as Labor Code § 218.7, makes a general contractor jointly liable for the failure of a subcontractor of any tier to pay the wages or fringe benefits owed to or on behalf of its workers.

The California Industrial Welfare Commission further regulates the wage and employment relationship, overseeing wages, hours and working conditions for certain on-site occupations in the construction, drilling, logging and mining industries.[326]

This wide-ranging order encompasses such new requirements as make up time, travel time, recording time, record-keeping, deductions from pay, uniforms and equipment, meal periods, rest periods and alternative work week schedules. Employees governed by collective bargaining agreements are exempt from certain provisions of the Wage Order, so long as they are paid at least 30 percent more than the California Minimum Wage.[327]

In *Small v. Super. Ct.*, the Court of Appeals upheld Wage Order No. 16-2001, including those portions that require a new alternative

---

[325] In 2012, the California Legislature enacted Labor Code §1771.3 to enhance DLSE's ability to monitor and enforce prevailing wage compliance, primarily on public works projects which are paid for with funds derived from bonds issued by the state, *as cited in* California Labor Commissioner Julie A. Su, "Public Works Manual," State of California Department of Industrial Relations Division of Labor Standards Enforcement, (June 2014), available at http://www.dir.ca.gov/dlse/PWManualCombined.pdf.

[326] Wage Order No. 16-2001(effective January 1, 2002, as amended, Sections 4(A) and 10(C) amended and republished by the Department of Industrial Relations, effective July 1, 2014, pursuant to AB 10, Chapter 351, Statutes of 2013 and AB 1835, Chapter 230, Statutes of 2006).

[327] *Id.*§ 3(H)(1).

workweek schedule election when employees in a work unit increase by 50 percent or more.[328]

Another case involved plaintiff painting subcontractor, who was working under a public works contract between a county and a general contractor, which violated the prevailing wage law.[329] According to the wage law, Labor Code § 1775, a public entity which has contracted for a public works project had to withhold statutory penalties and underpaid wages upon learning that a contractor or subcontractor violated the law by paying less than prevailing wage to its employees.[330] The Labor Commissioner issued an initial "notice to withhold," directing the county to withhold payment and penalties assessed at $50 per worker per day, the maximum statutory rate, from the general contractor based on the subcontractor's wage law violations.[331]

Although the Commissioner ultimately concluded that the subcontractor's wage law violations were deliberate and fraudulent and again assessed the maximum statutory penalty, the Trial Court granted the subcontractor's petition for a writ of mandate and set aside the initial notice to withhold as premature.[332]

The Court of Appeal reversed the Trial Court's decision, holding that the painting subcontractor possessed a "beneficial interest" and standing sufficient to maintain the mandamus proceeding, and that no adequate remedy at law was available.[333] The Appeals Court reversed the decision, but not on the issue of standing.[334]

---

[328] 148 Cal. App. 4th 222, 239, 55 Cal. Rptr. 3d 410 (2007)

[329] *J & K Painting Co. v. Bradshaw*, 45 Cal. App. 4th 1394, 53 Cal. Rptr. 2d 496 (1996), as modified on denial of reh'g (June 21, 1996) Criticized by *Bostanian v. Liberty Savings Bank*, 52 Cal.App.4th 1075, 61 Cal.Rptr.2d 68, 97 Cal. Daily Op. Serv. 1198, 97 Daily Journal D.A.R. 1759 (Cal.App. 2 Dist. Feb 19, 1997) (NO. B102938), as modified (Feb 28, 1997), review denied (Dec 02, 1998). However, *Bostanian* was only criticizing the issue addressed in fn. 8 of whether a bankruptcy filing would interfere with the standing issue. The *J & K court* declined to reach the issue because it was not supported in the record.

[330] *J & K Painting Co., supra.*

[331] *Id.*

[332] *Id.*

[333] *Id.*; Code of Civ. Proc. § 1086.

[334] *Id.* at 1408.

The Labor Commissioner appealed, arguing that the painting company had no standing to bring a writ of mandamus and the Court of Appeal upheld the painting company standing to bring the suit. The reversal was on the issue of the labor commissioner's right to issue a withholding order before the determination of a penalty.

The Trial Court had held that the commissioner had no power to assess the penalty of a withholding order until a determination of the amount of the penalty.[335] The Court of Appeal held that the withholding was not a penalty, but merely a guaranty to assure future enforcement when a penalty was determined.[336] They said that the labor commissioner did not assess a penalty so much as he reduced the maximum penalty based on criteria that permit leniency.[337]

The Court of Appeal also held that the Trial Court erred in setting aside the notice to withhold as premature.[338] Although the commissioner did not determine the amount of penalties owed pursuant to Labor Code § 1775 before issuance of the initial notice to withhold, the subcontractor forfeited underpaid wages and penalties when it violated the prevailing wage law.[339] Hence, the County's power and duty to withhold penalties could be predicated on a preliminary or tentative estimation of penalties. Furthermore, the power to withhold funds is a device that can be used to aid in collection.

The purpose of the 1989 amendments to Labor Code § 1775 was not to impede the use of this device, but to increase the flexibility in its application.[340] There has been no overruling authority to J & K Painting. All subsequent references have been to the standing issue.

In another case, the Trial Court granted a surety's motion for judgment on the pleadings in an action by the State of California Department of Industrial Relations, Division of Labor Standards

---

[335] *Id.* at 1398.

[336] *Id.* at 1406.

[337] *Id.*

[338] *Id.* at 1396.

[339] *Id.* at 1404.

[340] Opinion by Kline, P.J., with Phelan, J., and Haerle, J., concurring. *J & K Painting Co.*

v. Bradshaw, 45 Cal. App. 4th 1394, 53 Cal Rptr 2d 496 (Cal. App. 1 Dist., 1996).

Enforcement (DLSE), brought on behalf of workers on a public works project for prevailing wages against the surety that had furnished the payment bond required for the project. [341] The Trial Court found that the action was barred by the ninety-day statute of limitations of Labor Code § 1775. [342]

The Court of Appeal reversed the decision, holding that the applicable limitations period was the six-month period of Civil Code § 3249 (action against surety, now Civil Code § 9558) and that the action was timely under that statute. [343] The DLSE has the authority to bring an action on behalf of workers whose statutory rights to prevailing wages allegedly have been violated. [344]

Statutory provisions other than Labor Code § 1775 also spell out the right to prevailing wages. [345] Thus, the Labor Code § 1775 remedy against the contractor is not the only means by which the DLSE may seek to collect prevailing wages under the prevailing wage law. Moreover, by its terms, Labor Code § 1775 becomes applicable when the DLSE's suit is against a contractor, not another entity such as a surety. The ninety-day limitation of Labor Code § 1775 does not apply to an action for payment of prevailing wages against a surety on a payment bond.

In yet another case, the Trial Court granted summary judgment for a contractor and related defendants in an action by the DLSE to recover unpaid wages for labor performed on a public works contract, based on the finding that the Employee Retirement Income Security

[341] Lab. Code §§ 96.7, 98.3, subd. (a); *Dep't of Indus. Relations v. Seaboard Sur. Co.*, 50 Cal. App. 4th 1501, 58 Cal. Rptr. 2d 532 (1996), as modified on denial of reh'g (Dec. 20, 1996)

[342] *Id.* at 1207. (Superior Court of San Diego County, No. 682725, Sheridan E. Reed, Judge).

[343] *Id.*

[344] *Id.*

[345] *E.g. Davis-Bacon Act (Davis-Bacon)* 40 U.S.C. §§3141 *et seq.* provides that contractors and subcontractors performing work on federally-funded or –assisted contracts in excess of $2,000 for the construction, alteration or repair of public buildings or public works pay their workers no less than the locally prevailing wages and fringe benefits for corresponding work on similar projects in the area as set by the U.S. Department of Labor (DOL).,

Act (ERISA) preempted California's prevailing wage law (Lab. Code § 1720, *et seq.*).[346]

The Court of Appeal reversed the judgment. The court held that in determining whether a state law relates to an ERISA plan because it has a "connection with" such a plan and is thus preempted, the court must consider whether the state law: (1) regulates the types of benefits in ERISA employee welfare benefit plans; (2) requires that a separate employee benefit plan be established to comply with the law; (3) imposes reporting, disclosure, funding, or vesting requirements for ERISA plans; and (4) regulates certain ERISA relationships, such as those between an ERISA plan and an employer or between an employer and employee.[347] Applying that test, the court held that the Trial Court erred in granting summary judgment for defendants.[348]

The defendants were liable under the prevailing wage law not because they failed to contribute to the employee benefit plan, but because they failed to pay their employees the prevailing wage.[349]

Where a legal requirement may be satisfied through means unconnected to ERISA plans, and relates only to ERISA plans at the election of an employer, it affects employee benefit plans in too tenuous, remote, or peripheral a manner to warrant a finding that the law "relates to" the plan so as to be preempted.[350] The prevailing wage law does not single out ERISA plans for special treatment, nor was it designed to affect such plans specifically. The provisions of the prevailing wage law at issue regulate wages generally and create no rights and restrictions predicated on the existence of any employee benefit plans.[351]

---

[346] *Dep't of Indus. Relations v. Nielsen Constr. Co.*, 51 Cal. App. 4th 1016, 59 Cal. Rptr. 2d 785 (1996); 31029 U.S.C. 1001 *et seq.*; Superior Court of San Diego County, No. 681931, Arthur W. Jones, Judge, Labor Code §1770 *et seq.*

[347] *Department of Indus. Relations*, citing WSB Elec., Inc. v. Curry (9th Cir. 1996) 88 F.3d 794. *See also Aloha Airlines, Inc. v. Ahue*, 12 F.3d 1498 (9th Cir. 1993)

[348] *Nielsen* (1996) at 10016.

[349] *Id.*

[350] *Id.*

[351] *Id.*

The prevailing wage law, which was designed to protect and benefit employees on public works projects, exemplifies the broad authority of States to protect workers.[352]

10.05 False Claims Acts

A final aspect of claims analysis that is critical for both the public entity and construction industry professionals are so-called "False Claims Acts." One example is the California False Claims Act of 1987 (FCA).[353] These Acts, which are similar to the Federal False Claims Act, provide for the regulation of false and fraudulent claims submitted to state and local public agencies.[354]

In the past, a contractor that knowingly submitted a false or fraudulent claim to a public entity was only subject to criminal fines and penalties.[355] The FCA, and similar state statutes, establish civil penalties and fines for the same conduct, thus making another remedy available to public entities.

If a contractor knowingly submits a false claim to a public entity, it will be liable for three times the amount of damages that the entity sustains, the costs of the suit and a civil penalty of up to $11,000 for each false claim.[356] Filing a false claim can also result in temporary or permanent debarment of a contractor from future business with one or more public entities. Debarment is often called "the death penalty for contractors."

An example of the debarment process is set forth in *Stacy & Witbeck, Inc. v. City and County of San Francisco*.[357] Pursuant to a section of a city administrative code, the city's public utilities commission (PUC) deemed a contractor to be an irresponsible bidder due to its filing of a false claim under a construction contract and banned it from bidding

---

[352] *Id.* at 1029.

[353] California Government Code §§ 12650 – 12655.

[354] Federal False Claims Act, 18 U.S.C. § 287.

[355] Penal Code § 72.

[356] *Id.*

[357] *Stacy & Witbeck, Inc. v. City & Cnty. of San Francisco*, 36 Cal. App. 4th 1074, 44 Cal. Rptr. 2d 472 (1995), as modified on denial of reh'g (Aug. 16, 1995).

on city public works projects for five years.[358] The contractor petitioned for injunctive relief. The Trial Court determined that the distortions in the claim did not violate any of the provisions governed by the city's administrative code section and, holding that the PUC lacked any legal basis for issuing its order, granted a preliminary injunction enjoining the city and the PUC from enforcing the order.[359]

The Court of Appeal reversed the order granting the preliminary injunction. The court held that the action of the PUC in deeming the contractor to be an irresponsible bidder was valid under the City's administrative code.[360] The city charter charged the PUC with the construction, management, operation, and control of all public utilities. The PUC carried out this charge pursuant to a chapter of the code entitled "Contract Procedure," which permitted the PUC to deem a contractor irresponsible for failing to abide by rules and regulations set forth in the chapter.[361] Further, the Court held the PUC properly ruled that the covenant for good faith and fair dealing was an implicit requirement of the clause of the contract under which the contractor's claim was made and of the code section governing payment of such claims.[362]Moreover, the Court held that the city's appeal of the Trial Court's injunction was not void even though the code section under which the order was made had been repealed, and that the code section was not facially unconstitutional, even though it did not specifically delineate that any procedures for notice and hearing followed by the PUC at the hearing were fair.[363] The Court also held that the claim for contract overages submitted to the city by the contractor could serve as the basis for the administrative action by the PUC to declare the contractor an irresponsible bidder, despite the contractor's contention that the claim was absolutely privileged under Civil Code § 47, subd. (B)(litigation privilege) because it had been filed in connection with

---

[358] *Id.*

[359] *Id.* at 1081.

[360] *Id.* at 1074.

[361] *Id.*

[362] *Id.*

[363] *Id.*

underlying litigation between the contractor and the city.[364] Finally, the Court held that state law did not preempt either: (1) the code section that provided for declaring a public works contractor an irresponsible bidder; or (2) the action of the PUC thereunder in declaring the particular contractor an irresponsible bidder.[365]

A second decision the following year, *Stacy & Witbeck, Inc. v. City and County of San Francisco*, addressed the Trial Court's granting of summary adjudication in favor of the contractor on an FCA cause of action. The court ruled that the alleged false claim was absolutely privileged under Civil Code § 47, subdivision (b) since it was submitted to the city in anticipation of litigation.[366] The Trial Court entered judgment accordingly.[367]

The Court of Appeal, thereafter, reversed the Trial Court's judgment.[368] The Court held that the city's cross complaint was not barred by the Civil Code § 47, subdivision (b), litigation privilege. Although the contract claim followed the contractor's presentation to the city of its claim under the Tort Claims Act (TCA) for material breaches of contract and subsequent rejection of the TCA claim, the contractor initiated its breach of contract action for the alleged damages detailed in the contract claim. The Court continued that the filing of the contract claim was also called for under the contract, and it stood wholly apart from any judicial action.[369] Further, they said even though Government Code § 12652, subdivision (e), excludes from liability claims made under TCA, the contractor had also filed a separate contract claim.[370]

While the TCA claim was an independent item with statutory requirements governing its contents (Government Code § 910), the contract claim did not resemble the claim described in Government Code § 910, and was required pursuant to both the terms of the contract

---

[364] *Id.*
[365] *Id.*
[366] *Id.*
[367] *Id.*
[368] *Id.* at 1081.
[369] *Id.* at 1093.
[370] *Id.*

and the course of dealing between the parties. Although the contract claim ultimately served a litigation purpose, it clearly was not a claim, record, or statement made pursuant to the TCA. The California Act has few defenses for contractors. This trend is also present in public works projects covered under the 2009 Federal Stimulus.[371]

---

[371] The American Recovery and Reinvestment Act of 2009 (ARRA) (Pub. L. 111-5).

CHAPTER 11

THE OPERATIONAL PHASE

11.01 Owner Buyback

The public owner may specify a owner buyback provision which the public owner may terminate the Concessionaire's interest before the end of the concession period. The P3 should set forth a formula or fair market valuation of the buyback price. Buybacks have also been negotiated when Concessionaires approach bankruptcy.

The public agency may do such a buyback of just the O & M contract, a way to bring the operational side of the project back to provide jobs for public union employees.

11.02 Liability of Concessionaire

The Concessionaire is an independent party in the partnership and may remain liable for contractual breaches if the contract so allocates such risks. In *Direct Supply, Inc. v. Specialty Hospitals of America, LLC,* the contract provided that the private company was solely liable for "the debts, liabilities, contract, or any other obligations of the Partnership."[372] After the government terminated the partnership, the private partner

---

[372] *Direct Supply, Inc. v. Specialty Hospitals of Am., LLC,* 878 F. Supp. 2d 13 (D.D.C. 2012)

remained liable to its supplier for expenses incurred during the partnership.

11.03 Liability of Designer

Under most statutes of repose, the Designer is barred from most types of liability exposure after a period of four, six, ten, or twelve years from substantial completion of the construction. In some states, those statutes of limitations or repose start with the completion of the plans, not the construction itself. In P3 projects, these phases often overlap.

It is always wise to consider a provision for A/E tail coverage.

11.04 Additional Statutes of Limitations

The P3 is unique in that the Concessionaire remains a contracting party with the public owner for twenty or more years. The Concessionaire would generally like to pass these claims along to the Design-Builder or the O & M. However, the structure of a P3 complicates the typical period for various parties asserting defect and warranty claims.

By way of example, the California Code of Civil Procedure contains a number of traditional limitation periods for filing various types of lawsuits by or against Construction Managers, A/E's, contractors, subcontractors, and suppliers.

Below is a partial list of the more frequently encountered statutes of limitations:

10 years from Substantial Completion for Latent Defects (CCP 337.15)*
4 years from Substantial Completion for Patent Defects (CCP 337.1)*
4 years from Breach of Written Contract (CCP 337)
4 years to Rescind Written Contract (CCP 337(c))
3 years for Relief from Fraud or Mistake (CCP 338)
3 years for Damage to Real Property (CCP 338)
2 years for Breach of Oral Contract (CCP 339)

2 years for Personal Injury & Death (CCP 335.1)
90 days for Administrative Mandamus (CCP 1094.6)
*Statutes of Repose are outside limits, not the shortest limitations periods.
In this regard, Code of Civil Procedure § 337 states the following:

"Within four years: (1) an action upon any contract, or obligation or liability founded upon an instrument in writing, except as provided in Section 336(a) (an action upon any bonds, notes or debentures issued by a corporation) of this Code."

Also, though not generally applicable, the "Oral Contract" statute is:

"Within two years: (1) an action upon a contract, obligation or liability not founded upon an instrument in writing . . ."[373]

Thus, for general use, a California party must bring a breach of written contract action within four years of the breach.[374] This, of course, begets the next question as to when the breach occurs.

In this regard, Civil Code § 337 states that an action based upon rescission of a contract that is in writing must be filed within four years.[375] The Code specifically states that the time begins to run from the date upon which the facts that entitled the aggrieved party to rescind occurred. Thus, there may be more than one breach of any given contract.[376]

It is important to document all of the acts and inactions that may or may not be tantamount to a breach so that the applicable date can be ascertained. For safety's sake, one should always utilize the earliest

---

[373] Code of Civ. Proc. §339.
[374] *Id.* §343.
[375] *Id.* §337(3).
[376] *Id.* §337(2).

possible date to protect oneself from the running of the statute of limitations.

The analysis of these limitations provisions is often very technical. In *Nelson v. Gorian & Associates, Inc.*, the Court held that Code of Civil Procedure § 337.15 (10-year statute of limitation for latent defects) begins to run as a bar to an action for soils subsidence when the work of the improvement (i.e., the grading of the specific lot) was finished, as opposed to a notice of completion for the entire tract.[377]

11.05 Tort Claims Issues

Contractors filing a tort claim on a public works project must comply with Government Code §§ 900-996.6, which sets forth the required claim procedures against public entities. An action involving a contract with a state agency must be filed within the time period specified in Public Contract Code § 19100.[378]

It is strongly recommended that a timely government claim be filed whenever a contractor seeks relief beyond the normal change order process or when negotiations stall. As a technical matter, the Public Contract Code provides that a Government Code claim need not be filed on a state contract claim as long as the Public Contract Code claim requirements are fulfilled.[379]

In *Schaefer Dixon Associates v. Santa Ana Watershed Project Authority*, the Court found that a government claim was required and barred the claim as untimely.[380] The Public Contract Code focuses on contract claims rather than the tort claims covered by the Government Code. Since many construction claims involve tort claims as well, it is appropriate to file a Government Code § 900, *et seq.*, claim as a precaution.

---

[377] 61 Cal. App. 4th 93, 71 Cal. Rptr. 2d 345 (1998).

[378] *See also*, Public Contract Code § 10265.

[379] *See* Public Contract Code §§ 10265 and 19100 (action or proceeding must commence within six months).

[380] 48 Cal. App. 4th 524, 526, 55 Cal. Rptr. 2d 698, 699 (1996).

In the case of *Arntz Builders v. City of Berkeley*, the court was again asked whether a formal presentation of a Government Code Claim is required in instances where the construction contract contains provisions governing the dispute resolution process.[381] The court held that a claims procedure established by agreement pursuant to Section 930.2 controls the claims to which it is related in instances where the contract did not expressly require presentation of a statutory claim in addition to contract claims process.[382]

Once again, the prudent contractor will submit the government claim at the right time, to the correct officer, and with the required statement of claim. The track taken will depend upon the nature of the filing, to whom and when the claim is filed. The appropriate strategies for claim submissions are technical legal issues requiring a careful legal review.

Legal action on the claim must be commenced within six months after the final decision of the agency, the determination of rights by the hearing officer, or the accrual of the cause of action if there are no applicable claim procedures in the contract.[383] However, the claim may be filed up to two years after the accrual of the cause of action if the agency does not respond at all. Since there is little hope that a contractor client will know of every piece of paper that has come into his office on a project, a better rule of thumb is to file within the six-month statute.

Always read the statute itself when calendaring these deadlines.

A claim involving a contract with a local agency must amount to no more than $375,000 in order for Public Contract Code §§ 20104–20104.6 to be applicable. Public Contract Code § 20104.2, relating to contracting by local agencies, provides an action for damages by unsuccessful bidders as part of the competitive bidding process.

As discussed above, an unsuccessful bidder may have an action for damages against the local entity if the unsuccessful bidder suffered bid preparation or other damages resulting from its bid not being accepted.

The foregoing is not meant to be an all-inclusive list of applicable notice provisions or statutes of limitations. It is provided for illustrative purposes only. Each claim situation involves specific requirements.

---

[381] 166 Cal. App. 4th 276, 284, 82 Cal. Rptr. 3d 605, 610 (2008).
[382] California Code §930.2.
[383] *See* Public Contract Code § 19100.

11.06 Statutes of Repose

The statutes that provide the construction industry with the most substantive protection are the special construction industry "statutes of repose."[384] They bar claims asserted more than four or ten years after substantial completion for patent or latent deficiencies, respectively.

However, the claim may be barred much earlier by government claims statutes or ordinary statutes of limitations. Thus, the four and ten-year statutes of repose may never come into play if the claim is already barred by the two, three or four-year statutes of limitations for specific remedies.

Additional protection is extended to trades and professions, such as architecture and engineering, such that "substantial completion" occurs when the trades people and professionals finish their work before the substantial completion of the entire improvement work.[385] These statutes have been generally upheld against constitutional attack on grounds of equal protection.[386]

---

[384] Code of Civil Proc. §§ 337.1 and 337.15.

[385] *Indus. Risk Insurers v. Rust Eng'g Co.*, 232 Cal. App. 3d 1038, 1043, 283 Cal. Rptr. 873 (Ct. App. 1991)

[386] E.g., *Eden v. Van Tine*, 83 Cal. App. 3d 879, 148 Cal. Rptr. 215 (Ct. App. 1978).

CHAPTER 12

US P3 PROJECTS

12.01 Project Examples

The FHWA has complied an extensive list of US P3 projects which are reproduced in the Appendix A.

In addition, these are a few significant projects that give the breadth and scope of P3 activity:

[A] Rapid Bridge Replacement Public-Private Partnership

Location: Pennsylvania

Summary: In October 2014, the Pennsylvania Department of Transportation awarded a P3 contract to Plenary Walsh Keystone Partners for the replacement of at least 558 state bridges within three and a half years, and 25 years of maintenance. This project was the first P3 in the nation to combine multiple assets and assign long-term maintenance responsibility to the private sector. The team's $899 million proposal averages to $1.6 million to design, construct, and maintain each bridge in the project. PennDOT's average cost per bridge would be $2 million. Work was scheduled to begin in the summer of 2015.[387]

---

[387] Pennsylvania Department of Transportation, *Rapid Bridge Replacement Project: Frequently Asked Questions*, (updated January 2015).

[B] City of Burlingame Wastewater Treatment Facility

Location: Burlingame, CA

Summary: In 1972, Burlingame, located just South of San Francisco, contracted with Veolia to provide full operations services for its 5.5 MGD (million gallons per day) wastewater treatment facility. This was the first time in U.S. history that the management of a municipally-owned wastewater facility was ever transferred to a non-public entity.[388] The contract has been continually renewed over past three decades. It received 1999 Winner of National Council for Public- Private Partnerships Award.[389]

Type of Project: O & M
Total Amount: Unknown
Private Sponsor: Veolia Water North America
Government Entity: City of Burlingame

[C] SR 91 Express Lanes

Location: Orange County, CA

Summary: State Route 91 is a four-lane toll facility in the median on a 16km section of the 91 Riverside Freeway between Orange and Riverside counties- one of the most heavily congested highways in the U.S. The privately-owned and operated project sought to relieve congestion by adding express lanes in the center of existing highway and through use of variable toll-way pricing.[390] SR 91 one of projects originally authorized under Assembly Bill 680 in 1988 (SR 125 below also included). Express lanes opened in December 27, 1995 and were

---

[388] The National Council for Public-Private Partnerships, *City of Burlingame, CA Wastewater Treatment Facility.*

[389] City of Burlingame California, *Waste Water Treatment Plant*, available at https://www.burlingame.org/departments/sustainability/wastewater_treatment.php.

[390] As of July 2019, tolls varied between $1.70 and $8.95, reflecting level of congestion delay avoided in the adjacent non- tolled freeway lanes. *See* 91ExpressLanes.com, *General Information*, available at https://www.91expresslanes.com/toll-schedules/.

subsequently purchased from CPTC by OCTA in January 2003 for $207M after a vote in April 2002. The purchase (and operation by a public agency) was the result over a hotly contested non-compete clause in the original agreement which ultimately postponed other surrounding projects and, in public opinion, created additional congestion and safety risks.

Type of Project: Build Operate Transfer; 35-year franchise agreement between California Private Transportation Company and the State of California. At the end of 35-year franchise agreement, Public Sponsor regains control of the facility.

Total Amount: $130 Million

Private Sponsor: California Private Transportation Company (CPTC), Level 3 Communications, Cofiroute Corp, Granite Construction.

Government Entity: $7 million loan from Orange County Transportation Agency

Lender: $65 million in 14 year variable rate bank loans, Banque Nationale de Paris, Deutsche Bank, Societe Generale, Citibank, $35 million in longer term loans (24 years) CIGNA Other Participants: $20 million private equity, $9 million subordinated debt to OCTA to purchase previously completed engineering and environmental work.

[D] South Bay Expressway (SBX)

Location: San Diego County, CA

Summary: The South Bay Expressway (SBX) toll road (the SBX Project) was a 9.2-mile, privately-developed southern extension of SR 125, extending from San Miguel Road in Bonita, CA near the Sweetwater Reservoir to SR 905 in Otay Mesa, near the International Border. The SBX Project connects the only commercial port of entry in San Diego to the regional freeway network.[391] It was constructed as a privately financed and operated toll road using FasTrak, an electronic

---

[391] U.S. Department of Transportation Federal Highway Administration, *South Bay Expressway (formerly SR 125 South Toll Road)*, available at http://www.fhwa. dot.gov/ipd/project_profiles/ca_southbay.aspx

collection system. South Bay Expressway, a limited partnership (LP), held a franchise with the State of California under which it financed and built the highway, then was to transfer the ownership to the State.[392]

On December 21, 2011 San Diego Association of Governments (SANDAG) purchased the SBX project from South Bay Expressway, LP.[393] The LP then leases back, operates, and maintains the facility for 35 years, at which point control goes back to the State at no cost.[394] Control of the project will revert back to CalTrans in 2042.[395]

Both the privately and publicly funded portions were built by the same contractor under two Design-Build contracts. California Transportation Ventures, Inc. (CTV), the general partner, managed the project and will administer the contracts. Washington Group International was the contractor with a joint venture of Parsons Brinckerhoff Quade and Douglas, Inc and J. Muller International as the design subcontractor. Construction began September 2003 and project opened to traffic in November 2007.[396]

Innovations: $140 Million TIFIA loan was the first-ever provided to a private toll road development.[397] The 38-year loan had a fixed rate borrowing cost equal to 30-year treasuries. Competitive (best value) bid, Design-Build procurement process was followed in which the same Designer, design subcontract, and design price were mandated to each proposer. The Designer was a joint venture composed of subsidiaries of the project sponsors.

Type of Project: Design-Build Finance Operate (DBFO)

Total Amount: $635 Million ($138 million for connector and interchange)

Private Sponsor: California Transportation Ventures, Inc. (a wholly owned subsidiary of Macquire Infrastructure Group), Washington Group (Design-Builder)

---

[392] Id.
[393] Id.
[394] Id.
[395] Id.
[396] Id.
[397] Id. See also U.S. Department of Transportation Federal Highway Administration, Transportation Infrastructure Finance and Innovation Act.

Government Entity/Sponsor: CalTrans

Lenders: TIFIA program, bond holders

Finance: $140 million TIFIA loan, $160 equity from Macquarie Infrastructure Group

Revenue Sources: Toll revenues

Other Participants: $48 million in right-of-way grants from local Developers, Commercial Debt (connector route: $132 million federal and local funding)

[E] Foothill/Eastern Transportation Corridor Agency (FETCA)

Location: Orange County

Summary: FETCA is a joint-powers authority formed by the California legislature in 1986 to plan, finance, construct, and operate the portion of Orange County's toll road system comprised of SR 133, SR 241 and SR 261 from the 91 freeway to south Orange County. [398] The public toll facility is owned and operated by the Orange County Transportation Authority (OCTA) and is comprised of two principal segments: Eastern Transportation Corridor (24-mile) and Foothill Transportation Corridor (27.7-mile upon completion).[399]

FETCA provides direct access between Riverside County's residential areas and Orange County's southeastern suburbs and northern San Diego County. Initially, SR 91 was constructed with two to three lanes in each direction and had auxiliary climbing lanes with future expansion capacity in the median available for general purposes, HOV lanes, or transit use. SR 241 is a tolled facility that interchanges with SR 91.[400] The SR 91 Corridor Improvement Project (SR 91 CIP)

---

[398] Transportation Corridor Agencies, *SR 241/91 Express Lanes Connector Technical Outreach Project Outreach Sheet.* The Transportation Corridor Agencies (TCA) is made up of two joint-powers agencies: the F/ETCA together with the San Joaquin Hills Transportation Corridor Agency (SJHTCA), operator of the SR 73 Toll Road.

[399] *Id.*

[400] *Id.*

will expand the existing SR 91 Express Lanes facility and include a new general purpose median in each direction.[401]

Type of Project: Design-Build consortium; turnkey; Design Bid; guaranteed maximum price and completion date.

Total Amount: $1.5 billion ($750 million in construction). The SR 91 CIP expansion estimated construction cost is $120 million with an additional $35 million in anticipated support costs.[402]

Potential Funding Sources: Toll revenue, federal loans and/or grants, and tax-exempt toll road revenue bond sales.[403] The north-to-east SR 241/91 connector will use dynamic pricing to balance traffic volumes from the connector with the eastbound traffic traveling in the SR 91 Express Lanes; connections between the FETCA, OCTA, and RCTC toll collection systems may be required; the west-to-south SR 241/91 Connector will be variable pricing.[404]

Private Partner: Flatiron Construction Corporation

Government Entity: Foothill / Eastern Transportation Corridor Agency (FETCA).

Project Partners: OCTA, Riverside County Transportation Commission (RCTC), CalTrans, and FHWA.

[H] California State University Sports Complex

In June 2001, the Board of Trustees approved the public/private partnership that led to the construction of the $150 million then named Home Depot Center sports complex on the campus of California State University, Dominguez Hills.[405] The existing partnership provided ASC with a lease of 85-acres for the major components of the development. There was also a 40-acre section of campus property on which the Developer renovated existing athletic facilities to allow for its programs' use when the University is not using the facilities.[406]

---

401 *Id.*
402 *Id.*
403 *Id.*
404 *Id.*
405 Dignity Health Sports Park, www.dignityhealthsportspark.com.
406 *Id.*

[I] University of California Merced 2020 - P3 Project

A further P3 project is UC Merced, a $1.3B expansion (for which I was a DRB panel member). In July 2016, the UC Regents approved a budget of $1.3 billion for the Merced 2020 Project. Of that total, $600 million will come from UC external financing; the Developer, Plenary Properties Merced, will invest $590.35 million; and campus funds will account for $148.13 million.[407]

The University's ability to afford the project was determined based on a holistic, long-range financial model. The model includes a combined estimate of design and construction costs as well as preventative maintenance lifecycle costs.[408]

The Merced 2020 Project is a type of public-private partnership known as an "availability-payment concession," in which a single private development team designs, builds, operates and maintains major building systems and partially finances the entire project under a single contract known as the "Project Agreement".[409]

During construction, the university will make predetermined progress payments to the Developer. Once the buildings become available for use, the university will make performance-based "availability payments" that cover remaining capital costs, as well as the operations and maintenance of major building systems. From start to finish, the duration of the agreement is 39 years.[410]

As structured, this hybrid model captures the time and cost advantages of the familiar "Design-Build" method of developing buildings and effectively adds a preventative capital-maintenance program and capital-renewal program. It does not transfer the university's property rights, does not assign revenue streams and is not a lease.[411]

A further list of P3 projects is available in Appendix E.

---

[407] Project Funding – Construction of the Merced 2020 Project Represents a major financial commitment by the people of California to fulfill the mission of UC Merced, available at: https://merced2020.ucmerced.edu/financestructure.
[408] Id.
[409] Id.
[410] Id.
[411] Id.

CHAPTER 13

CANADIAN P3 PROVISIONS

The development of P3 contracts in Canada has led to substantial success in completing exceptional projects and attracting private investment. As such, it is useful to examine the types of contract clauses and relief offered Concessionaires in Canada in contrast to some of the more stringent clauses in US P3 practice.

Once such project is the Golden Ears Bridge. The Golden Ears Bridge is a six-lane extradosed bridge in Metro Vancouver, British Columbia. It spans the Fraser River, connecting Langley on the south side with Pitt Meadows and Maple Ridge on the north side. The bridge opened to traffic on June 16, 2009.

The following clauses are typical of many Canadian P3 Agreements:

13.01 Developer Compensation

Example from Vancouver's Golden Ears Bridge[412]

After receiving the award, the contractor pays a $50,000,000 "license fee" for the exclusive right to design, build, finance and

---

[412] TransLink, *Golden Ears Bridge & Tolling Info*. The Golden Ears Bridge connects the western Canadian Pitt Meadows and Maple Ridge to Langley, Surrey, and beyond.

operate the project.[413] After substantial completion, the Developer is paid availability payments (here called "Capital Payments") to pay the lump sum bid price over approximately 30 years and a monthly stipend for operational expenses ("OMR Payments").[414] These are the only payments to the contractor; the owner keeps the toll revenue.[415]

The following provisions are from the Project Agreement Article 7 – Payment or related:

7.1 Payment of Capital Payments and OMR Payments

"Subject to the terms and conditions of this Agreement and the other DBFO Agreements, TransLink will pay the DBFO Contractor in accordance with Schedule PA-7 and Schedule PA-8."[416]

7.2 Limitation on Payments

"Other than any payments specifically provided for in this Agreement, the DBFO Contractor will have no right to any further payment from TransLink in connection with the DB Work, the OMR Work or the Project."[417]

Schedule PA-7

This schedule sets the monthly Capital Payments based upon the construction cost bid in the Developer's proposal, a fixed interest rate, and a thirty-two year amortization period.[418] The monthly payments are adjusted for changes in the Consumer Price Index

---

[413] TransLink, *Golden Ears Bridge Project Agreement Between Greater Vancouver Transportation Authority and Golden Crossing General Partnership.*
[414] *Id.* at Article 7.1.
[415] *Id.*
[416] *Id.*
[417] *Id.* at Article 7.2.
[418] *Id.* at Article 7.1.

indexed to the date of the Developer's proposal. Additionally, the owner does not make any Capital Payments until substantial completion, and makes reduced payments at the beginning of the operations period with the assumption that the toll income received by the owner will start low and increase.[419] Liquidated Damages for delayed "Total Completion" are deducted from Capital Payments. Bridge-Closure Deductions are deducted from Capital Payments.

Schedule PA-8

This schedule sets monthly OMR Payments, which are intended to cover the ongoing costs of operations, maintenance and rehabilitation. Deductions are made for Non-Availability Events (i.e. unexcused lane closures) and Non-Conforming Event Points (i.e. failure to repair potholes within 4 hours of detection).[420]

Definitions

"Capital Payment Period" means each period of 1 month during the OMR Term, the first such period commencing on the Substantial Completion Date.

"Inflation Index" for any period n, means the ratio of the Reference CPI applicable to that period n divided by the Reference CPI_0, and which ratio, expressed as a fraction, is Reference CPI_n/Reference CPI_0.[421]

"Reference CPI_0" means the value of the Reference CPI for the Base Date.[422]

---

[419] *Id.* at Article 16.8.
[420] *Id.* at Article 18.10.
[421] *Id.* Article 1.2(p).
[422] *Id.*

13.02 Relief Events

[A] Example from Golden Ears Bridge

For this project a Relief Event causes an excusable but non-compensable delay. A Change Event is excusable and compensable. The impacts of a Change Event are Change Consequences and, after a notice of Change Event, relief is provided by approval of a Design, Build, Finance Operate (DBFO) Contractor Change (the contractor's request for a change order) or a TransLink Change (owner change order).[423]

(a) **Definitions**

"Relief Event" means the occurrence after October 18, 2005 of an earthquake, tornado, flood, lightning, or typhoon/hurricane of category 3 or higher according to the United States System of Typhoon/Hurricane Classification, or a fire or explosion not caused by or resulting from any Non-Excusable Event of the party claiming relief from such event.[424]

"Change Event" means any of the following events or circumstances occurring or existing before the end of the License Term, if and for so long as neither party has exercised a right to terminate the DBFO Agreements as a result of such event or circumstance: [edited for length]

    (b)   a Change in Law;
    (c)   a Force Majeure;
    (d)   a Labour Dispute;
    (e)   a Protest Action;
    (f)   any failure of TransLink to make any Facility Lands available to the DBFO Contractor in accordance with the Facility Lands Availability Schedule;
    (g)   any amendment, supplement or replacement, after October 18, 2005, of any Facility Lands Interest, Facility Lands Agreement or Facility Lands Encumbrance [. . . .];

---

[423] *Id.* at Article 10.10.
[424] *Id.* at Article 10.11.

(h) any failure of:
  (i) any party to any Facility Lands Agreement or Facility Lands Encumbrance to materially comply with the provisions thereof; or
  (ii) any third party to an agreement that TransLink is obligated under section 6.12(b) to use reasonable efforts to enforce, to materially comply with the obligations of such third party under such agreement; other than a failure of the DBFO Contractor to comply with the terms of this Agreement;

(i) TransLink's inability to obtain a Rail Crossing Agreement from a Railway, on terms at least as favourable to TransLink as those set out in Schedule PA-28 for such Rail Crossing Agreement, or within 13 months after making application therefor in accordance with section 6.13(d), or both, provided the DBFO Contractor has complied with its obligations under section 6.13;

(j) any replacement of the Tolling Gantries required as a result of a change in tolling technology;

(k) any challenges to the validity of . . . the Environmental Assessment Certificate [. . . .];

(l) the discovery on any Facility Lands of any Contamination (other than Disclosed Contamination), that:
  (i) existed on such Facility Lands at the time such Facility Lands were made available to the DBFO Contractor pursuant to section 6.1; or
  (ii) migrated onto such Facility Lands from lands other than Facility Lands after the time such Facility Lands were made available to the DBFO Contractor pursuant to section 6.1;

(m) the discovery after October 18, 2005 on the Facility Lands of any Heritage Object;

(n) any factual inaccuracy in the Geotechnical Data;

. . .

(o) any failure by TransLink to perform or observe any of its material obligations under any of the DBFO Agreements, if such failure substantially frustrates or renders it impossible for the DBFO Contractor to perform the DBFO Contractor's material obligations [. . . .]; that impacts (whether positively or negatively) the carrying out of the DB Work or the OMR Work, as the case may be, or impacts (whether positively or negatively) the cost of carrying out the DB Work or the OMR Work, provided none of the foregoing events or circumstances shall constitute a Change Event that a party hereto may rely on, to the extent such events or circumstances arise or result (directly or indirectly) from any Non-Excusable Event in respect of such party.[425]

10.11   Relief Events

Where, due to the occurrence of a Relief Event, TransLink or the DBFO Contractor is prevented from or limited in the performance of any of its respective obligations under any of the DBFO Agreements with respect to DB Work and/or the OMR Work:

(a) subject to section 10.11(c), TransLink or the DBFO Contractor, as the case may be, shall be excused from the performance of such obligations and relieved from its liability (including the risk of termination of the DBFO Agreements under Article 12 or Article 11, as the case may be) in respect of any breach of such obligations, but only for the period during which and to the extent such Relief Event so prevents or limits performance of such obligations; and

subject to section 10.11(c):

(b) the DBFO Contractor will be entitled to an extension to the time provided for the performance of such obligations in

---

[425] *Id.* at Article 10.2.

accordance with the Project Schedule, if any, that is reasonable and necessary in the circumstances; and

(i) if such extension affects any task on the critical path of the DB Work, the DBFO Contractor will be entitled to an extension to the Substantial Completion Target Date and the Substantial Completion Longstop Date that is reasonable and necessary in the circumstances; and in order to receive the benefit of sections 10.11(a) and (b), the party affected by a Relief Event must, as soon as practicable following the date on which it first became aware of such Relief Event, notify the other party in writing of:

(ii) the occurrence of the Relief Event;

(iii) particulars of the obligations of the notifying party the performance of which is prevented or limited by the Relief Event, and particulars of the impact thereof, if any, on the performance of any tasks on the critical path of the DB Work; and

(iv) particulars of the period during which the Relief Event so prevents or limits performance of such obligations; provided, however, that in the case of a Relief Event that is continuing, only one notice shall be necessary with respect to that Relief Event."

10.2   Change Events

(a) Either the DBFO Contractor or TransLink may deliver to the other party notice of the occurrence of a Change Event, to be evaluated and addressed by the parties pursuant to this Article 10.

(b) No notice of the occurrence of a Change Event may be delivered by either party more than 18 months after the date of the occurrence or commencement of such Change Event.

(c) As a result of any Change Event, including any Change Event in respect of which notice has previously been delivered by the DBFO Contractor to TransLink pursuant to section 10.2(a), TransLink may (to the extent that it is reasonable to do so in light of the relevant Change Event) issue a TransLink Change pursuant to section 10.1(a)(i), and the Change Consequences shall thereupon be determined, without duplication, for both the Change Event and the resulting TransLink Change.

(d) Notwithstanding any other provision of this Article 10, neither party hereto shall be entitled to receive compensation and/ or other relief in respect of Change Consequences under this Article 10 in respect of a Change Event, to the extent that the events or circumstances constituting the Change Event arise or result (directly or indirectly) from any Non-Excusable Event in respect of such party.

13.03 Developer Permitting Obligations

Example from Golden Ears Bridge

20.00 Governmental Authorizations

20.01 Subject to Article 23.00, the DBFO Contractor shall take or cause to be taken, at the DBFO Contractor's expense, all such actions as are necessary to:

(a) obtain all Governmental Authorizations, other than the Environmental Assessment Certificate and the Authorizations contained in the GVRD Agreement and the Fraser River Port Authority Lease, as are necessary in order for the DBFO Contractor to carry out its responsibilities and obligations in connection with the DB Work; and

(b) comply with, promptly renew and maintain in good standing all such Governmental Authorizations (except as provided in the DBFO Agreements with

(c) respect to the Environmental Assessment Certificate, the Authorizations contained in the GVRD Agreement and the Fraser River Port Authority Lease).

20.02 In obtaining Governmental Authorizations, the DBFO Contractor will make complete and timely application to the relevant Governmental Authorities in compliance with such Governmental Authorities' procedures and requirements, and with regard to the critical path of the DB Work, so as not to delay any task on the critical path of the DB Work.

20.03 In carrying out the DB Work, the DBFO Contractor will comply with the terms and conditions of the Environmental Assessment Certificate and any Authorization issued with respect to the Environmental Assessment Certificate.

20.04 The DBFO Contractor, if required by TransLink, and TransLink will sign any Authorization issued by the Department of Fisheries and Oceans (Canada) with respect to the Project and abide by the terms and conditions of such Authorization.

20.05 The Table of Commitments and Assurances describes commitments and responsibilities of the DBFO Contractor in connection with the DB Work. In carrying out the DB Work, the DBFO Contractor will comply with and perform all of the DBFO Contractor's commitments and responsibilities described in the Table of Commitments and Assurances and in a manner that meets all requirements of Governmental Authorizations.

21.00 Utilities

21.01 Subject to Article 23.00, the DBFO Contractor shall, at its own cost as part of the DB Work:

(a) be responsible for making all necessary arrangements with utility companies and Governmental Authorities for the supply of Utilities used in or supplied to the Facility, both temporary and permanent as required for the DB Work, including applying for and obtaining all necessary Authorizations for all necessary connections and services of Utilities in connection with the DB Work;

(b) coordinating or ensuring the coordination with utility companies, Governmental Authorities, including the GVRD, and persons having service lines, pipelines, transmission lines and other equipment, cables, systems and other apparatus in, on, under or over the Facility Lands required for the temporary or permanent relocation of any lines, pipes, equipment, cables, systems and other apparatus affected by the DB Work and securing or causing to be secured any necessary Authorizations in connection therewith; and

(c) causing provision to be made for the removal, accommodation or temporary or permanent relocation and restoration of Utilities, including lines, pipes, equipment, cables, systems or other apparatus, which intersect, interfere, interface with or otherwise affect any DB Work and arranging for temporary rights of entry and access to Utilities to be made available, as may be necessary for the performance of the DB Work and as may be required pursuant to applicable Design, Authorizations and Laws, and shall comply with, promptly renew and maintain in good standing all such Authorizations.

21.02 In obtaining Authorizations from a utility company or Governmental Authority for Utilities work required in connection with the performance of the DB Work, the DBFO Contractor will make complete and timely application to the relevant utility company or Governmental Authority in compliance with such utility company's or Governmental Authority's procedures and requirements and with regard to the critical path of the DB Work, so as not to delay any task on the critical path for the DB Work.

21.03 In addition to the terms and conditions of the GVRD Agreement, any adjustment, relocation or replacement of services or infrastructure of Utilities in connection with the DB Work, will be performed by the DBFO Contractor in a manner that protects the Utilities and maintains Utilities service operation throughout the course of the DB Work.

21.04 The DBFO Contractor shall preserve and protect the infrastructure affected by the DB Work carried out pursuant to Article 21.00.

21.05 The DBFO Contractor shall confirm the location of all Utilities and ensure that all of its labour force, employees, Principal Contractors, Subcontractors, owner/operators and any other workers on the Facility Lands:

(a) are made aware of the location of all Utilities in connection with the DB Work and the Facility and the importance of avoiding damage to those underground or above ground Utilities; and

(b) observe all instructions in connection with those Utilities issued by the owners or operators of Utilities.

21.06 Neither TransLink nor TransLink's Consultant is responsible or liable for the accuracy of information regarding Utilities provided to the DBFO Contractor from any source.

22.00 Railways

22.01 Subject to Article 23.00, the DBFO Contractor shall, at its own cost as part of the DB Work, be responsible for making all necessary arrangements with Railways, except for the Rail Crossing Agreements as provided for in Project Agreement section 6.13, including obtaining any Authorizations required to carry out the DBFO Contractor's responsibilities and obligations in connection with the DB Work, and shall comply with, promptly renew and maintain in good standing all such Authorizations.

22.02 In obtaining Authorizations from a Railway pursuant to the applicable Rail Crossing Agreement, the DBFO Contractor will make complete and timely application to the relevant Railway in compliance with such Rail Crossing Agreement and such Railway's procedures and requirements, and with regard to the critical path of the DB Work, so as not to delay any task on the critical path of the DB Work.

23.00 TransLink Assistance with Governmental and Other Authorizations

23.01 Without derogating from the DBFO Contractor's responsibilities under sections 20.01, 21.01 and 22.01 to obtain all necessary Governmental Authorizations and other Authorizations from utility companies and Railways, TransLink shall in response to any reasonable request by the DBFO Contractor provide the DBFO Contractor with such reasonable assistance as TransLink is able to offer in connection with obtaining such Authorizations.

23.02 In the event that the DBFO Contractor, despite acting reasonably and prudently and making all commercially reasonable efforts, including making complete and timely application as provided for in sections 20.02, 21.02 and 22.02, and despite taking all commercially reasonable mitigation measures (including, to the extent practicable, considering modifications to the Design) experiences a delay in respect of any task on the critical path of the DB Work as a result of:

(a) any unreasonable delay by a Governmental Authority, utility company or Railway in issuing; or

(b) any unreasonable refusal by a Governmental Authority, utility company or Railway to issue;

(c) any necessary Governmental Authorization or other Authorization from a utility company, or from a Railway pursuant to the applicable Railway Crossing Agreement, such delay in respect of any task on the critical path of the DB Work shall be a Change Event, and the relevant Change Consequences in respect thereof shall be addressed in accordance with Project Agreement Article 10.

23.03 Subject to the DBFO Contractor having made a complete and timely application as provided for in section 21.02 for the removal, accommodation (other than the mere issuance of an Authorization without any other work to be performed by the relevant utility company), temporary or permanent relocation and restoration of Utilities described in such application, required in connection with the performance of the DB Work (each a "Requested Action" in this section 23.03) to the following entities (or their respective successors in interest):

(a) British Columbia Hydro and Power Authority

(b) British Columbia Transmission Corporation

(c) Telus Corporation

(d) Shaw Cable Systems Limited

(e) Terasen Inc.

(f) Terasen Pipelines Inc.

(each a "Utility Company" in this section 23.03)

In compliance with each Utility Company's procedures and any other applicable requirements of such Utility Company, if a Utility Company does not carry out the Requested Action within 270 days from the date on which the DBFO Contractor submitted a complete application in compliance with such Utility Company's procedures and other requirements and the DBFO Contractor experiences a delay in respect of any task on the critical path of the DB Work as a result, such delay in respect of any task on the critical path of the DB Work shall be a Change Event, and the relevant Change Consequences in respect thereof shall be addressed in accordance with Project Agreement Article 10.

"Governmental Authorizations" means all Authorizations conferred under applicable Laws or other requirements of any Governmental Authority (excluding TransLink), which are necessary in order for the DBFO Contractor to carry out its responsibilities and obligations:

(a) for the DB Agreement, in connection with the DB Work; and

(b) for the OMR Agreement, in connection with the OMR Work;

(c) and includes the Environmental Assessment Certificate, the Table of Commitments and Assurances, and the Authorizations contained in the GVRD Agreement.

(From Project Agreement) ARTICLE 6 - REAL PROPERTY AND RELATED AGREEMENTS

6.1 Facility Lands Availability

TransLink shall use all commercially reasonable efforts to make the Facility Lands available to the DBFO Contractor for the purposes and on the terms and conditions set out in the DBFO Agreements, in accordance with the Facility Lands Availability Schedule and, in the case of railway lines and associated properties of the Railways, in accordance with section 6.13.

(from Design-Build Agreement)

4.00 Conflict Between Agreements and Documents

4.01 If there is any conflict between the provisions of the documents mentioned below the following order of precedence shall apply for interpretation purposes:

(a) the provisions of applicable Laws shall take precedence over the provisions of this Agreement, the DB Requirements and the Governmental Authorizations;

(b) the provisions of Governmental Authorizations shall take precedence over the provisions of this Agreement; and

(c) the provisions of this Agreement (excluding the Schedules) shall take precedence over the Schedules to this Agreement unless otherwise expressly stated in this Agreement or any Schedule.

(From Project Agreement) ARTICLE 6 - REAL PROPERTY AND RELATED AGREEMENTS

6.1 Facility Lands Availability

TransLink shall use all commercially reasonable efforts to make the Facility Lands available to the DBFO Contractor for the purposes and on the terms and conditions set out in the DBFO Agreements, in accordance with the Facility Lands Availability Schedule and, in the case of railway lines and associated properties of the Railways, in accordance with section 6.13.

6.2 Facility to be Constructed on Facility Lands

The DBFO Contractor confirms and agrees that no portion of the Facility shall be constructed or located on any lands that are not Facility Lands or on any Facility Lands that are Temporary Easement Areas.

6.3 Performance of Agreements

Subject to section 6.4, during the Licence Term the DBFO Contractor shall, at its own cost and expense (subject to Article 10 in respect of Change Events):

(a) perform in all material respects, those obligations of TransLink under:

(i) the Master Municipal Agreement;

(ii) the GVRD Agreement;

(iii) the Onni Statutory Right-of-way;

(iv) the Mutual Materials Statutory Rights of Way; and

(v) the Fraser River Port Authority Lease;

(together, the "Specified Agreements and Encumbrances"), that are specified in Schedule PA-31 as being the obligations of the DBFO Contractor; and

(b) not do or omit to do, and not cause or permit to be done or omitted by any person for whom the DBFO Contractor is in law responsible, anything on or with respect to the Facility Lands or the TransLink Lands or any improvements thereon, that would cause TransLink to be in material default under any of the Facility Lands Agreements or the Facility Lands Encumbrances.

The End

AUTHOR BIOGRAPHY

Ernest C. Brown, Esq, P.E. graduated in Civil Engineering from the Massachusetts Institute of Technology (MIT) and earned a Master's Degree in Construction Management and a Law Degree with distinction from the University of California at Berkeley. He served as Corporate Counsel for Fluor Corporation and as a construction and real estate partner in several large law firms.

In 1989, he founded Ernest Brown & Company, specializing in construction law and dispute resolution. Mr. Brown's firm grew to 50 people and served as Owner's Counsel for the design and construction of the John Wayne Airport ($300 million) and the Honda Center (Anaheim - $100 Million), as well as counsel for the Carquinez Suspension Bridge ($300 Million) and numerous other large civil engineering, infrastructure and development projects.

He served as Joint Venture Counsel for the Presidio Parkway Project, a $1.2 Billion Public Private Partnership (P3) Project in San Francisco, California. He served in a similar capacity for the Oakland Connector Project, a $500 million, Design-Build people mover system linking BART and the Oakland International Airport. It included a twenty year operations and maintenance agreement (Completion 2014).

Mr. Brown has widely shared his expertise in P3 formation, design-build contracts and project execution. He currently serves as Chair of the P3 Working Group for ConsensusDocs. In that role he has participated in shaping ConsensusDocs policy on P3s and drafted and lead the committee in completing a standard Public Private Partnership (P3) Agreement and an Operations and Maintenance Agreement (O & M) for use in P3 Projects.

His thirty years of construction law practice includes five airports, bridge and highway projects, high rises, hotels, hospitals, refineries, pipelines, storage tanks, water and wastewater treatment plants and a myriad of other civil engineering, power plant, environmental and defense projects in the US and 26 foreign countries. He has been a Mediator, Arbitrator and Special Master for the California Superior Courts, the American Arbitration Association and the California Office of Administrative Hearings for over thirty years.

He is also the author of *California Infrastructure Projects, 4th Edition* (2020), *California Public Works: Contracts & Litigation* (1999), and *Architect/Engineer Malpractice*, Federal Publications, 1980 (co-author) and dozens of professional articles.

APPENDIX A

THE FEDERAL HIGHWAY ADMINISTRATION CURRENT P3 PROJECTS, UPDATED - OCTOBER 2019

Design–Build Finance Operate Maintain (DBFOM) Toll Concessions:

- **91 Express Lanes** *-* *Orange County, California*
- **395 Express Lanes** *- Alexandria and Arlington, Virginia*
- **Belle Chasse Bridge and Tunnel Replacement** *- Plaquemines Parish, Louisiana*
- **Capital Beltway High Occupancy Toll (HOT) Lanes (I-495)** *- Fairfax County, Virginia*
- **Dulles Greenway** *- Loudoun County, Virginia*
- **Elizabeth River Tunnels (Downtown / Midtown Tunnel)** *- Cities of Norfolk and Portsmouth, Virginia*
- **Foley Beach Express** *- Baldwin County, Alabama (local road project)*
- **I-77 Express Lanes** *- Charlotte, North Carolina*
- **I-95 Express Lanes Fredericksburg Extension** *- Stafford County, Virginia*
- **I-95 HOV/HOT Lanes** *- Fairfax, Prince Williams, and Stafford Counties, Virginia*
- **LBJ Express/IH 635 Managed Lanes** *- Dallas County, Texas*
- **North Tarrant Express I-820 and SH 121/183 (Segments 1 and 2W)** *- Dallas-Fort Worth Metroplex, Texas*
- **North Tarrant Express 35W (Segments 3A, 3B and 3C)** *- Dallas-Fort Worth Metroplex, Texas*
- **SH 130 (Segments 5-6)** *- Austin, Texas Metropolitan Area*
- **SH 288 Toll Lanes Project** *- Houston, Texas*

- **South Bay Expressway (formerly SR 125 South)** * - *San Diego County, California*
- **Teodoro Moscoso Bridge** - *San Juan to Carolina, Puerto Rico*
- **Transform 66 - Outside the Beltway** - *Fairfax and Prince William Counties, Virginia*
- **US 36 Express Lanes (Phase 2)** - *Denver Metro Area, Colorado*

Build Finance Operate Maintain (DBFOM) Availability Payment Concessions:

- **Central 70** - *Denver, Colorado*
- **Eagle Project** - *Denver Metro Area, Colorado (transit project)*
- **Goethals Bridge Replacement** * - *Staten Island, New York to Elizabeth, New Jersey*
- **Gordie Howe International Bridge** - *Windsor, Ontario to Detroit, Michigan*
- **I-4 Ultimate** - *Orlando, Florida*
- **I-69 Section 5** - *Bloomington to Martinsville, Indiana*
- **KentuckyWired** - *Kentucky (statewide)*
- **I-75 Modernization Project Segment 3** * - *Detroit Metropolitan Region, Michigan*
- **I-595 Corridor Roadway Improvements** - *Broward County, Florida*
- **Metro Region Freeway Lighting P3 (Michigan)** - *Detroit Tri-County Area*
- **Northampton County Bridge Renewal Program** * - *Northampton County, Pennsylvania*
- **Ohio River Bridges East End Crossing** - *Southern Indiana/Louisville, Kentucky*
- **Pennsylvania Rapid Bridge Replacement Project** * - *Pennsylvania (statewide)*
- **Port of Miami Tunnel** - *Miami, Florida*
- **Presidio Parkway (Phase II)** - *San Francisco, California*
- **Purple Line Project** - *Washington DC Metro Region / Central Maryland (transit project)*
- **Southern Ohio Veterans Memorial Highway (Portsmouth Bypass)** - *Portsmouth to Lucasville, Scioto County, Ohio*
- **State Street Redevelopment Project** * - *West Lafayette, Indiana (local road project)*

Long-Term Lease Concessions:

- **Chicago Skyway** - *Chicago, Illinois*
- **Indiana Toll Road** - *Indiana*
- **Luis Muñoz Marín International Airport Privatization** - *San Juan, Puerto Rico (aviation project)*
- **Maryland I-95 Travel Plazas Redevelopment** - *Cecil County and Harford County, Maryland*
- **Moynihan Train Hall** - *New York, New York (transit project)*
- **Northwest Parkway** - *Denver Metro Region, Colorado*
- **Ohio State University Parking Facility** - *Columbus, Ohio*
- **Pocahontas Parkway/Richmond Airport Connector** - *Greater Richmond, Virginia*
- **Puerto Rico PR-22 & PR-5 Lease** - *Northern Puerto Rico*
- **Seagirt Marine Terminal** - *Baltimore, Maryland*

APPENDIX B

FHWA - STATE P3 ENABLING STATUTES

State	Category	Allows for Unsolicited?	Statute(s)	Overview
Alabama	Broad	No	Ala. Code §§ 23-1-40	Effective November 2018, this statute describes the state DOT duties and powers generally. The statute gives the DOT the authority to enter into contracts with public or private entities for the construction of a public road, bridge, or tunnel. The DOT may use Design-Build, Design-Build-operate, Design-Build-own-operate, Design-Build-own-operate-maintain, Design-Build-finance-operate-maintain, or other similar project delivery models in which "the design, right-of-way acquisition, relocation of structures or utilities, construction, financing, ownership, management, maintenance, and operation, or any combination thereof, of a public road, bridge, or tunnel project is accomplished by the department or on behalf of the department by any of the aforementioned entities or methods." The DOT may also enter leases, licenses, franchises, concessions, or other agreements for the development, operation, management, or undertaking of all or any part of a public road, bridge, or tunnel project.

Alabama	Broad	No	Ala. Code §§ 23-1-81	Authorizes county commissions and the state DOT to license private entities to establish or operate toll roads, toll bridges, ferries or causeways. Allows the authorization of a licensee to establish and fix the rates of toll.
Alabama	Broad	No	Ala. Code §§ 23-2-140 to 163	Authorizes the Alabama Toll Road, Bridge and Tunnel Authority to enter into agreements for Design-Build, Design-Build-operate, Design-Build-own-operate or Design-Build-own-operate-maintain contracts, or other similar arrangements or agreements; also allows for leases, licenses, franchises, concessions or other agreements for the development, operation, management or undertaking of all or any part of a project. Allows any entity that owns, leases or otherwise operates a toll facility to set and collect tolls, subject to such conditions as the authority and the state DOT may establish. Allows bids to be awarded by best value or qualifications. Sets the bond issue date at 75 years.
Alaska	Limited	No	Alaska Stat. §§ 19.75.011 to 990	Authorizes the Knik Arm Bridge and Toll Authority to enter into P3s in any form to finance, design, construct, maintain, improve or operate the Knik Arm Bridge. Allows the authority to issue bonds or incur other forms of indebtedness to finance the project and to fix and collect tolls for the use of the bridge; these tolls may exceed operating costs.
Arizona	Broad	Yes	Ariz. Rev. Stat. §§ 28-7701 to 7710 A	Comprehensive statute that authorizes P3s for transportation projects. Under legislation enacted in 2009 (Senate Bill 2396; 2009 Ariz. Sess. Laws, Chap. 141), authorizes the state DOT to enter into agreements with private entities to design, build, finance, maintain, operate, manage and/or lease transportation facilities, or for any other project delivery method that the DOT determines will serve the public interest.

				Allows for availability payments and revenue sharing. Limits agreements to no more than 50 years, which may be extended by the DOT. Requires any foreign entity that submits a concession agreement to provide satisfactory evidence of compliance with certain requirements. Prohibits noncompete clauses, in that a P3 agreement must include a provision that bars a private partner from seeking relief to hinder the DOT from developing or constructing any facility that was planned at the time the agreement was executed. However, an agreement may provide for reasonable compensation to the private partner for adverse effects on revenues resulting from the development and construction of a then-unplanned facility. Allows for solicited and unsolicited proposals.
Arkansas	Limited		Ark. Stat. Ann. § 14-305-102	The law authorizes the use by counties of P3s for the development of unpaved roads.
Arkansas	Limited	No	Ark. Stat. Ann. §§27-86-201 to 211; Ark. Stat. Ann. §27.76.402	Sections 27-86-201 to 211 allows counties to grant franchises to private entities to build toll bridges, turnpikes or causeways over or along swamps, watercourses, lakes or bays whenever it is in the public interest. Requires consent from the federal government for construction of the bridge. Gives counties superintending authority on rates. Prohibit granting a franchise to operate a toll road on the state highway system. Section 27.76.402 prohibits a regional mobility authority from selling a toll facility project to a private entity or entering into a lease or concession agreement for a toll facility.
Arkansas	Broad		Ark. Code §§ 22-10-101 to 22-10-505	The Partnership for Public Facilities and Infrastructure Act authorizes county and local government to use P3 for projects that have a long-term operations agreement. Eligible projects include: ferry, mass transit facility, vehicle parking facility, port facility, power generation facility, fuel

				supply facility, combined heating and power facility, central utility plant facility, distributed generation facility, oil or gas pipeline, water supply facility, water treatment intake and distribution facility, waste water treatment and collection facility, waste treatment facility, hospital, library, school, educational facility, medical or nursing care facility, recreational facility, administrative facility, law enforcement facility, fire department facility, public administrative office, toll road, correctional facility, technology infrastructure facility, public building, and transportation system. Projects must be approved by the Arkansas Economic Development Commission and Arkansas Development Finance Authority. The statue does not apply to the DOT.
California	Limited	Yes	Cal. Gov. Code §§ 5956 to 5956.10	Authorizes local governmental agencies to enter into agreements with private entities to study, plan, design, construct, develop, finance, maintain, rebuild, improve, repair and/or operate a variety of fee-producing infrastructure facilities, including rail, highway, bridge, tunnel or airport projects. Allows for solicited and unsolicited proposals. Prohibits using the authority in this section to design, construct, finance or operate a toll road on a state highway.
Colorado		No	Colo. Rev. Stat. § 32-9-128.5	Regional Transportation District has authority for mass transit projects. This statute describes how the Regional Transportation District may load net proceeds of private activity or exempt facility bonds to a private entity to finance all or a portion of a project.
Colorado		Yes	Colo. Rev. Stat. §§ 43-1-1201 to 1209	Allows the state DOT to enter into agreements for public-private initiatives, including for the design, financing, construction, operation, maintenance, and/or improvement

				of toll roads, turnpikes and high-occupancy toll lanes. Allows for solicited and unsolicited proposals.
Colorado			Colo. Rev. Stat. § 43-2-219	Authorizes a board of county commissioners to enter into public-private initiatives for county highways and bridges, to privatize any county highway or bridge, or to charge tolls for such facilities.
Colorado			Colo. Rev. Stat. §§ 43-3-202.5	Authorizes the state DOT to make or enter into contracts or agreements with one or more public or private entities to design, finance, construct, operate, maintain, reconstruct or improve a turnpike project by means of a public-private initiative. Finds that privately-developed transportation projects can result in time and cost savings, risk reduction and new tax revenues. Requires that the public or private entity secure and maintain liability insurance coverage.
Colorado			Colo. Rev. Stat. §§ 43-4-413-414	Authorizes the Transportation Commission, with the approval of the governor, to enter into a contract with a private individual, firm or corporation for construction, maintenance and operation of one or more toll tunnels. Requires all rates for tolls or fees to be charged by a private contractor to first be approved by the commission.
Colorado			Colo. Rev. Stat §§ 43-4-801 to 812	Creates and authorizes a Statewide Bridge Enterprise to enter into P3s to design, develop, construct, reconstruct, repair, operate or maintain bridge projects. Also creates the High-Performance Transportation Enterprise (HPTE) to seek out and enter into P3s and other innovative means of completing surface transportation infrastructure projects. Both enterprises shall operate as government owned businesses within the state DOT.
Connecticut	Limited	No	Conn. Gen. Stat. §§ 4-255 to 4-263	This statute authorizes the Governor to approve up to 5 projects to be implemented as P3 projects prior to January 2016. Eligible facilities

				include early childcare, educational, health or housing; transportation systems including ports, transit-oriented development; or any other facility designated by an act of the General Assembly. The statute limits state support of a partnership agreement to 25% of the cost of the project.
Delaware	Broad	Yes	Del. Cod. Ann. Tit. 2, §§ 2001 to 2012	Comprehensive statute that authorizes P3s for transportation projects. Authorizes the secretary of transportation to enter into agreements with private entities to study, plan, design, construct, lease, finance, operate, maintain, repair and/or expand transportation systems. Establishes the Public-Private Initiatives Program Revolving Loan Fund, which provides funds for financing such projects. Allows for solicited and unsolicited proposals.
Florida	Broad	Yes	Fla. Stat. Ann. § 334.30	Comprehensive statute that authorizes P3s for transportation projects. Authorizes the state DOT, with legislative approval, to enter into agreements with private entities to build, operate, own or finance transportation facilities. Creates evaluation criteria for such projects. Prohibits noncompete clauses. Exempts private entities from certain taxes. Allows the DOT to lease existing toll facilities (except the Florida Turnpike System) through P3s with legislative approval; the DOT also may develop new toll facilities or increase capacity on existing toll facilities through P3s. Requires provisions in the P3 agreement that ensure a negotiated portion of revenues from tolled or fare generating projects are returned to the DOT over the life of the agreement. Allows a private entity to impose tolls or fares, subject to DOT regulation and certain limits. Allows for availability payments or shadow tolls, subject to annual appropriation by the Legislature.

				Limits P3 terms to no more than 50 years; however, the secretary of transportation may authorize a term of up to 75 years, and the Legislature may approve a term exceeding 75 years. Limits the total obligations for all projects under this section to no more than 15 percent of total federal and state funding for the State Transportation Trust Fund in any given year. Allows for solicited and unsolicited proposals.
Florida	Broad	Yes	Fla. Stat. Ann. § 337.251	Authorizes the state DOT to lease to public or private entities, for a term not to exceed 99 years, the use of DOT property, including rights-of-way. Also authorizes the DOT to lease the use of areas above or below state highways or other transportation facilities for commercial purposes. Leases under this section may not interfere with the primary state transportation needs nor be contrary to the best interests of the public. Allows for solicited and unsolicited proposals.
Florida	Broad	No	Fla. Stat. Ann. § 338.22 to 2511	Creates the Florida Turnpike Enterprise, which operates like private-sector business within the state DOT, in order to plan, develop, own, purchase, lease or otherwise acquire, demolish, construct, improve, relocate, equip, repair, maintain, operate and manage the Florida Turnpike System. Allows the enterprise to cooperate, coordinate, partner and contract with other entities, public and private, to accomplish its purposes.
Florida	Broad	Yes	Fla. Stat. Ann. § 343.962	Tampa Bay Area Regional Transportation Authority Act authorizes the regional transportation authority to receive or solicit proposals and enter into agreements with private entities or consortia thereof for the building, operation, ownership, or financing of multimodal transportation systems, transit-oriented development nodes, transit stations, or related facilities

Florida	Broad	Yes	Fla. Stat. Ann. § 343.875	Authorizes the Northwest Florida Transportation Corridor Authority to enter into agreements with private entities to build, operate, own or finance transportation facilities within its jurisdiction. Sets criteria for proposed projects. Allows for solicited and unsolicited proposals. Allows a private entity to impose tolls or fares, but rates and use of funds must be regulated by the authority to avoid unreasonable costs to facility users.
Florida	Broad	Yes	Fla. Stat. Ann. § 348.0004	Authorizes any expressway authority, transportation authority, bridge authority or toll authority to enter into agreements with private entities to build, operate, own or finance transportation facilities within the jurisdiction of the authority. Creates evaluation criteria for such projects. Prohibits noncompete clauses. Allows a private entity to impose tolls or fares, but rates and use of funds must be regulated by the authority to avoid unreasonable costs to the users of the facility. Requires all P3 facilities to be consistent with state, regional and local comprehensive plans. Allows for solicited and unsolicited proposals.
Florida	Broad	Yes	Fla. Stat. Ann § 287.05712	County, municipality, or special district has authority to establish P3 for project that serves a public purpose, including, but not limited to, any ferry or mass transit facility, vehicle parking facility, airport or seaport facility, rail facility or project, fuel supply facility, oil or gas pipeline, medical or nursing care facility, recreational facility, sporting or cultural facility, or educational facility or other building or facility that is used or will be used by a public educational institution, or any other public facility or infrastructure that is used or will be used by the public at large or in support of an accepted public purpose or activity. The statute describes the project qualification process and procurement procedures,

214

Florida	Broad		Fla. Stat. Ann § 255.065	including the development of interim and comprehensive agreements. Allows for solicited and unsolicited proposals. Exempts unsolicited proposals for P3 projects from public record and public meeting requirements for 180 days after receipt, if the public entity does not issue a competitive solicitation, or until the end of any competitive solicitation or promptly reissued competitive solicitation. These temporary exemptions are intended to protect the P3 process by "encouraging private entities to submit such proposals, which will facilitate the timely development and operation of a qualifying project."
Georgia	Broad		Ga. Code Ann. §48-5-41; Ga. Code Ann. §48- 5-421.1	This statute exempts property that qualifies as a public-private transportation project from ad valorem taxes, and section 48-5-421.1 provides that such projects shall not constitute special franchises.
Georgia			Ga. Code Ann. § 32-10-76	This statute establishes a grant program for P3 streetcar development and provides assistance to local government entities.
Georgia			Ga. Code Ann. §32-2-41(b)(6)	This statute allows the commissioner to establish a Public-Private Initiatives Division within the state DOT.
Georgia	Broad	No	Ga. Code Ann. §§ 32-2-78 to 80	Authorizes the DOT to solicit and accept proposals for projects that are funded or financed in part or in whole by private sources. Require all future P3 projects to be solicited by the DOT. Include public comment requirements and criteria for the DOT to use in awarding contracts. Authorizes contracts to include tolls, fares, or other user fees and tax increments for use of the project. Final approval of P3 contracts shall be by action of the State Transportation Board. The Partnership for Public Facilities and Infrastructure Act establishes guidelines for local government for

Georgia	Broad	Yes	Ga. Code. Ann. §§ 36-91-110 to 36-91-118	P3 procurement. The statute also outlines procedures for the review and analysis of each proposal. 'Qualifying project' means any project selected in response to a request from a local government or submitted by a private entity as an unsolicited proposal and subsequently reviewed and approved by a local government, within its sole discretion, as meeting a public purpose or public need. This term shall not include and shall have no application to any project involving a) the generation of electric energy for sale, b) communication services, c) cable and video services, d) water reservoir projects.
Illinois	Limited		Ill. Rev. Stat. ch. 20, § 2705/2705-450	Authorizes the state DOT to enter into agreements with any public or private entity for the purpose of promoting and developing high-speed rail and magnetic levitation transportation within the state.
Illinois	Limited		Ill. Rev. Stat. ch. 620 § 75/2-35	The South Suburban Airport Act provides gives general powers to the airport authority, specifically for P3. Any combination of design, build, finance, operate, and maintain are authorized. The term of a P3 agreement is lifted to 75 years, though the term may be extended by the General Assembly by law. The statute describes the prequalification and procurement processes. The statute also describes the provisions to be included in the P3 agreement. The P3 Developer is unable to impose user fees outside of the P3 agreement.
Illinois	Limited		Ill. Rev. Stat. ch. 605, § 5/10-802	Authorizes municipalities to make contracts "of every kind and nature" to acquire, construct, reconstruct, improve, enlarge, better, operate, maintain and/or repair any bridge within five miles of the corporate limits of the municipality, and to fix and apply tolls and fees for use of such a bridge.

State			Statute	Description
Illinois	Limited		Ill. Rev. Stat. ch. 605 §§ 130/1 to 130/999	Authorizes the state DOT to enter into a P3 to develop, construct, manage or operate the Illiana Expressway. Limits the contract term to 99 years, including extensions. Requires legislative approval for all extensions. Chapter 820 section 130/2 makes a P3 for the Illiana Expressway subject to the state Prevailing Wage Act (this section is also applicable to a lease of facility property at Chicago Midway International Airport).
Illinois	Broad		Ill. Rev. Stat. ch. 630 §§ 15/5	The Public-Private Partnership Act provides broad authority for the development of new P3 projects by the DOT and Tollway Authority. Eligible projects include roads, bridges, intermodal facilities, intercity or high-speed passenger rail or other transportation facilities. Airports and toll roads are not eligible unless authorized by law. The Act can be applied toward reconstruction or expansion of existing assets. The Act describes project identification processes and the need for legislative authorization by joint resolution of the Illinois House and Senate. The Act describes three types of procurement processes: sealed bidding, sealed proposals, and Design-Build. A preferred proponent's proposal will be reviewed by the State's Commission on Government Forecasting and Accountability. The Governor makes the final award decision.
Indiana	Broad	No	Ind. Code Ann. §§ 5-23-1-1 to 5-23-7-2	Authorizes governmental bodies to enter into P3 agreements with private entities for the acquisition, planning, design, development, reconstruction, repair, maintenance or financing of public facilities. Applies to the state, a political subdivision in a county containing a consolidated city, or a political subdivision in a county that adopts these provisions by resolution or ordinance. Limits original terms of P3 agreements to no more than five

				years with board approval; a term in excess of five years requires approval from the board, the governor and/or the fiscal body of a political subdivision. Requires a public hearing. Allows for solicited proposals only.
Indiana	Broad	No	Ind. Code Ann. §§ 8-15.5-1-1 to 8-15.5-13-8	Authorizes the Indiana Finance Authority to enter into P3 agreements with private entities to plan, design, acquire, construct, reconstruct, improve, extend, expand, lease, operate, repair, manage, maintain or finance toll road projects. Prohibits the state DOT or the authority from issuing a request for proposals or entering into a P3 for a toll road after Aug. 1, 2006, unless the General Assembly adopts a statute authorizing the imposition of tolls. Exempts certain projects from the legislative approval requirement, including the Illiana Expressway under legislation enacted in 2010 (Senate Bill 382; 2010 Ind. Acts, P.L. 85). Requires public hearings to be held in affected counties; also requires certain preliminary studies. Limits lease terms to no more than 75 years. Allows for solicited proposals only.
Indiana	Broad	No	Ind. Code Ann. §§ 8-15.7-1-1 to 8-15.7-16-8	Authorizes the state DOT to enter into P3s to develop, finance or operate transportation projects, including tollways, roads and bridges, and some rail projects. Prohibits the DOT or the Indiana Finance Authority from issuing a request for proposals or entering into a P3 agreement unless the General Assembly adopts a statute authorizing that activity. Exempts certain projects from the legislative approval requirement, including an Interstate 69 project and the Illiana Expressway under new legislation enacted in 2010 (Senate Bill 382; 2010 Ind. Acts, P.L. 85). Allows for solicited proposals only.

Kentucky	Broad	No	Ky. Rev. Stat. § 45A.077	The statute establishes an 11-member Kentucky Local Government Public Private Partnership, which will approve review and approve certain P3 agreements. The law also directs the Secretary of Finance and the Administration Cabinet to establish regulations in order to determine when a P3 may be used for a particular project, as well as those local governments must follow concerning P3 agreements. The law sets forth regulations as to what should be contained in an RFP and establishes procedures regarding unsolicited proposals.
Louisiana	Broad	No	La. Rev. Stat. Ann. § 48:250.	Authorizes the DOT to solicit and enter P3 contracts for a transportation facility. Twenty-five percent of P3 projects undertaken by the DOT should be located outside the boundaries of a metro area. Rural projects are subject to approval of the House and Senate committee on agriculture and rural development.
Louisiana	Broad	No	La. Rev. Stat. Ann. § 48:1660.1	Competitive bidding on contracts provides broad authority to the Regional Transit Authority to enter into P3 contracts for transportation facilities. RTA is unable to accept an unsolicited proposal. The statute refers to the procedural requirements previously enacted.
Louisiana	Broad		La. Rev. Stat. Ann. §§48:2020 to 2037	Encourages parishes and municipalities to use P3s to help the state finance improvements to the state highway system and meet local transportation needs. Authorizes parishes and municipalities to create transportation authorities, which may enter into agreements with public or private entities to construct, maintain, repair and/or operate transportation projects. Allows transportation authorities to authorize investment of public and private money to finance such projects, subject to compliance with state law relative to use of public funds.

Louisiana	Broad	Yes	La. Rev. Stat. Ann. §§48:2071 to 2074; La. Rev. Stat. Ann. §48:2077; La. Rev. Stat. Ann. §§48:2084 to 2084.15	Creates the Louisiana Transportation Authority to pursue alternative and innovative funding sources - including P3s, tolls and unclaimed property bonds - to supplement public revenue sources and to improve Louisiana's transportation system. Allows the authority to contract with a public or private entity to construct, maintain, repair or operate authority projects, and to authorize the investment of public and private money to finance such projects, subject to compliance with state law relative to the use of public funds. Allows a private entity to impose user fees, but prohibits a private entity from imposing tolls or user fees on any existing free transportation facility unless the facility is improved or expanded. Allows for solicited and unsolicited proposals.
Maine	Broad	Yes	Me. Rev. Stat. Ann. Title 23, § 4251	Authorizes the state DOT - with legislative approval - to enter into P3s for transportation projects with an estimated cost of more than $25 million or when a project proposal includes tolling existing transportation facilities that were not previously subject to tolls. Allows for solicited and unsolicited proposals. Sets standards and requirements for P3 proposals, including completion of certain studies. Requires P3 proposals to limit the use of state capital funding to less than 50 percent of the initial capital cost of the facility and, to the extent practicable minimize use of public transportation funding sources. Allows a P3 agreement to authorize a private entity to impose tolls or fares, subject to certain requirements. Limits term length to 50 years unless the Legislature, upon the recommendation of the commissioner of transportation, approves a longer term.

Maryland	No		Md. Code Regs. § 23.3.05.05	County or local educational agencies can establish P3 for shared use arrangements of school facilities in exchange for school property enhancements and/or revenue
Maryland	Broad		Md. Code Ann., State Fin. & Proc. §§ 10a-101 to 10a-403	Statute provides authority to reporting agencies to State Finance and Procurement to pursue P3 project delivery. The statute allows agencies to determine their own regulations and processes for the procurement, development and delivery of P3 projects. Eligible projects are those that "develop and strengthen a public infrastructure asset in conjunction with a public-private partnership."
Maryland	Broad	Yes	Md. Code Regs. §§ 11.07.06.01 to 14	The law establishes a Maryland Transportation Authority program for P3. It describes the steering committee, identification process, screening process, procurement steps, and delivery procedures. Allows for unsolicited proposals only.
Massachusetts	Broad	Yes	Mass. Gen. Laws Ann. Ch. 6C, §§1 to 74	MassDOT may solicit proposals and enter into contracts for Design-Build-finance-operate-maintain or Design-Build-operate-maintain services with the responsible and responsive offeror submitting the proposal that is most advantageous to the department through the sale, lease, operation and maintenance of a transportation facility within the commonwealth. A Special Public-Private Partnership Infrastructure Oversight Commission is established, which must comment on and approve all requests for proposals.
Michigan	Broad	No	Mich. Comp. Laws § 124.401 to 426	This statute provides broad procurement authority to metro transportation authorities to implement P3 for transportation facilities.
Michigan	Broad		Mich. Comp. Laws Ann. §§ 125.1871 to 125.1883	The Private Investment Infrastructure Funding Act authorizes the department of transportation, county road commission, drain commissioner, city, village or township with

				jurisdiction of a public facility to establish a negotiating partnership to develop and finance public facilities. While not explicitly recognizing P3 in the traditional sense, this has allowed agencies to negotiate with private entities on the development and financing of public facilities.
Minnesota	Limited	Yes	Minn. Stat. Ann. §§ 160.84 to 98	This statute generally authorizes state and local road authorities to solicit or accept proposals from and enter into development agreements with private entities to develop, finance, design, construct, improve, rehabilitate, own and/or operate toll facilities. It also authorizes user fees for as high-occupancy vehicle lanes or dynamic shoulder lanes. The extent to which a private entity can operate and maintain a road is significantly limited. Section 160.845 prohibits a road authority or a private operator from converting, transferring or utilizing any portion of a highway to impose tolls or for use as a toll facility (excepting dynamic shoulder lanes or HOV/HOT lanes); and section 160.98 prohibits a road authority from selling, leasing, executing a development agreement for a build-operate-transfer or build-transfer-operate facility that transfers an existing highway lane, or otherwise relinquishing management of a highway.
Mississippi	Limited	Yes	Miss. Code Ann. §§ 65-43-1 to 85	Authorizes the Mississippi Transportation Commission, county boards of supervisors and/or the governing authorities of municipalities to contract with other governmental agencies or private entities for the purpose of designing, financing, constructing, operating and maintaining one or more new toll roads or toll bridges in the state. Prohibits noncompete clauses by authorizing toll roads or bridges at and along only those locations where an alternate untolled route exists.

Missouri	Broad	Yes	Mo. Rev. Stat. §§ 227.600 to 669	Limits contract terms to 50 years, which cannot be extended or renewed. Allows for solicited and unsolicited proposals. The Missouri Public-Private Partnerships Transportation Act authorizes the Highways and Transportation Commission to enter into agreements with private partners to finance, develop and/or operate any pipeline, ferry, river port, airport, railroad, light rail or other mass transit facility. Any project not mentioned previously cannot be financed, developed or operated by a private partner until it is approved by a vote of the people. Allows for solicited and unsolicited projects.
Missouri			Mo. Rev. Stat. §§ 238.300 to 367	Authorizes creation of special purpose, nonprofit "transportation corporations" by private parties, which may enter into agreements with the Highways and Transportation Commission in order to fund, promote, plan, design, construct, maintain and operate one or more transportation projects. Authorizes such corporations to issue bonds and to establish and charge user fees for projects. No part of the earnings or assets of a transportation corporation shall inure to the benefit of any private interests, person or entity.
New Jersey	Limited	Yes	TBD; SB 865	This law authorizes local government entities to enter into P3 agreements for the "development, construction, reconstruction, repair, alteration, improvement, extension, operation, and maintenance of any building, road, structure, infrastructure, or facility constructed or acquired by a local government unit to house local government functions, including any infrastructure or facility used or to be used by the public or in support of a public purpose or activity; provided that, with respect to a roadway or highway project, a qualifying project shall include an expenditure of at

least $10 million in public funds, or any expenditure in solely private funds." P3 lease terms are limited to 30 years. Qualifying projects will be submitted to the New Jersey Economic Development Authority for its review and approval. The law allows for unsolicited proposals.

State			Citation	Description
Nevada	Limited		Nev. Rev. Stat. §§ 338.161 to 167	The law authorizes counties with a population exceeding 700,000 to enter into P3s for transportation projects, including mass transit facilities.
Nevada	Limited	Yes	Nev. Rev. Stat. §§ 338.161 to 168	Allows private entities to submit a request to a public body to develop, construct, improve, maintain or operate, or any combination thereof, a transportation facility. Excludes toll roads and toll bridges.
Nevada	Limited		Nev. Rev. Stat. Chapter 277A	This statute defines powers for regional transportation commissions and section 280 allows for the use of turnkey procurement and competitive negotiation procurement processes.
New Hampshire	Broad		NH Rev. Stat. Ann. 228:107 to 228:115	Establishes a P3 oversight commission to recommend projects to the transportation commissioner using DBFOM or DBOM delivery models. The commission functions as an advisory board during P3 project implementation by helping to develop the RFP and preparation of agreements.
North Carolina	Limited	No	NC Gen. Stat. § 136-18	Allows the state DOT to enter into a contract with a private Developer to accomplish the engineering, design or construction of improvements to any transportation infrastructure under its jurisdiction. Sets restrictions on such projects, including that DOT participation is limited to the lesser of 10 percent of the engineering contract and any construction contract or $250,000, and that, in any case, DOT costs must not exceed normal practices. Requires projects to be constructed in accordance with DOT-approved plans and specifications. Terms must be less than 50 years. Solicited proposals only.

			Allows the state DOT to enter into a contract with a private Developer to accomplish the engineering, design or construction of improvements to any transportation infrastructure under its jurisdiction. Sets restrictions on such projects, including that DOT participation is limited to the lesser of 10 percent of the engineering contract and any construction contract or $250,000, and that, in any case, DOT costs must not exceed normal practices. Requires projects to be constructed in accordance with DOT-approved plans and specifications. Terms must be less than 50 years. Solicited proposals only.
North Carolina	Limited	No	NC Gen. Stat. §§ 136-89.180 to 198	Authorizes the North Carolina Turnpike Authority to enter into agreements with the state DOT, political subdivisions and private entities, and to expend such funds as it deems necessary pursuant to such agreements, to finance the acquisition, construction, equipping, operation or maintenance of any turnpike project. Authorizes the authority to fix and collect tolls and fees for the use of a turnpike project. Prohibits noncompete clauses by requiring the DOT to maintain an existing, alternate, comparable nontoll route corresponding to each turnpike project constructed pursuant to this article. Allows the authority to study, plan and conduct preliminary design work on up to nine projects and then to design, establish, purchase, construct, operate and maintain five identified projects only. Any additional projects require legislative approval.
Ohio	Broad	Yes	Ohio Rev. Code Ann. § 5501.71 to 5501.75	This statute defines the authority of the state DOT to enter public-private initiatives, including guidelines for solicitation and selection. The state DOT can use P3 for public or private highway, road, street, parkway, public transit, aviation, or rail project, and any related rights-of-way, bridges or

				tunnels. The DOT may use sealed bidding and the selection of proposals using qualifications or best value (or both).
Oklahoma	Limited		Okla. Code Ann. Tit. 74 § 5151 to 5158	The Oklahoma Public and Private Facilities and Infrastructure Act establishes a Partnership Committee to determine potential P3 projects. The statute requires that the Committee provide a public sector comparator for each project. The OK Office of P3 is responsible for procurement practices. The state DOT and Turnpike Authority are exempt from the law.
Oregon			Or. Rev. Stat. § 184.631	OR DOT's Research and Development Program can use P3 for state highways
Oregon	Broad	Yes	Or. Rev. Stat. §§ 367.800 to 826	Establishes the Oregon Innovative Partnerships Program within the state DOT, which is authorized to enter into agreements with private entities to plan, acquire, finance, develop, design, construct, reconstruct, replace, improve, maintain, manage, repair, lease and/ or operate transportation projects. Lists specific goals for the program, including to speed project delivery, maximize innovation and develop partnerships with private entities. Lists specific requirements for P3 agreements, including financing, risk management, penalties for nonperformance and incentives for performance. Allows for solicited and unsolicited proposals.
Oregon	Broad	Yes	Or. Rev. Stat. §§ 383.001 to 075	Authorizes the state DOT to enter into agreements with private entities and/or units of government to acquire, design, construct, reconstruct, operate or maintain and repair tollway projects. Includes lease agreements. Allows the DOT or a private entity that operates a tollway project pursuant to an agreement with the DOT to impose and collect tolls. Allows for solicited and unsolicited proposals.

Pennsylvania	Broad	Yes	Penn. Conso. Stat.74 §§ 9101 to 9124	The law allows state or local public entities to enter into P3s for the design, construction, operation, maintenance, financing or lease of transportation facilities. All partnerships must be approved by a Public-Private Transportation Partnerships Board. The bill also allows the legislature to block P3s for state-owned facilities and requires legislative approval for P3s on the Pennsylvania Turnpike.
Puerto Rico	Broad	No	PR Laws Ann. Tit. 9, §§ 2001 to 2021	Creates the Puerto Rico Highway and Transportation Authority. Empowers the authority or the Department of Transportation and Public Works to contract with private parties to design, construct, operate and maintain new highways, bridges, avenues, expressways and ancillary transit facilities, and informative electronic signboards or billboards. Limits contract terms for the operation, administration and maintenance phases to 50 years. Requires the secretary of transportation and public works or an official designated by him to be the representative of the public interest and to ensure the private entity fulfills its contractual obligations, among other duties. Creates a negotiated competitive bidding process. In case an existing road is converted into a toll road, requires an alternate road that is not tolled.
Puerto Rico	Broad	No	PR Laws Ann. Tit. 9, §§ 2001 to 2021P.R. Laws Ann. tit. 27, §§ 2601 to 2623	Comprehensive statute that authorizes P3s, passed in 2009 (Senate Bill 469). States the commonwealth's motives and goals for authorizing P3s. Establishes the Public-Private Partnership Authority as an entity of the Government Development Bank. Empowers the authority to establish P3s for infrastructure projects, and makes the authority the sole government entity responsible for implementing public policy on P3s as set forth in this act. Limits term lengths to 50 years,

				with extensions subject to legislative approval. Creates guidelines for evaluating, approving, contracting for and overseeing P3 projects. The authority will form a separate committee for each proposed project; authority members and the project committee will assess the credentials of each project, and the committee will be able to issue RFQs and negotiate contracts. Final approval of P3 contracts rests with the governor.
South Carolina	Broad		SC Code Ann. §§57-5-1310 to 1495	Allows the state DOT to construct and operate turnpike facilities. Section 57-5-1330(1)(4) appears to allow the use of P3s for these facilities by allowing the DOT to exercise such authorizations as are granted by the provisions in other statute law to designate, establish, plan, abandon, improve, construct, maintain and regulate turnpike facilities.
South Carolina	Broad		SC Code § 57-3-200	Authorizes the state DOT to expend such funds as it deems necessary to enter into partnership agreements with private entities to finance, by tolls and other methods, the cost of acquiring, constructing, equipping, maintaining and operating highways, roads, streets and bridges in the state.
Tennessee	Limited		Tenn. Code §§ 54-3-101 to 54-3-113	Authorizes tolling as an additional and alternative method for funding or financing transportation facilities. Authorizes the state DOT to enter into agreements with private parties to develop or operate a tollway, toll facility or any part thereof. Limits authorization for tolling initially to a pilot program of two projects. Provides that existing highways cannot be converted into toll roads, but additional lane capacity constructed on or along an existing highway or bridge may be developed and operated like a tollway. Requires legislative approval.
Tennessee	Limited	Yes	Tenn. Code §§ 54-6-101 to 54-6-121	This law enables the DOT to use P3 delivery for a tollway or toll facility. The law outlines procedures for project procurement, and the metrics

				that the DOT may consider when evaluating a proposal. Allows for unsoliciting proposals.
Texas			Tex. Transportation Code Ann. §§222.001 to 107	Relates generally to funding and federal aid, with provisions pertaining to P3s. Prohibits the state DOT from using state highway funds to guarantee loans or insure bonds for costs associated with a toll facility of a public or private entity. Authorizes the DOT to otherwise participate in the cost of acquiring, constructing, maintaining or operating a toll facility of a public or private entity. Allows the DOT to enter into an agreement with a public or private entity to pay pass-through tolls (also known as shadow tolls) to that entity as reimbursement for the design, development, financing, construction, maintenance or operation of a toll or nontoll facility on the state highway system.
Texas	Limited	Yes	Tex. Transportation Code Ann. §§ 366.401 to 409	Authorizes regional tollway authorities to use comprehensive development agreements with private entities to design, develop, finance, construct, maintain, repair, operate, extend or expand turnpike projects.
Utah	Limited	Yes	Utah Code Ann. § 63G-6-503; § 63G6a-103; § 6 3G-6a702; § 63G6a-703; § 63G-6a-707	Authorizes the state DOT to accept proposals for, and enter into, tollway development agreements with public or private entities to study, predevelop, design, finance, acquire, construct, reconstruct, maintain, repair, operate, extend or expand tollway facilities. Defines the terms that must be included in such agreements. Tollway development agreements must be approved by the Utah Transportation Commission. Allow for solicited and unsolicited proposals.
Utah	Limited		Utah Code Ann. §72-6-118; Utah Code Ann. 72-2-120	Authorizes the state DOT to establish, expand and operate tollways and related facilities. Authorizes the DOT to enter into contracts, agreements, licenses, franchises, tollway development agreements, or other arrangements for tollway projects. Prohibits

the DOT or other entity from establishing or operating a tollway on an existing state highway unless approved by the Transportation Commission and the Legislature, except for high occupancy toll lanes or additional capacity lanes. Requires revenue generated from tollway development agreement projects to be deposited into the Tollway Special Revenue Fund created in section 72-2-120 and used for transportation facilities within the corridor served by the tollway, unless the revenue is to the private entity or identified for a different purpose under the agreement.

| Vermont | Limited | Yes | 19 V.S.A. § 26 | This statute establishes, in 2019, a pilot program for P3s. The program will accept unsolicited proposals and will also solicit proposals to undertake a P3 project. The statute describes the elements by which proposals are evaluated and requires the total estimated State funding over the lifetime of the project to be less than $2,000,000.00. Eligible projects requiring legislative approval are projects that has not been approved in the most recently adopted Transportation Program or projects with an estimated State funding of greater than $2,000,000.00 over its lifetime. The statute also describes legislative oversight requirements and the report to be delivered on the pilot program's impact. |
| Virginia | Broad | Yes | Va. Code §§ 33.2-1800 | The Public-Private Transportation Act of 1995 (subsequently modified) is a comprehensive P3 statute intended to encourage private investment in transportation facilities. Authorizes a private entity to develop and/or operate a qualifying transportation facility, subject to approval from and a comprehensive agreement with the responsible public entity. Contains detailed implementation guidelines, |

Washington	Broad	Yes	Wash. Rev. Code §§ 47.29.010 to 900	including specific requirements for comprehensive agreements. Stipulates the powers and duties of a private entity in a P3 and provides financing mechanisms. Allows for solicited and unsolicited proposals. Authorizes the state DOT to enter into P3s for transportation projects, whether capital or operating, where the state's primary purpose for the project is to facilitate safe transportation of people or goods via any mode of travel. Defines terms that must be included in agreements. Requires review by and approval of the Transportation Commission for P3 contracts or agreements. Requires an advisory committee for any project that costs $300 million or more. Authorizes the DOT to solicit or accept unsolicited proposals after Jan. 1, 2007, for eligible transportation projects.
Washington, D.C.	Broad	Yes	D.C. Code §§ 2-271.01 to 2-275.01	Establishes an Office of Public-Private Partnerships within the City Administrator's office and specifies its duties, including an established fun from which to fund the Office's activities. The statute details the procurement process, including for the receipt of unsolicited proposals. Section § 2–273.09 describes transparency measures and the Office's relationship to the City Council.
Washington, D.C.	Broad		D.C. Code § 2-356.01	This statute provides general authority for construction projects and related management services. Authorized delivery models include architectural and engineering services; construction management; construction management at risk; design-bid-build; Design-Build; Design-Build-finance-operate-maintain; Design-Build-operate-maintain; and operations and maintenance.

State				Description
West Virginia	Broad	No	WVa. Code §§ 17-28-1 to 12	Authorizes Division of Highways to enter into comprehensive agreements with private entities to acquire, construct or improve transportation facilities. Sets guidelines for soliciting proposals. Specifies what comprehensive agreements shall contain. Allows a private Developer to charge user fees if they are consistent with the rate of return specified in the agreement; requires the schedule and amount of initial user fees and any fee increase to be approved by the Commissioner of the Division of Highways. Original bill expired in 2011 and was reenacted in 2013.
Wisconsin	Limited	No	Wis. Stat. Ann. § 84.01 (30)	Authorizes the state DOT to enter into build-operate-lease or transfer agreements with private entities for construction of transportation projects and for maintenance or operation of projects that are not purchased by the state upon their completion. Lists specific provisions that must be included in every agreement. An agreement may not be entered into unless the DOT determines that it advances the public interest and the private entity meets certain criteria.

APPENDIX C

BUILDING A STRONGER AMERICA: PRESIDENT DONALD J. TRUMP'S AMERICAN INFRASTRUCTURE INITIATIVE

INFRASTRUCTURE & TECHNOLOGY

Issued on: February 12, 2018

BUILDING AMERICA'S INFRASTRUCTURE: Today, President Donald J. Trump released his legislative goals to rebuild our Nation's crumbling infrastructure. The six principles include:

- $200 billion in Federal funds to spur at least $1.5 trillion in infrastructure investments with partners at the State, local, Tribal, and private level.
- New investments will be made in rural America, which has been left behind for too long.
- Decision making authority will be returned to State and local governments.
- Regulatory barriers that needlessly get in the way of infrastructure projects will be removed.
- Permitting for infrastructure projects will be streamlined and shortened.
- America's workforce will be supported and strengthened.

STIMULATE INFRASTRUCTURE INVESTMENT: President Trump's plan will lead to at least $1.5 trillion in investments to rebuild our failing infrastructure and develop innovative projects.

- $200 billion in Federal funds will spur at least $1.5 trillion in new infrastructure investments.
- Federal infrastructure spending will promote State, local, and private investments and maximize the value of every taxpayer dollar.
- Of the $200 billion, $100 billion will create an Incentives Program to spur additional dedicated funds from States, localities, and the private sector.
- Applications for the Incentives Program will be evaluated on objective criteria, with creating additional infrastructure investment being the largest factor.
- The Incentives Program will promote accountability, making Federal funding conditional on projects meeting agreed upon milestones.
- $20 billion will be dedicated to the Transformative Projects Program.
- This program will provide Federal aid for bold and innovative projects that have the potential to dramatically improve America's infrastructure.
- The program will focus on projects that could have a significant positive impact on States, cities, and localities but may not attract private sector investment because of the project's unique characteristics.
- $20 billion will be allocated to expanding infrastructure financing programs.
- Of the $20 billion, $14 billion will go to expanding a number of existing credit programs: TIFIA, WIFIA, RRIF, and rural utility lending.
- $6 billion will go to expanding Private Activity Bonds.
- $10 billion will go to a new Federal Capital Revolving Fund, which will reduce inefficient leasing of Federal real property which would be more cost-effective to purchase.
- A new fund will allow some incremental revenues from energy development on public lands to pay for the capital and maintenance needs of public lands infrastructure.

INVEST IN RURAL AMERICA: Rural America's infrastructure has been left behind for too long, and President Trump's plan will make sure it is supported and modernized.

- $50 billion of the $200 billion in direct Federal funding will be devoted to a new Rural Infrastructure Program to rebuild and modernize infrastructure in rural America.
- The bulk of the dollars in the Rural Infrastructure Program will be allocated to State governors, giving States the flexibility to prioritize their communities' needs.

- The remaining funds will be distributed through rural performance grants to encourage the best use of taxpayer dollars.

INCREASE STATE AND LOCAL AUTHORITY: President Trump's proposal will return decision-making authority to State and local governments, which know the needs of their communities.

- Funds awarded to State and local authorities, such as through the Incentives Program and the Rural Infrastructure Program, will be allocated to infrastructure projects they prioritize.
- This empowers States and localities to make more infrastructure investment decisions and prioritize projects based on the needs of their communities
- The plan will expand processes that allow environmental review and permitting decisions to be delegated to States.
- The plan will also allow Federal agencies to divest assets that can be better managed by State or local governments or the private sector.

ELIMINATE REGULATORY BARRIERS: The President's plan would eliminate barriers that prevent virtually all infrastructure projects from being efficiently developed and managed.

- The President's plan will:
- Provide more flexibility to transportation projects that have minimal Federal funding but are currently required to seek Federal review and approval.
- Incentivize the efficient development and management of water infrastructure, in part, by providing more flexibility to the U.S. Army Corps of Engineers and its partners.
- Give the Department of Veterans Affairs the flexibility to use its existing assets to acquire new facilities by allowing it to retain property sale proceeds and exchange existing facilities for construction of new facilities.
- Expand funding eligibility for land revitalization projects through the Superfund program and establish tools to help manage their legal and financial matters.

STREAMLINE PERMITTING: President Trump's infrastructure proposal will shorten and simplify the approval process for infrastructure projects.

- Working with Congress, we will:
- Establish a "one agency, one decision" structure for environmental reviews.
- Shorten the lengthy environmental review process to two years while still protecting the environment.
- Eliminate certain redundant and inefficient provisions in environmental laws.
- Create two new pilot programs to test new ways to improve the environmental review process.

INVEST IN OUR COUNTRY'S MOST IMPORTANT ASSET – ITS PEOPLE: The President is proposing reforms so Americans secure good-paying jobs and meet the needs of our industries.

- The President's plan would reform Federal education and workforce development programs to better prepare Americans to perform the in-demand jobs of today and the future. This includes:
- Making high-quality, short-term programs that provide students with a certification or credential in an in-demand field eligible for Pell Grants.
- Reforming the Perkins Career and Technical Education Program to ensure more students have access to high-quality technical education to develop the skills required in today's economy.
- Better targeting Federal Work-Study funds to help more students obtain important workplace experience, including through apprenticeships.

APPENDIX D

CONSENSUSDOCS – P3 AGREEMENTS

    A. Public Private Partnership Agreement 900 (Sample – Not for Reuse)

    B. Operations & Mantenance Agreement 910 (Sample – Not for Reuse)

Order from: https://www.consensusdocs.org/ contract_category/publicprivatepartnership/

APPENDIX E

ADDITIONAL P3 PROJECTS

FHWA – Center for Innovative Finance Support

Project sample contracts and procurement

> *https://www.fhwa.dot.gov/ipd/p3/p3_projects/*

Design–Build Finance Operate Maintain (DBFOM) Toll Concessions:

- 91 Express Lanes *- *Orange County, California*
- 395 Express Lanes - *Alexandria and Arlington, Virginia*
- Belle Chasse Bridge and Tunnel Replacement - *Plaquemines Parish, Louisiana*
- Capital Beltway High Occupancy Toll (HOT) Lanes (I-495) - *Fairfax County, Virginia*
- Dulles Greenway - *Loudoun County, Virginia*
- Elizabeth River Tunnels (Downtown / Midtown Tunnel) - *Cities of Norfolk and Portsmouth, Virginia*
- Foley Beach Express - *Baldwin County, Alabama (local road project)*
- I-77 Express Lanes - *Charlotte, North Carolina*
- I-95 Express Lanes Fredericksburg Extension - *Stafford County, Virginia*
- I-95 HOV/HOT Lanes - *Fairfax, Prince Williams, and Stafford Counties, Virginia*
- LBJ Express/IH 635 Managed Lanes - *Dallas County, Texas*
- North Tarrant Express I-820 and SH 121/183 (Segments 1 and 2W) - *Dallas-Fort Worth Metroplex, Texas*

- North Tarrant Express 35W (Segments 3A, 3B and 3C) - *Dallas-Fort Worth Metroplex, Texas*
- SH 130 (Segments 5-6) - *Austin, Texas Metropolitan Area*
- SH 288 Toll Lanes Project - *Houston, Texas*
- South Bay Expressway (formerly SR 125 South) * - *San Diego County, California*
- Teodoro Moscoso Bridge - *San Juan to Carolina, Puerto Rico*
- Transform 66 - Outside the Beltway - *Fairfax and Prince William Counties, Virginia*
- US 36 Express Lanes (Phase 2) - *Denver Metro Area, Colorado*

Build Finance Operate Maintain (DBFOM) Availability Payment Concessions:

- Central 70 - *Denver, Colorado*
- Eagle Project - *Denver Metro Area, Colorado (transit project)*
- Goethals Bridge Replacement * - *Staten Island, New York to Elizabeth, New Jersey*
- Gordie Howe International Bridge - *Windsor, Ontario to Detroit, Michigan*
- I-4 Ultimate - *Orlando, Florida*
- I-69 Section 5 - *Bloomington to Martinsville, Indiana*
- KentuckyWired - *Kentucky (statewide)*
- I-75 Modernization Project Segment 3 * - *Detroit Metropolitan Region, Michigan*
- I-595 Corridor Roadway Improvements - *Broward County, Florida*
- Metro Region Freeway Lighting P3 (Michigan) - *Detroit Tri-County Area*
- Northampton County Bridge Renewal Program * - *Northampton County, Pennsylvania*
- Ohio River Bridges East End Crossing - *Southern Indiana/Louisville, Kentucky*
- Pennsylvania Rapid Bridge Replacement Project * - *Pennsylvania (statewide)*
- Port of Miami Tunnel - *Miami, Florida*
- Presidio Parkway (Phase II) - *San Francisco, California*
- Purple Line Project - *Washington DC Metro Region / Central Maryland (transit project)*
- Southern Ohio Veterans Memorial Highway (Portsmouth Bypass) - *Portsmouth to Lucasville, Scioto County, Ohio*
- State Street Redevelopment Project * - *West Lafayette, Indiana (local road project)*

Long-Term Lease Concessions:

- Chicago Skyway - *Chicago, Illinois*
- Indiana Toll Road - *Indiana*
- Luis Muñoz Marín International Airport Privatization - *San Juan, Puerto Rico (aviation project)*
- Maryland I-95 Travel Plazas Redevelopment - *Cecil County and Harford County, Maryland*
- Moynihan Train Hall - *New York, New York (transit project)*
- Northwest Parkway - *Denver Metro Region, Colorado*
- Ohio State University Parking Facility - *Columbus, Ohio*
- Pocahontas Parkway/Richmond Airport Connector - *Greater Richmond, Virginia*
- Puerto Rico PR-22 & PR-5 Lease - *Northern Puerto Rico*
- Seagirt Marine Terminal - *Baltimore, Maryland*

Pending New P3 Airport Projects – Airports (Courtesy of Levelset):

Denver International Airport

The city of Denver recently agreed on a $1.8B P3 project on the Denver International Airport. This is not the first time the Denver airport has done the P3 dance – just one year ago a commuter rail project was completed using the P3 format. This P3 will improve security and modernize the layout of the ticketing and entryway.

La Guardia

La Guardia airport in New York upped the ante on its P3 agreement. Last June, LaGuardia entered into a $4B P3 to completely overhaul a terminal. Under the project, their private partner will also complete infrastructure and an entryway.

Kansas City

The Kansas City International Airport is currently reviewing P3 proposals to build a new terminal. Four groups bid on the $1B project.

Printed in the United States
By Bookmasters